Home as Found

ERIC J. SUNDQUIST

Home as Found

Authority and Genealogy in Nineteenth-Century American Literature

The Johns Hopkins University Press
Baltimore and London

Part of Chapter 1 originally appeared as "Incest and Imitation in Cooper's *Home as Found*," © 1977 by The Regents of the University of California, and is reprinted from *Nineteenth-Century Fiction*, Vol. 32, No. 3, pp. 261–84, by permission of The Regents.

Manufactured in the United States of America

The Johns Hopkins University Press, Baltimore, Maryland 21218
The Johns Hopkins Press Ltd., London

Library of Congress Catalog Number 79-4949

ISBN 0-8018-2241-6

Library of Congress Cataloging in Publication data will be found on the last printed page of this book.

For my parents

MEN EXECUTE nothing so faithfully as the wills of the dead, to the last codicil and letter. *They* rule this world, and the living are but their executors. . . . like some Indian tribes, we bear about with us the mouldering relics of our ancestors on our shoulders. . . . All men are partially buried in the grave of custom.

—Thoreau, *A Week on the Concord and Merrimack Rivers*

EXTRAORDINARY, we say to ourselves on such occasions, the amount of formal tribute that civilization is after all able to gouge out of apparently hopeless stuff; extraordinary that it can make a presentable sheath for such fangs and such claws. The mystery is in the *how* of the process, in the wonderful little wavering borderland between nature and art, the place of the crooked seam where, if psychology had the adequate lens, the white stitches would show.

—James, *The American Scene*

Contents

Preface

"Act, if you like—but you do it at your peril," writes Emerson in the essay on Goethe in *Representative Men.* "Men's actions are too strong for them. Show me a man who has acted, and who has not been the victim and slave of his action. What they have done commits and forces them to do the same again. The first act, which was to be an experiment, becomes a sacrament."[1] Emerson's remarks could stand with ease as an epigraph to many literary texts, though that is not to say that documents of a political, sociological, or scientific nature would not be as well illuminated and constrained by the tension between experiment and sacrament, as the range of *Representative Men* itself suggests. Perhaps, though, only an American could have made such a statement; this is, of course, not literally the case, but just as it has belonged to the American experience that its construction of institutions and fables has gathered power from experimentation, from starts both fresh and false, clumsy and energetic, so it has also been the case that the gap between experiment and sacrament in America has often been slight, whether by necessity or by the token of its unwitting effacement at the hands of statesmen and literati. Against the spirit of repudiation that upholds any revolutionary performance there must weigh an anxiety over the loss of those forms of practical or ceremonial behavior in which are dramatized the sacraments of a culture, and any new culture will consequently be marked by a longing, a *desire,* to return to those sacraments or to place in their stead others that are yet more potent and binding. To the degree that a representative of the new culture—an author, say—takes his personal situation to be as much at stake as that of his country and makes his own career *representative,* we may find that his own *desire* creates the materials on which he works as much as he takes those materials from the shunned and shattered institutions behind him or the incipient institutions around him. In this case the actions that are "too strong" for him may be of serious intimacy, and the conflict between experiment and sacrament may wrench apart his allegiances, welding devotion and rebellion inextricably together.

The kind of desire that produces such a conflict, it could be argued, belongs generally to the large arena of human experience in which cultures, or generations within a culture, are pitted against one another; but it may also be the case that *desire,* as Leo Bersani has noted, is more particularly "a phenomenon of the literary imagination," that because it is "an appetite stimulated by an absence" which entails "a hallucinated satisfaction in the absence of the source of satisfaction," the "activity of desiring is inseparable from the activity of fantasizing."[2] I want to accept Bersani's theory and propose that for each of four nineteenth-century American writers the source of satisfaction found wanting is tied in an urgent way to his family or genealogy, which by virtue of either their instability or their unwanted pressure act as surrogates for a more abstractly envisioned "past," and to this extent stimulate the writer's *desire* to find in the family a model for the social and political constructs still so much in question for a recently conceived nation. Whether that act takes the form of idealization or criticism, calm veneration or violent attack, what is at issue is the authority generated by dependence upon, or independence of, a genealogy; and it is precisely in the very personal terms of such a question that authorship may find its own power. Desire and authority, then, are yoked together, as are desire and authorship, though as Emerson's remarks remind us, experiments in authorial desire must risk the possibility that they too will either become repetitive commemorations in the name of an overthrown authority, or else find themselves at a loss before the very absence of that authority. Precisely because the two cannot be untangled, however, the genealogical conflict presumed in Freud's "family romance" acquires central importance as the paradoxical crisis around which the desires of authorship must turn.

That paradox finds its most precarious and rewarding configuration in the notion of the sacramental totem meal adumbrated by Freud. Since at the heart of the totemic celebration Freud finds the Oedipal conflict in condensed form, the festive observance, even while it celebrates a seizure of authority appropriate to the advance of the community, suppresses—or rather, represses—the violent and suspect incestuous desires that have generated that seizure. We will have occasion to examine more closely the contradictory impulses arising from the fact that, although the crime of parricide reenacted in the totem meal has an incestuous intent (whether the act is one of identification or usurpation), the murder ostensibly takes place in the name of democratizing the community and forestalling a dynasty built on incest; but it should be noted here that the crime issues at length in a festive repetition of the act which at once celebrates the community's ominous achievement and allays its own sense of guilt by paying homage to the fallen ancestor. As a covenant with the father, says Freud, the totem meal must thus balance "expressions of remorse and attempts at atonement" against "a remembrance of the triumph over the father," and consequently entertain the risk that "the dead father [will become] stronger than the living one had been," even to the extent that he is finally transfigured into a god from whom the community can claim descent.[3] In the totem meal, then, an act that was once a rebellious "experiment" has become a commemorative "sacrament," and because any account or reenactment of the crime must have a view toward both considerations, the authority which the present community has gained will be extremely ambiguous: the ritual remembrance of the crime unnervingly augments the slain father's power at the same time it celebrates the seizure of that power.

When the sacrificial observance is transposed into a domain of literary performance where authority is so closely linked with authorship, this tension, even though it is figurative, is consequently magnified. For if we take account of the etymological kinship between *author* and *augere* proposed by Edward Said (following Eric Partridge),[4] and say that an author's own authority derives from his roles as "begetter" or "father" and as "increaser" or "founder," then we must be prepared to hazard the eventuality that the kind of authority achieved by the act of writing will not only locate its own power in rebellion and seizure but also paradoxically augment the power of the ancestor whose downfall has become the subject of the sacrament of writing. Mockery and tribute will be fused in the craft of narrative, and the authority a writer's own performance implements will be sanctioned by violence at the same time it is hedged by his unconscious invocation and veneration of the ancestors whose place he has usurped. That veneration need not be unconscious or unintended, however, for in the most potent confrontations with the past, the measure of a writer's own success must lie exactly in his willingness to meet such a crisis. To the degree that he finds his own authority impeded and qualified by a requisite tribute to vanquished power, he may take the ratio between repudiation and commemoration, or destruction and augmentation, embodied in his public performance to be the juncture of a further crisis, one legislated by the conflicts that surround the gratification of anterior Oedipal desires and grant the self a more immediate authority. When taken as a communal model, the family must represent a source of both security and conflict; and the superimposition of these crises, the intimately personal and the decisively public, is perhaps analogous to the tension registered in Thoreau's observation in the *Week* that "inside the civilized man stand[s] the savage still in a place of honor,"[5] for the transition between private and public, like that between primitive and civilized, is often a clouded one in which repression must be poised against triumph and sacrifice against achievement.

To be sure, the record of this conflict takes different forms, and without rehearsing individual cases at length I would only point out that the notion of an American Eden is crucial to the readings I propose, particularly to the extent that the Edenic appears as a prelapsarian moment when, as Thoreau remarks in his journal, man could "simply wonder, without reference or inference," free from the dangerous "network of speculations" cast over post-Adamic America.[6] As a number of critics have noted, the "simple wonderment" advocated in many nineteenth-century conceptions of the Edenic not only took its initiative from the Rousseauvian longing for return to a "state of Nature," but also resembled an infantile fantasy that impinged precariously upon the erotic, and more particularly, upon the incestuous. Against the bad or wasted mother of England was set the virgin land of America,[7] the blank page of Nature on which could be written the story of a fresh settlement. Reflecting on this commonly noted difference, Emerson remarked in *English Traits* that in the "great sloven continent" of America "still sleeps and murmurs and hides the great mother, long since driven away from the trim hedge-rows and over-cultivated garden of England."[8] The femininity or maternity of Nature that had been a dominant metaphor among writings on America since its earliest discoverers took increased sanction from both the familial rhetoric of the Revolution and the changes in the social function of the family that followed. In response to the loosening of feudal family ties and the collapse of an aristocratic ideal of patriarchy that accompanied the expansion of the nation, family and work became more separate, and "the home," as Michael Paul Rogin points out, "became in Jacksonian America an isolated repository of virtue; mother was its symbol."[9] Paternal energies were directed toward the clearing of land and the founding of a nation "conceived" in liberty. But the settlement of America, even while it promised a beneficent, pastoral reunion with the state of Nature, also had to account for the more primitive and violent impulses that the dream of a "free" land promoted; and as often as not, the very methods employed to cultivate the continent—the plowing of fields, land speculation, the building of trading posts, railroads, or towns—were most responsible for undermining the dream they hoped to fulfill. Because the pastoral dream tallied with the nineteenth-century cult of sentimentality, the violence of its desires often reflected a paradoxical attitude toward both Nature and the family. The same fantasies that pushed the frontier ever farther kept society fragmented and the family sequestered, and just as the cultivation of the virgin land took the figurative form of masculine domination or even rape, so the sentimental ideal governing the family required feminine submission. Yet while "the sentimental family activated fears of domination by women," Rogin remarks, the "idealization of wife and mother also expressed hidden violence against her,"[10] and in this respect the attitudes toward the family and toward Nature were complimentary and upheld one another in paradoxical suspension.

Taking their metaphors from the family—a family whose centrality and inherent instability were endorsed by the fact that it was often taken to be a figure for equally unsettled social or political institutions—the writers engaged in documenting the settlement of "the great mother" thus had to balance sentiment and glorification against violence and domination. The link between the sentimental cult of family and the Edenic ideal in Nature made the yoking of the two inevitable as a powerful field for the work of the literary imagination, whether in practical or theoretical terms. Thoreau's joining of "reference" and "speculation" is not fortuitous in the least, then, for as he and other perceptive observers noticed, the literary craft took a hand in the settlement of America, and its fusion of the imaginative and the commercial was subject to the same social and political constraints as any other enterprise. For the very reason that cultivation and commercial speculation broke up the dream of the virtuous state of Nature, the writer was in jeopardy of the same irony as the pioneer or statesman: the dissolution of the Edenic was as much bound up with his craft as the proclamation of the Edenic had been, and his funneling of desires and impulses that belonged to the family into a narrative of Nature's conquest became an astute commentary on not only the complexities of the American dream but also his own psychological propensities and sense of career. If he made his own dreams those of a nation, he had also to accept the consequences of those dreams, however anxious or dangerous they might be. Within the construct of the "family romance" the disruption of the Edenic corresponds figuratively to the shattering of the narcissistic relationship between child and mother or their metaphoric equivalents: for example, the safe and innocent relationship between man and Nature of the nostalgic pastoral. The fact that any such moment can appear only as fantasy or projection, though, is what allows it to be held forth or "remembered" as a scene of harmony in demand of erotic repossession, a scene supported by social idealization of the maternal and one in which the entanglements of reference and speculation that Thoreau feared are not ostensibly at work. The American Eden is thus assumed not only to contain those mytho-historical connotations that have long been ascribed to it, but moreover to embody the rather explicit set of psychological forces so well distilled by Emily Dickinson:

Eden is that old-fashioned House
We dwell in every day
Without suspecting our abode
Until we drive away.

How fair on looking back, the Day
We sauntered from the Door—
Unconscious our returning,
But discover it no more.[11]

Dickinson's Edenic "house," however, like Poe's morbid abodes, is often transfigured into a haunted dwelling, and likewise the *home* sought out by Cooper, Thoreau, Hawthorne, and Melville is each in its own way startlingly *unheimlich*, "uncanny," in the broad sense described by Freud: "an uncanny experience occurs when infantile complexes which have been repressed are once more revived by some impression, or when primitive beliefs which have been surmounted seem once more to be confirmed."[12] Insofar as the *Heim* (home) Freud associates with the maternal ("the place where each of us lived once upon a time and in the beginning"[13]) represents an Edenic moment that has been buried or effaced, and the act of settling a wilderness produces a potent confrontation between savage impulse and inherited constraints, the conjunction of the infantile and the primitive is what lends the Freudian scenario a peculiar power for nineteenth-century American writers.

The balked nostalgia implicit in Dickinson's "unconscious return" not only turns the Edenic into an unsatisfied fantasy of pastoral compulsion but also provides a measure of the degree to which experiment and rebellion give way to, or find contained within themselves, sacrament and repetition, the uncanny recurrence of repressed desires. In borrowing Cooper's *Home as Found* for my own title, then, I am interested at once in assessing the play of experiment and sacrament that goes into the settling or "founding" of a home in an era when that very action is challenged by a hostile terrain or an inadequacy of social and political models, and in defining the dangerous transaction of desires inherent in the act of "finding" a home lost in memory and "settling" an ancestral account on that home's behalf. Because the web of speculation and reference consequent upon the disruption of that psychological home represents the anxious uncertainty of an illicit power acquired through transgression or usurpation, any attempt to balance the account with the past will find itself constantly in debt—a debt in whose payment repetition and sacrament ironically endorse a retrieval of the lapsed Edenic moment even as they threaten the rebellious intent of that retrieval. Whether the moment of crisis in which the American "fall" occurs is presented as the decay or destruction of a virtuous natural aristocracy that can only be rescued by incest (Cooper), the paradox-riddled *cultivation* of Nature (Thoreau), the sexual transgression against ancestral law (Hawthorne), or the nightmare of self-generation embodied in a bizarre incest fantasy (Melville), the recovery of *home* is shot through with eruptions of recollected danger that make any narrative, any "account," of the moment an extremely hazardous enterprise.

In the essays that follow I am taking Cooper, Thoreau, Hawthorne, and Melville to be "representative men" whose victimization at the hands of their own projects is a measure of personal commitment as well as a result of

the traumatic assumption of the public role of authorship. The tension between experiment and sacrament, if it begins in a moment of psychological
crisis whose familial roots lie partially exposed to remembrance, is nonetheless refracted into the elements of a larger drama, one in which the family is
not so much the "real" family as the constellation of forces generated
within a dramatic communal context. And although the model for the conflicts under examination is the sacrificial totem meal Freud finds so strikingly fused with the Oedipal situation, I want to offer two methodological
qualifications: first, that I do not wish to imply—indeed I wish strongly to
resist the conclusion—that the writers under consideration are being judged
neurotic; and second, for a related reason, that I take Freud the cultural
historian to be of more immediate interest, and perhaps of more lasting
significance, than Freud the clinician. Of course the two roles are not easily
separated, and it is precisely in their conjunction that Freud's most valuable
insights lie, a fact to which *Totem and Taboo,* whatever its shortcomings,
clearly attests. I hedge the issue in the hope of qualifying the charge of "psychoanalytic criticism" and the constraints that accompany such a charge.
Both the accusation and the constraints have a place and a force to be carefully judged; and readers or critics who pursue a psychoanalytic course
should be prepared in advance to admit into their dialogue the deflating
criticism offered by Wyndham Lewis when he remarked that Freud's psychology is one "appropriate to a highly communized patriarchal society in
which *the family* and its close relationship is an intense obsession, and the
obscene familiarities of a closely-packed communal sex-life a family joke, as
it were."[14] But having allowed Lewis's own joke, sincere and acute though it
is, we should note that it is exactly the obsession and familiarities he describes that make the family and personal lives of the American writers before us amenable to psychological analysis. Yet whether any of them is
"neurotic" is at once difficult, if not impossible, to ascertain and aside from
my purposes; or, more accurately, their neuroses, even if they were that, are
not necessarily signs of failure or deviance, but rather are the materials of
real creative powers, the very source of those fantasies in which authority
finds its own desires achieved.

Psychological criticism will have its advocates and detractors regardless
of the degree to which it purports to be either clinical or cultural, and in any
case the reader will have to judge for himself on this score. I accept the
Freudian model, with limitations and questions that will be raised along the
way, because the complicated relationship it introduces between the challenge and commemoration of authority—or between "experiment" and
"sacrament," as Emerson has it—helps define the scenes of crisis that com-
pel some of the best American literature of the nineteenth century. Whether

or not the family or the institutions of the nation were or should be those of a "highly communized patriarchal society" was precisely the question taken up by Cooper, Thoreau, Hawthorne, and Melville. Quite clearly, they reacted to the question differently, and the difference in their reactions is an index of both the answers that were possible and the peculiar situation each faced. But for all four the desire to revolt against the past was countered by the need to invoke or even repeat the past, in the same way that in Freud's totemic sacrifice the slaying of the "father" instills in the community both a triumphant freedom and a form of guilt that issues in a need to commemorate the slain ancestor. The paradox of this situation is crucial to the conflicts that at once produce and sustain the totemic observance and, moreover, to the Oedipal struggle which that observance so often seems to represent. And it is also the case that this "representation" is integral to the structure of the authorial sacrifice, for when the examples before us are makers of literature, those constraints which in the totemic drama require the participants to act in the place of the dead ancestor, as his *representatives,* are thrust upon the very craft of the author, bringing his own *representations* into a complex and intimate relationship with the authority that is being both disavowed and invoked. Thus, if Cooper, Thoreau, Hawthorne, and Melville are "representative men," it is not only because they pursue common themes and stand out among their generation as articulate analysts of a cultural problem, but also because their own acts of *representation* are at stake in their work. This entails the risk, as Emerson recognized, that they become victims of their own action and by involving themselves in a sacrifice of commemoration undermine the rewards which their own experimentation and rebellion have projected.

Richard Poirier has argued that "the strangeness of American fiction has less to do with the environment in which a novelist finds himself than with the environment he tries to create for his hero, usually his surrogate."[15] I want to endorse and extend this claim by adding that the questions of style and representation Poirier demonstrates to be so important to American authors are indeed critically bound up with the notion of fictional or figurative surrogacy, though not only because American writers have been compelled to create in stylistic extravagance "a world elsewhere," but also because their attempts at such experimental creation have been qualified by their acting as "representatives" in a drama—indeed, a *trauma*—in which filial anxiety prompts the writer's participation and challenges his power of independent self-representation. The penchant of American authors for casting fictional characters in the role of authorial surrogate belongs in part to the fear Melville voiced when he complained that "we are all sons, grandsons, or nephews, or great-nephews of those who go before us. No one is his own sire,"[16] and in part to the kind of genealogical pressure that induces in Hawthorne "a sort of home-feeling with the past" and compels him to take the shame of his ancestors upon himself "as their representative."[17] Writing a narrative about oneself may represent an extremity of Oedipal usurpation or identification, a bizarre act of self-fathering, at the same time that it pays homage to an ancestry that is in need of *representation,* either legally or artistically. The "father" in question is not necessarily the "real" father of Cooper, say, or Melville; rather, he is the symbolic father upon whose overthrow the totemic sacrament depends. In this sense the writings before us are more than personal confessions, even though confession is at the heart of the sacrament which the writings have become in their attempt to mediate the conflicting drives and desires behind them. If American authors have been particularly obsessed with *fathering* a tradition of their own, with becoming their "own sires," they have also had to answer to the doubts about the control of, and responsibility for, their craft voiced by Twain when he remarked of his own "methods" in "The Art of Authorship" that, since they seemed to have "begot themselves," he was "only their proprietor, not their father."[18] The struggle between proprietorship and fatherhood, like that between sacrament and experiment, is central to the crisis of representation, and hence of style, that allows American authors to find in their own fantasies those of a nation and to make of those fantasies a compelling and instructive literature.

The choice of "representative" men and women in such a study must, of course, run its own risk. If I do not take up Whitman, Dickinson, Emerson, and Poe at length, it is quite clearly not because they are any less concerned with similar crises of genealogical authority; rather, it is because Cooper, Thoreau, Hawthorne, and Melville, insofar as they provide us with sustained narratives which are to some extent autobiographical and in which the family and the career are very evidently at stake, offer a more dramatic opportunity for appreciating and detailing genealogical conflict. Thoreau will appear to some the odd man out, but I take his writings on the Indian, the West, and the cultivation of an American garden to be vital to the questions handled by all American writers up until the Civil War; and perhaps *because* the actual family is not an obvious issue for Thoreau, the intricate psychological problems of settling a home are more pointedly exposed. The record of his own attempts at settlement provides a theoretical framework for the issues of familial crisis taken up in nonetheless personal fashion by Cooper, Hawthorne, and Melville. And to the same extent that one can read their fiction as autobiography, Thoreau's work may well be a powerful essay in fiction.

Among likely American candidates, my list is short, even for a fertile thirty-year period from the 1820s to the 1850s; and one could make a very fine case for, say, Faulkner's *Absalom! Absalom!* and *Go Down Moses* within the thematic limitations proposed. Nor are the writers of so-called ''realistic'' or ''naturalistic'' narratives unavailable to psychological analysis; indeed, in certain respects their proximity to Freud makes them *more* available, for Freud is nothing if not a storyteller himself torn between naturalism and romanticism. We may take *Pierre* to be the climax of a phase, though, for after the Civil War at least, the fantasy of an American Eden was more demonstrably shattered and the family became more noticeably an institution under pressure from social, industrial, and commercial forces outside its control. Aside from the piercing irony of Twain's retrospective narratives, the major writers of the later nineteenth century neither look very often to internal genealogical conflicts for their most compelling examinations of the family, nor are they engrossed by the same myths as their precursors, except in haunting but fading echoes. The crisis of settlement gives way to very different crises, and the totemic myth of the beast as Father so potent in Cooper or Melville, for example, is at length analytically transfigured into a skeptical legend like that of Henry Adams's *Pteraspis:* ''To an American in search of a father, it mattered nothing whether the father breathed through lungs, or walked on fins, or on feet.'' James to the contrary, America's history had finally increased to the point where, as Adams remarks in a larger context, it became ''a tangled skein that one could take up at any point, and break when one had unravelled enough'' and still find that ''the *Pteraspis* grins horribly from the closed entrance.''[19] Though Darwin and industrialism alone did not prohibit the recurrence of questions faced by an earlier generation, they certainly changed the shape of the answers and crippled the illusions upon which the ancestors of the new realism had thrived. But this is not the place to take up the issue of Romance versus Realism so important in American literature. If the following essays are able to suggest the remarkable extent to which ''family romance'' infuses the careers and concerns of four writers often situated in the camp of Romance, we may hope to feel more at home with the problems of authority and genealogy that first helped to generate the issue.

Acknowledgments

Taking account of critical debts must be a misleading and sketchy action, and the author of any study may not be in the best position to know what he has learned from whom, whether he has gotten it right, or whether such citations will even be welcomed. In the hope of recording tribute not adequately reflected in footnotes, I want to call attention to some books from which I, among others, have learned very much and which in one way or another have given focus to my own study. This admittedly incomplete genealogy would have to include Henry Nash Smith, *Virgin Land: The American West as Symbol and Myth;* R. W. B. Lewis, *The American Adam: Innocence, Tragedy, and Tradition in the Nineteenth Century;* Leo Marx, *The Machine in the Garden: Technology and the Pastoral Ideal in America;* Edwin Fussell, *Frontier: American Literature and the American West;* Richard Slotkin, *Regeneration Through Violence: The Mythology of the American Frontier, 1600-1860;* Annette Kolodny, *The Lay of the Land: Metaphor as Experience and History in American Life and Letters;* Frederick Crews, *The Sins of the Fathers: Hawthorne's Psychological Themes;* and John T. Irwin, *Doubling and Incest/Repetition and Revenge: A Speculative Reading of Faulkner.* The extent to which their critical experiments have become sacraments we repeat and transform reflects the importance of their vision.

More immediately I must thank Laurence B. Holland and Avrom Fleishman for their initial and implementing direction of this study. Their incisive comments and corrections often rescued me when my own experimentation threatened to stray blindly and always kept the value of critically acceptable sacraments before me. I would also like to thank William Cain, Eric Cheyfitz, John Irwin, and Barry Weller for their sound advice on various portions of the manuscript. Last, but certainly not least, I should thank Betty Carroll for her expert help in preparing and typing the manuscript. Always first, and certainly most, I will thank those to whom the book is dedicated.

Home as Found

ONE

"The home of my childhood"

Incest
and Imitation
in Cooper's
Home as Found

It's far easier to call names than to shoot a buck on the spring...
—Cooper, *The Pioneers*

No man, unless he puts on the mask of fiction, can show his real
face or the will behind it. For this reason the only real biographies
are the novels, and every novel, if it is honest, will be the autobiography of the author and biography of the reader.
—Howells, *Years of My Youth*

While Cooper is deservedly praised for exploring that "area of
possibility,"[1] in the words of R.W.B. Lewis, represented by the American
frontier, no one would deny that his dramatizations can be both penetrating
and ludicrous on the same page, that the frontier can at times become an
area of impossibility populated by stick figures mouthing stylized handbook
creeds. In the case of the Leatherstocking Tales we quietly utter the word
"romance" and tend to forgive, if only to salvage Natty Bumppo as the totem (whether hero or scapegoat) of our literature. What to do with Cooper's
"Silk-Stocking Tales,"[2] as *Homeward Bound* and *Home as Found* have
been called, is another thing altogether. It is precisely the point of the second and third Effingham novels, *The Pioneers* being the first, that Natty
Bumppo has vanished over the western horizon and that the area of possibility has become a scene of both chaos and constriction. Moreover, Cooper's
staginess, always a crucial issue in his work, seems in *Home as Found* to have
slipped off the steep edge of pathos. What was once in *The Pioneers* a difficult tension between the natural virtue of Natty and the civic virtue of

Marmaduke Temple, has become an inflexible stand-off between the un-harnessed democracy of language and manners in Steadfast Dodge, Arista-bulus Bragg, and the general population of Templeton on one hand, and the inbred self-importance of the socially aristocratic Effinghams on the other.

David Noble has convincingly argued that in the long run Judge Tem-ple in *The Pioneers* is Cooper's truly intended archetypal hero and that the aim of the Leatherstocking series is finally to depict the collapse and passage of the nostalgic Adamic myth represented by Natty.[3] One must add to this that *Home as Found* portrays the consequent near failure of the Judge Tem-ple myth, the myth, that is, of the public figure whose leadership is resolute and just, both civically responsible and privately compassionate. What is at stake in the two books is the issue of authority in America, particularly the legal authority of the country's fledgling institutions, but by the same token the authority of the family. If we tentatively offer the premise, one to which most readers would consent, that Cooper is the "father" of American fic-tion, we will be in a better position to gauge the importance of *Home as Found,* not just among Cooper's works but among the best of nineteenth-century American documents as well. For if the question of paternal author-ity undergoes a striking change between *The Pioneers* and *Home as Found,* it is both a change that was acutely personal for Cooper and one that he turned into a compelling examination of the role of American literature as an instrument of social power.

The middle ground represented by Judge Temple (who was, of course, modeled on Cooper's father) has evaporated in *Home as Found.* Whatever is wooden in the Judge's character or harsh in his policies in *The Pioneers,* Cooper exaggerates, if in part unintentionally, in the later generations of Ef-finghams. As abstractions they show up quite well against the uncouth pup-pet of public opinion, editor Dodge, and the fauning, unmannered land agent Bragg; but in the flesh the Effinghams seem finally, as James Gross-man puts it, to be little more than "trained mechanisms of recoil from the vulgar."[4] While this is the case, however, it is still not exactly to the point. The rancorous pride that the family displays is a transparent substitute for Cooper's own, and the Effinghams thus occupy a somewhat privileged posi-tion among Cooper's fictional automata. *Home as Found* is not only a fierce social satire—one of the finest, despite disastrous sections, in American liter-ature—but also an absorbing exhibition and defense of Cooper's own psy-chological vagaries and social tastes, tastes which inform the most pressing questions posed by the settlement of America. In this respect, D. H. Law-rence's overblown observation that the "Effinghams are like men buried naked to the chin in ant-heaps, to be bitten into extinction by a myriad

ants'' which secrete ''the formic acid of democratic poisoning,''[5] is more indicative of the drastic situation Cooper portrays under the cover of a novel of
manners.

The strangulated self-esteem of the Effinghams is perhaps just as much
the object of Cooper's ridicule as the frenzied Templeton populace, though
in an intensely covert and sublimated fashion. What is generally brushed
aside as one more piece of rather obtrusive machinery—the disclosure of the
mysterious identity of Paul Effingham and his fairytale marriage to his
cousin Eve—is the very heart of the book, not only because the resolution of
the plot hinges upon it, but because aristocratic incest and inbreeding is the
last, and most extreme, bulwark against the chaos of mob rule which Cooper
found threatening himself and his country. I want to suggest too that his
treatment of incest is intimately tied to the peculiarly American question of
imitation in its relation to social and literary authority. Yet if incest and imitation are part of Cooper's defensive posture, that defense also bears the
marks of a repression that cannot be sustained but bursts into violent self-
parody.

I

While the degree to which *Home as Found* is autobiographical has
often been presented, it may be well to summarize the pertinent parallels.[6]
The Effinghams, like Cooper's own family who resided abroad from 1826 to
1833, return to find their homeland intoxicated by wildcat speculation and
an inflated faith in democratic ''go-aheadism;'' their ancestors' language
degenerating into a discordant medley of cant phrase and barbarous slang;
and their fondly remembered Templeton populated by ''birds of passage''
(165)[7] for whom '' 'always' means eighteen months, and...'time im-
memorial' is only since the last general crisis in the money market'' (212),
and who consider anything not nailed down to be public property. John Effingham characterizes the home Cooper found on his return when he tells
his own returning family that ''the whole country is in such a constant state
of mutation, that I can only liken it to the game of children, in which, as
one quits his corner another runs into it, and he that finds no corner to get
into, is the laughing-stock of the others. Fancy that dwelling [that is] the residence of one man from childhood to old age; let him then quit it for a year
or two, and on his return he would find another in possession, who would
treat him as an impertinent intruder, because he had been absent two
years'' (118). The trigger for Cooper's satire is the controversy over Three-
Mile Point, a picnic area on Lake Otsego which by law belongs to the Effinghams, but which in their absence the ''public'' has claimed as its own, upon

the authority of a universally acknowledged rumor that from "time im-memorial," and by right of the will of Edward Effingham's father, the Point has been owned by the public. Though the will specifically names the Ef-fingham family as heirs, Edward's publication of a warning against trespass-ing is greeted by a town assembly in which resolutions are passed condemn-ing the Effinghams as aristocratic snobs and denouncing their claim to ownership.

Cooper lifted the incident almost directly from his own life, and *Home as Found* is in some respects but the second installment of his vendetta with Cooperstown, the first being his letters that appeared in the *Freeman's Jour-nal* after the Point controversy, explaining the actual ownership and attack-ing the public. The two main differences between the real affair and the fic-tionalized version are not great but still worth remembering. While Cooper did defend his claim to the land in public print, Edward Effingham only reports the facts of the will to Bragg and counts on him to make them known to the populace, thus leaving himself open to even greater abuse on the grounds of his unwillingness to face the people. Cooper, moreover, did not in fact own the Point by himself; rather, Judge Cooper's will left the land in his son's trust, designating that it remain the mutual property of the Cooper family until 1850, at which time it would pass solely to the youngest descen-dant bearing the name of Cooper. While the distinction between ownership and guardianship does not in any way negate Cooper's own claim, it does grant that of Edward Effingham more force and eclipse what would have been a stickier question, given the rhetorical purpose of the novel.

Since his father's will bears directly on the central issues of *Home as Found,* it is worth examining one of Cooper's letters of defense in detail:

> In 1850, there will be descendants of Judge Cooper in the fifth generation. The family tie, even, is broken by time, and the connexion between these children would be getting to be remote. Intermarriages and females would interpose other names between that of the family of the testator and those of these descen-dants, and it is only in the direct line that feelings of the sort I have described are long continued. The testator would seem to have foreseen this, and that the traditions and feelings of other families might take the place of his own. He makes a remainder, therefore; and with what intention? To abandon the Point to the public? So far from this, he recalls it to his name and blood, bringing it as near himself, again, as circumstances will at all allow. He even bestows it on the *youngest* of his name, as if expressly to keep it as long as possible in his direct line. In short, he made one of these [sic] dispositions of that spot, that men are apt to make, who desire to associate themselves with their remote posterity...[8]

What is at stake here personally for Cooper is the intention and honor of his father; what he sees to be at stake publicly is whether or not a man's will shall be respected and his family and property safe from the rapacious democratic fever sweeping the nation. But Cooper's letter also reveals a protective, even obsessive, regard for the sacrosanct family *name,* as though insuring that the authority of Judge Cooper would prevail even from beyond the grave. More important, though, is the fact that it is Cooper's attention to the letter of his father's will which is responsible in *Home as Found* for the elaborate ruse by which Paul Powis becomes an Effingham, thus protecting the continuance of the patriarchal name.

The affair of Three-Mile Point does not dominate *Home as Found,* yet the issues it raises about the authority of the past in America, and the way in which it affects present and future settlement, pervade the book, either in recognizable displacements of Cooper's personal conflicts or in more general inquiries into American customs and manners. When, for example, Bragg upbraids Sir George Templemore over the fact that in England "industry and enterprise are constantly impeded by obstacles that grow out of its recollections" (23) and goes on to "rejoice in being a native of a country in which as few impediments as possible exist to onward impulses" (24), the satire on American progress at the expense of a usable past is hardly exceptional. After Bragg continues by adding that "the man who should resist an improvement in our part of the country, on account of his forefathers, would fare badly among his contemporaries" (24), Cooper's hand is beginning to show. But when Cooper plants a question about preference in trees, to which Bragg can reply, "the pleasantest tree I can remember was one of my own, out of which the sawyers made a thousand feet of clear stuff, to say nothing of middlings" (25), Cooper's muted rage is getting uncomfortably close to home. The figure of the tree not only embraces the overall desecration of the wilderness which American settlement entailed, but for Cooper it has a profoundly personal significance: one of the incidents that finally brought him to issue the trespassing warning for the Point was that, along with damage done to several cabins on the property, a certain tree, which, Cooper enigmatically reported, "had a *peculiar association connected with my father,*"[9] had been flagrantly cut down. Perhaps the psychic scar was not as strong for Cooper as the emblem of the severed tree might suggest, but his reticence on the manner of "association" may indicate more than a bashfulness over its frivolity. When Bragg goes on to say, "the house I was born in was pulled down shortly after my birth, as indeed has been its successor" (25), we have only to recall Henry James' remark in *The American Scene,* upon returning from abroad to find his birthplace demolished, that the effect "was of having been amputated of half of my history,"[10] to gauge the anxiety Cooper has funneled into a relatively innocuous piece of dialogue and the simple symbols of house and tree, symbols which, as we will see, recur in the book in more dramatic roles.

This is not to say that *Home as Found* has interest only as a case history; it has interest too as an historical case. The figure of the severed tree stands at a personal level for the repudiation of the past that seems to govern the country at a national level. On returning from Europe Cooper was confronted with what James early in the next century would designate "the monstrous form of Democracy"[11]—a society split between an idle aping of European manners on the one hand and a wholesale repudiation of the past on the other, between subservient mimicry and arrogant speculation and invention. Cooper's cutting picture of the New York exchange is a somewhat tamer forerunner of James's nightmare of commerce; and the mock "green turban" which a visit to Paris entitles Cooper's American "Hajji" to wear (5) performs a function much like that James would find in fashionable headdress at the Metropolitan Opera: "In worlds otherwise arranged . . . the occasion itself, with its character fully turned on, produces the tiara. In New York this symbol has, by an arduous extension of its virtue, to produce the occasion."[12] James's remark enunciates with economic precision the singular importance of symbol in the American tradition, the importance of the American writer's reliance upon a scarlet *A*, a whale, or a blade of grass (to name obvious instances) to create a metaphoric center around which previously undefined experiences can cluster; but more particularly it raises the question of form, of show and imitation, which Cooper met so bluntly at home and which in a country to a large degree cut loose from a history of institutionalized forms is the persistent question behind all manner of political and social desires for documentation and control. The New York society to which Cooper subjects the Effinghams is called by Eve Effingham "an excrescence of society; one of its forms; but by no means society itself" (7). What Eve has hit upon but not quite understood, is that it is precisely the case in America that although there is no standard of society, because available standards have been renounced, rival imitations still flourish, each hoping to become the new standard. Society in America is now a virtual wilderness of contending forms, none of which is yet secure in its authority.

For Cooper, the fact that Americans have no "social capital" and thus "possess no standard for opinion, manners, social maxims, or even language" (xxviii), is directly responsible for the cultural breach which has opened between him and his countrymen during his years abroad and which has permitted the name and authority of his father to be sullied by a mindless mob. The disrespect for private property, the wrenching daily changes in conventional language, and the blind financial fury of "Western fever" (22) are the most manifest signs of a general "mania of mutations" (130) infecting American life at every juncture. The country is bloated by false ostentation, by the strutting language of Bragg and Dodge, and by mad speculation. Cooper's vignette of New York finance is as penetrating a critique of commerce as sheer game as anything in Emerson or Dreiser, indicating the extent to which the founding of the new country, even in its presumably most concrete dimension, depends on arbitrary form and fantasy. John Effingham takes a somewhat cynical glee in showing Sir George how the increases in value have no foundation whatever, but are "all fancy," all based on the "imaginary estimate" of the auctioneer. In a country where the impediments of recollection have been abolished, speculation is unmoored, its ground lost (101–2).

A passage in *The American Democrat* makes clearer why the commercial binge is the disease and an affair like that of Three-Mile Point but a symptom: "Every transfer of title causes an indebtedness, and consequently a necessity for a circulating medium to represent it. The earth does not probably contain a sufficiency of the precious metals, at their present value, to represent all the debts of this one country.... The unrestrained issue of paper-money, with its attendant contractions, keeps the value of property unsettled, creates pressures and bankruptcies, and otherwise produces the instability that so peculiarly marks the condition of American trade."[13] Cooper's assessment points up a bothersome paradox in the America of 1838, one which is more elaborately articulated in Thoreau's economic puzzles—that the very act of settlement is what most keeps the affairs of the nation *un*settled, what insures that values will skyrocket and stagger unpredictably, that debt, whether to previous owners, to ancestors, or even to an abstractly conceived history, cannot be conveniently tallied up but rather may become exorbitantly multiplied or else be shunned altogether. Mad speculation and paper towns, a new country built flimsily on "a capital of hopes" (21), a populace that regards the past as an obstacle to progress and history an exercise in repudiation—these are the upshot of a spirit Cooper is barely able to admit as democratic. Cooper's remarks on transfer of title also, of course, corroborate his desire to maintain a family hold on the title to Three-Mile Point and help to justify the strange way he goes about it in the fictional setting; and as I will want to suggest shortly, the question of indebtedness and the transfer of representative currency is equally a part of the problem confronting American fiction and its authority.

Marvin Meyers has put more succinctly than Cooper the case for believing that "society organized by the middling standard was a precarious creation: its mobility could run wild, its naturalness give way of oafishness, its decency decay into an arrant philistinism, its subtly graded order sink into a false equality."[14] This nightmare has come true in Cooper's Templeton, crowding out not only the fading dream of Natty Bumppo but Cooper's dream of a cultural aristocracy as well. And though Cooper insisted that "aristocracy" was a political term, not a social one, and that the true democrat was *not* an aristocrat,[15] his Effinghams can hardly escape the stricture. Critics have labeled the family variously and located their beliefs at different distances from a line running between Jefferson and Jackson; but Marius Bewley probably comes nearest their hybrid nature when he designates them a "queer combination of Adams's aristocracy, Jefferson's liberal faith in the democratic possibilities of America, with more than a perceptible taint of Hamiltonian snobbishness and financial acuteness."[16] Yet their particular creeds, which are never very obvious in the book (Cooper saved his most dogmatic statements for *The American Democrat*), are not as important as their joint attempt at a stolid representation of correct form in the face of rampant social disintegration. The wall of manners and breeding thrown up by the Effinghams barely keeps out the surrounding chaos, and it does so only by cutting them off into a restricted world where purity comes to equal artificiality in the most disturbing fashion. In *Home as Found*, as in all his fiction, Cooper is concerned with the social clashes and the barriers that keep one group clean and cast out another. Natty Bumppo is only the most obvious example of the tragedy which the legitimization of society entails, for what continually haunts Cooper is that too far outside of society is lawlessness and anarchy, but too deep inside it is denial of freedom if not outright suffocation. Natty can survive only on the outside, beyond the fringes, while the Effinghams can only survive, though deadeningly, at the very core. Living at the center of Templeton, they are the fixed standard, while the surrounding riffraff are the human equivalent of that deceitful network of "opinion always vibrating around the centre of truth" (374). The Effinghams stand still, or attempt to, but America gyrates wildly about them.

II

Most glaringly deviant from the center of truth is the American language, which, like public opinion, rules by fiat and undergoes daily transformation. The Effinghams "live in an age when new dictionaries and vocabularies are necessary to understand each other's meaning" (380), when "a change of administration, the upsetting of a stage, or the death of a cart-horse. . . are all equally crisises, in the American vocabulary" (219). The fact that public opinion is "sapping the foundations of society, by undermining its virtue," Cooper contends in *The American Democrat,* is due primarily to disrespect for the English language, which in America suffers every possible outrage: "the common faults of the American language are an ambition of effect, a want of simplicity, and a turgid abuse of terms. . . . Many perversions of significations also exist, and a formality of speech, which. . . seriously weakens the power of language, by applying to ordinary ideas, words that are suited only to themes of gravity and dignity."[17] This is much the same complaint Tocqueville voiced after his visit to America. Unlike aristocracies, where language often rests in a comfortable state of repose, Tocqueville noted, democracies are marked by a penchant for altering their language even when there is no apparent need. Since persons in a democracy "are apt to entertain unsettled ideas...they require loose expressions to convey them. As they never know whether the idea they express today will be appropriate to the new position they may occupy tomorrow, they naturally acquire a liking for abstract terms. An abstract term is like a box with a false bottom; you may put in it what ideas you please, and take them out again without being observed."[18]

The false bottom of American language is closely akin to the imaginary foundation upon which the country's speculated growth is based; both substitute a fancied surface for an authorized structure and build on future risk rather than the grave of the past. So much did Cooper worship the grave and abhor the risk, that it would not be out of line to suggest that part of the woodenness of his own language and that of his characters is an over-compensation, conscious or not, for the abuse which surrounded him. But the fact remains that Cooper is met on the issue of language with the same paradox that, as John McWilliams points out, arises in his attitude toward the Constitution: "if the true republic is to be maintained, the Constitution cannot be changed, but unless change is permitted, the very meaning of American liberty is lost."[19] Cooper continually hangs himself on this paradox. He makes his characters speak as though from prepared social and political texts precisely to the degree that he feels none exists or that the ones which do are threatened with molestation if not outright destruction; and it would be a critical mistake blithely to divorce Cooper's seemingly stilted fictional maneuvers from his anxious concern with legal or documentary models of performance.

The deterioration of value in the American language is also at the heart of Cooper's obsession with names and naming in *Home as Found*. As we have seen, the desire of Cooper's father to perpetuate the yoke of his *name* and his *land* is what governs Cooper's novel from the start and what places the issue of authority so squarely before us. Cooper understood as well as Whitman that "all the greatness of any land, at any time, lies folded in its names," that "names are the turning point of who shall be master."[20] It is nearly facile to point out that naming has been particularly important in America, not only because the mixing of languages and customs has always produced some odd results, but more so because the task is in itself an exhilarating codification of discovery and revolution, of achieved originality.

Yet the unlegislated invention of names also has its drawbacks, for as George Stewart points out, it was the case after the Revolution that "every man was as good as another to give a name. Freedom ran wild, and under the banner of democracy arose an unfortunate repetition of the more popular names. . . . The demand for names outran the supply, and the result was both monotony and confusion."[21] The problem of giving names, of keeping and repeating them, and of making them respectable, is for Cooper intimately bound up with the backsliding of American values, the country's rampaging commercialism, and the decay of the English language. This combination of concerns is hardly new; Samuel Johnson raged at the influx of foreign words and phrases which accompanied the expansion of England's trade in the eighteenth century, and periodic manias for shoring up language against malign influences have appeared ever since language first was. Still, American language, stuffed with slang, technological jargon, and frontier braggadocio, is particularly threatening to the aristocratic social dream Cooper and his Effinghams represent, and even more threatening because it would presume to violate the sanctity of a time-honored name. The Effinghams find on their return that "even the names of a place undergo periodical mutations, as well as everything else" (117), and that those who have emigrated to the Middle States in the last thirty years "are not satisfied with permitting any family or thing to possess the name it originally enjoyed, if there exists the least opportunity to change it" (51).

Names have ceased to mean anything in America (or perhaps have not yet begun to mean anything) and function merely as badges of convenience. The nadir of linguistic democracy, one imagines, is reached in the scene in which Ordeal Bumgrum wants to borrow Mrs. Abbott's name for his mother's use on a trip to Utica. Mrs. Bumgrum complains that "folks don't treat her half as well when she is called Bumgrum as when she has another name," and she decides to try Mrs. Abbott's this time (232). This is ludicrous enough, especially in view of the fact that Mrs. Abbott spends the day sending her children around town to borrow one utensil or another as a pretext to cull the current gossip. In divesting Mrs. Abbott of her name, though, Cooper is setting up a specific effect, which is revealed soon after when Dodge and Mrs. Abbott debate Edward Effingham's ownership of Three-Mile Point:

> "But he does not own it," interrupted Mrs. Abbott. "Ever since I have known Templeton the public has owned it. The public, moreover, says it owns it, and what the public says in this happy country is law."
> "But, allowing that the public does not own—"
> "It does own it, Mr. Dodge," the nameless repeated positively. (237)

This is an irritatingly effective example of Cooper's contention in *The American Democrat* that " 'They say,' is the monarch of this country in a social sense."[22] It intimates as well that in Cooper's America legal rights threaten not to issue from an identifiable authority but to arise almost magically from a nameless repetition of rumor and hearsay as unfounded as the riskiest of speculations.

Just as ridiculous as Mrs. Abbott's borrowed name are the mock hybrid names of the Abbott children—Orlando Furioso, Bianca-Alzuma-Ann, Roger-Demitrius-Benjamin, and Rinaldo-Rinaldini-Timothy (227–31). Cooper's satire is not without its problems, though, for who, after all, is his hero?—a character who is first identified by the townspeople as a poet because he has *no* name at all (133), who admits in his marriage proposal to Eve that he bears "a name to which I have no legal title" (349), and who must, when all is told, carry around the ponderous appellation of Paul Blunt-Powis-Assheton-Effingham, the first surname being his disguise in *Homeward Bound,* the second his stepfather's, the third his true father's false married name, and the last his father's true name. Two things might be suggested here: either Cooper is a fool and does not recognize that his hero ends up in as absurd a plight as the Abbott children; or, since Paul's name ends up at Effingham, all must be naively well in Cooper's eyes. The usual procedure is to pronounce Cooper rather dim whenever a muddle crops up in his books; but it would seem that if in one sense Cooper is completely at a loss before this problem, he is in another keenly incisive. In effect, the Abbotts illustrate one side of the issue, as Cooper put it in *The American Democrat:* "some changes of the language are to be regretted, as they lead to false inferences, and society is always a loser by mistaking names for things"; and Paul Effingham illustrates the other: "nothing is. . . gained, while something is lost in simplicity and clearness by the substitution of new and imperfect terms, for the long established words of the language. In all cases in which the people of America have retained the *things* of their ancestors, they should not be ashamed to keep the *names.*"[23] The Abbotts violate decorum by an unlegislated and corrupt imitation of age-old European names, while they at the same time represent that grafting so integral to American naming. Paul Effingham fulfills his function as hero precisely by escaping a tangle of names and assuming the name with a history of respect; but he at the same time exists perilously close, if not to burlesque, at least to taboo, for his role is to imitate *exactly,* to bind and secure the sacred family name by incest. How important this problem is for Cooper ironically appears in the most tossed-off but unnerving speech in the book, that delivered by Eve when she is playfully miffed to discover that her almost husband is also her blood cousin: "You abridge me of my rights, in

denying me a change of name. . . . What a happy lot is mine! Spared even
the pain of parting with my old friends, at the great occurrence of my life,
and finding my married home the same as the home of my childhood!"
(396). This is *home as found* with a vengeance.[24]

The problem of naming, and the right to a name, is always a central one
for Cooper. Natty's reply in *The Deerslayer* when Hetty Hutter asks his
name is the famous example: "That's a question more easily asked than it is
answered." It is a question answered with difficulty because Natty, as he
proves, has "borne more names than some of the greatest chiefs in all
America."[25] But the difficulty lies too in the fact that for Natty and Cooper,
as for Thoreau, a name should reveal something essential about one's
character; the Indian's language appears to retain this metaphorical correlation between thing and name more closely than does the white man's language, so that Natty's name changes with his prowess as he in effect undergoes an extended initiation ritual reaching a preliminary climax at "Deerslayer." Employing the metaphor of the hunt as a sacrificial marriage,
Richard Slotkin has described well the totemistic process which Natty goes
through: "since the hunter becomes one with the prey at the moment of the
kill, he must prepare himself to be a fit and equal opponent for it. In the kill
itself he assumes the powers of the thing he has dominated and slain and
therefore takes his new name and his character from his victim. Each new
name thus reflects a newly revealed or achieved quality of character and is
closer to being the true or authentic name that will express the initiate's
whole and ultimate character."[26]

Since *The Deerslayer,* following *The Pathfinder,* was written three years
after *Home as Found* and can be read at least in part as a last desperate
recuperation of the Leatherstocking myth (especially since Natty gets
younger), the emphasis Cooper puts on Natty's names not only romanticizes
him as a mysterious patriarchal figure but also opens an enormous ironic rift
between the nostalgic wilderness and the settled Templeton. Natty's string
of names, gained by ordeal, is juxtaposed to the foolish hybrids of the Abbott children; but more significantly, it highlights the trap Cooper lays with
Paul's palimpsest of names. As Dodge replies when Mrs. Abbott complains
of Eve's having so many married names, "the Effinghams hold their heads
very much up. . . and the more names the better, perhaps for such people"
(416). The names wielded by the hero of *Home as Found* set him alongside
Natty in one respect, but deflate him as quickly in another. If we keep in
mind Slotkin's metaphor of the hunt as a symbolic marriage, Cooper's satire
is even more acute. Paul's preparation to be a fit partner in the marriage
means discovering his own identity, but discovering his own identity also

means discovering that his "prey" already bears his own name and vice versa. There is more to be said about the intricacies of the Effingham marriage ritual, but for now it is enough to emphasize the perplexing distance which arises between Natty's totemic name, earned by wilderness trial and consecrated in a symbolic marriage to nature, and Paul's final name, earned by the sublimated hunt for an identity which turns out to mimic that of his prey and consecrated in an incestuous marriage. Something drastic has occurred between Natty's chaste marriage to "nature" and the bond of Paul and Eve, who first by blood and now by sacred ceremony are one another's "natural heirs" (444).

Lewis Leary has maintained that "it would be monstrous to suspect that [Cooper] considered the possibility that a union between two young people, so closely kin and so much of a kind, might lead to sterility. In advance of his time or behind it, Cooper did not maneuver well within conscious subtleties."[27] What must be said about Leary's assessment is that, aside from its probable accuracy regarding Cooper's knowledge of physiology, it plainly skirts the issue. Cooper may be clumsy at times, but the question of incest in *Home as Found* cannot be dismissed so lightly. What is most remarkable in Leary's statement is that his own allusion to *Hamlet* ("A little more than kin, and less than kind!") does not lead him to ponder one of the book's strangest scenes and to reflect on the fact that both Shakespeare's play and Cooper's novel are concerned with revenge on behalf of a wronged father.[28] The relevance of the scene in question—actually it is not a scene at all, but a two-line epigraph—is not immediately evident. What is crucial is the acting off stage, that is, Cooper's own acting marginally unveiled in the few terse words from the soliloquy closing the second act of *Hamlet* which form the epigraph for chapter twenty-seven: "What's Hecuba to him, or he to Hecuba, / That he should weep for her?" It is true that one can spend hours negotiating Cooper's epigraphs without discernible headway, and on the face of it this is just such another throwaway; yet a consideration of the epigraph's context yields some rather striking forces at play. Referring to the player who has just delivered Aeneas's tale of Priam's slaughter, Hamlet's speech mocks his own balked motivation and speculates on how convincing the player would be if he only had Hamlet's reason for despair. Cooper's point is not so clear. The action of the chapter includes John Effingham's confession of his dark past—that he is Paul's father—and Paul's and Eve's congratulation of themselves on the fact that Paul has turned out to be an Effingham. There is little of Hecuba in this. But a glance at Hamlet's speech at greater length brings to the surface Cooper's fullest, if perhaps unconscious, intentions:

Is it not monstrous that this player here,
But in a fiction, in a dream of passion,
Could force his soul so to his own conceit
That from her working all his visage wanned,
Tears in his eyes, distraction in his aspect,
A broken voice, and his whole function suiting
With forms to his conceit? And all for nothing!
For Hecuba!
What's Hecuba to him, or he to Hecuba,
That he should weep for her? What would he do
Had he the motive and the cue for passion
That I have? He would drown the stage with tears
And cleave the general ear with horrid speech,
Make mad the guilty and appal the free,
Confound the ignorant, and amaze indeed
The very faculties of eyes and ears.
Yet I,
A dull and muddy-mettled rascal, peak
Like John-a-dreams, unpregnant of my cause,
And can say nothing. No, not for a king,
Upon whose property and most dear life
A damned defeat was made....
. . . .
Why, what an ass am I! This is most brave,
That I, the son of a dear father murdered,
Prompted to my revenge by heaven and hell,
Must like a whore unpack my heart with words
And fall a-cursing like a very drab...

Hamlet goes on, of course, to plan the entrapping play-within-the-play and closes with the lines, "The play's the thing / Wherein I'll catch the conscience of the king" (II, ii).[29]

The epigraph in context becomes a startling revelation of Cooper's own anxiety and self-consciousness about his novel and the actions it portrays, for it raises pointedly the spectres of incest and paternity which haunt *Home as Found;* and it is in the chapter in question that Eve, as we have seen, revels in finding her childhood and marriage homes to be the same. Behind Cooper's invocation of Hamlet's speech is the affair of Three-Mile Point and Cooper's sense of the violation done his father, so much so that he might well have amended Hamlet's lines to read, "The novel's the thing wherein I'll catch the conscience of the town." Of course he did catch the conscience of the town, was harshly rebuked in the Whig newspapers, counterattacked on his own with libel suits, and spent years in court with barely more gains than losses. What is important to note, though, is Cooper's recognition of his own Hamlet-like impotency and, moreover, of the degree to which his players, like *Hamlet*'s player, or even Hamlet himself, have become but strutting actors, figures geared up in a fiction, yet painfully far removed from his own "motive and cue for passion." And it is exactly at the point where the plot of Cooper's novel, with the unraveling of Paul's identity, has become most stupifying and nakedly contrived, that he calls attention to it as an elaborate ruse, a tale which in its preposterousness is nearly like the harangue of Aeneas spoken by the player.

Cooper's stark plunge into incest as a means of saving the honor of Paul and Eve's marriage is not strictly necessary; any honorable past would have done for Paul. Turning him into an Effingham is Cooper's desperate ploy, conscious or not, for guarding, even in fiction, his father's desire to perpetuate the bond between his name and his property. More than a mere trick of plot on Cooper's part, as may be the case when Oliver Edwards turns out to be an Effingham in *The Pioneers,* the discovery of Paul's identity in *Home as Found* is a last-ditch effort at *founding* a true and lasting *home* that will withstand the turmoil of mob democracy. That Cooper had *Hamlet* on the brain and applied its lesson not only to his own situation but also to the country at large, is also evident in a somewhat veiled allusion to the play in *The American Democrat*: "power always has most to apprehend from its own illusions. . . . in a democracy, the delusion that would elsewhere be poured into the ears of the prince, is poured into those of the people."[30] The delusion—that is, the lies that Claudius and Gertrude pour into Hamlet's ears, just as poison has been poured into the ear of Hamlet's father—is in America generated by demagogues who, according to Cooper, have the people to deceive rather than a suspicious prince. Yet given the affair of Three-Mile Point and given too Cooper's seeming identification with Hamlet in *Home as Found,* the passage takes on a grimly personal meaning. If Cooper has drawn a partial analogue between *Hamlet* and the situation of Templeton-Cooperstown, though, the issue of incest, which bothers Hamlet more than the murder, has veered off on an irksome course, for Cooper has placed it squarely in the middle of his dramatic resolution of the conflict and awarded it to his hero and heroine like a grand prize.

But as I have suggested, the incestuous marriage is a last defense on Cooper's part, a skewed protection against the chaos without. In this respect, Freud's theory that the idea of a democratic social contract and the taboo of incest arose simultaneously is of particular interest here. According to Freud,[31] a group of sons driven out of the family of the primal horde band together and overcome the father; cannibalize him to achieve identification and take on his powers; form a social contract whereby each renounces his desire of gaining the father's privileged position of authority and thus possessing his mother or sister; and hence agree to a taboo of incest. Granted first that Freud's primal horde is a small group, not a mass of men, and that one would hardly point to the America of 1838 as a primitive society in any exact sense, Freud's theory, precisely because it works to collapse the distinction between primitive and civilized, animates the structure of power in *Home as Found* as well as the foundation of America itself. The Templeton populace stand arrogantly for equality and for the right to rebuke authority, in this case that represented by the Effinghams' legal ownership of Three-Mile Point, and their seizure and use of the Point is in effect a symbolic overthrow and cannibalizing of Edward Effingham's (or Cooper's) father, just as the cutting down of the tree amounts, in Cooper's eyes, to a figurative emasculation of the father. Moreover, their objection to the Effingham marriage corresponds to Freud's belief that the disavowal of incestuous desires initially marks a detachment from parental authority that insures the opposition between generations and thus promotes the "progress" of civilization. In order to "defend itself against the danger that the interests which it needs for the establishment of higher social units may be swallowed by the family," says Freud, the democratic social community establishes a taboo against incest; the danger of violating the taboo "lies in the risk of imitation, which would quickly lead to the dissolution of the community. If the violation were not avenged by the other members they would become aware that they wanted to act in the same way as the transgressor."[32]

Yet the opposition between the community and the transgressor is no simple one, and the equilibrium of the democratic community has at best a short life, for the power of the father, far from being obliterated by his murder, is in fact transfigured and augmented through the community's guilt over its complicity in the deed. As a result, a totem meal is instituted which represents the cannibalization and serves at once as a remembrance of the triumph over the father and as a covenant that allays the sense of guilt; in the repetition of the commemorative meal the community's identification with the slain father eventually is reenforced to the point that he is elevated into a god from whom descent can be claimed. I want to suggest, then, that Cooper and the Effinghams, in their attempt to subvert an overthrow they find illicit, represent that stage in the community's development at which the exhilaration of democratic equality will give way to a ritual veneration of the founding fathers of the country, whether Washington and Judge Cooper or Natty Bumppo. And if it is argued that Natty stands for regression to a primitive condition, what must be noted is that the totemic process by which he acquires his power and status as a patriarchal figure is not entirely different from that totemization by which the Effinghams themselves repeat and commemorate the name of their father. In this respect, there is a complicated tension in Freud's admonition that the risk in violating the incest taboo lies in an "imitation" that would dissolve the democratic community; for though this is initially true, it is precisely the case that in the long run the very coherence of the community, once it has reinstated the slain father as an ancestral god, depends upon a repeated commemoration in which the father's power is guaranteed by a form of imitation that merges with the totem meal but necessarily goes against the prohibition of incest. The paradox of Cooper's position thus lies in the fact that he and the Effinghams make the family ancestor a community god (whether the community will or not), and in so doing justify the violation of taboo as a means of reasserting the power of the father by imitation. While the self-enclosed perpetuation of the family may in one sense swallow up the power necessary to "the establishment of higher social units," it insures as well that the covenant with the ancestral father will be maintained and his power increased in the interest of the establishment of that tradition equally necessary to guarantee the advance of the community and the maintenance of democratic rights. The repudiation of incestuous desires, rather than marking a break between a primitive (infantile) condition and a more advanced (adult) society, is no sure one at all, but instead undergoes an inversion in the interests of the community and under the auspices of the name of the father. Perhaps, then, the distance between Natty and the Effinghams is not as great as it might seem. We must postpone this question, though, and look first at one of the book's most compelling domestic actions.

III

The weight Cooper places on the family bond could not be clearer than it is in the proposal scene of chapters 22 and 23, where a bizarre ritual is played out to secure the marriage. During the waning hours of the Fourth of July celebration, the "Fun of Fire," Eve and Paul walk leisurely through the mazelike, carefully landscaped (though unfinished) garden grounds surrounding the Effingham "Wigwam." After several interruptions and his own hopelessly stylized stammering, Paul gets out what amounts to a proposal, which Eve of course accepts. Elated, Paul continues, "But your father?"—at which point Edward Effingham emerges from the shrubbery, where he has been listening to their conversation, and announces he "is here to confirm what his daughter has just declared" (350). When Edward later refers to the marriage as a "contract" and a "treaty" of which he was the "negotiator" (383), we are hardly surprised, so candidly, even stiltedly, ritualized has the marriage become, the father handling the daughter like property or the stake in a game.

Again, we may be tempted to dismiss the scene as one more bit of heavy-handed staging on Cooper's part. But the *staging* of the scene is very much to the point. The Effingham grounds stand in the middle of Templeton, a weird labyrinth in which the family entourage promenade in two's and three's, crisscrossing each others' paths and watching or listening to one another from behind the bushes, almost in self-mockery of their abhorrence of the gossip and lack of secrecy ruling Templeton. Outside, the celebration of independence sputters to an end, providing a pretty backdrop for the party—except for a stray rocket here or there, like the one that whizzes past at the very moment Paul begins to churn out flowery praise of Eve, sublimating the patriotic rhetoric of his spoken courtship. Yet it is no more an accident that Cooper's proposal scene is enacted on the Fourth of July than it is that Thoreau takes up his abode on that day; both play out the meaning of independence by making desperate statements to their audiences (and Thoreau would no doubt have endorsed Cooper's declaration in *The American Democrat* that "he is the purest democrat who best maintains his rights, and no rights can be dearer to a man of cultivation, than exemptions from unseasonable invasions on his time, by the coarse-minded and ignorant"[33]). But if Thoreau's pure democrat would seek to break out of the constricted circle of Concord, Cooper's would draw the circle, in the face of the Templeton populace, ever more snugly about himself.

Cooper's date is no accident, and as he remarks at the opening of the scene, "we shall not say it was an accident that brought Paul and Eve side by side" in the imperfect garden (319); but it is "no accident" in more than the obvious sense that Paul and Eve are attracted to one another and paired off by Cooper. One thing at stake for Cooper throughout the novel is whether it is aristocracy or democracy which is based on *accident*. But since Eve maintains exactly contrary opinions within the space of five pages—on the one hand holding that "the instant you do away with the claims of hereditary power, the door is opened to a new chapter of accidents" (30), and on the other that "one has more reason to be proud of ancestors who have been chosen to fill responsible positions, than of ancestors who have filled them through the accidents, *heureux ou malheureux,* of birth" (35)— the question only becomes more dense. Cooper, moreover, has Mrs. Bloomfield remark to Sir George at one point that it is "accident that has liberated us [Americans] from trammels that still fetter you [English]" (56); but he allows John Effingham to say at another that the "American system... has been deliberately framed," while the institutions of other countries "are the results of time and accidents" (313).

What can sensibly be said in view of Cooper's confusion, deliberate or otherwise, is not clear; but the inordinate concern expressed for Paul's legitimacy, for clearing the name of his mother, and not least for discovering his paternity, reveals Cooper's own dread of the possibility that Paul himself is an "accident," that is, a bastard. The issue is purity of stock, whether in the family or in the institutions of government; the fear of misrule by public opinion is translated into fear of illegitimacy in the family. That the equation of family and government continued to obsess Cooper is evident even in the sketch of New York he was writing at the time of his death in 1851: "marriage, contracted by any ceremony whatever, is held to be a contract for life. The same is true of governments: in their nature they are intended to be indissoluble."[34] Both the family and the nation are threatened by the common tyranny of the public; and the incest of the Effinghams is thus in the end as much a political as a social statement. Keeping the Constitution pure and respecting the letter of the law are actions tantamount to rigorously guarding the family structure, and it is for this reason that the ritual of the marriage proposal is enacted on the Fourth of July.

But Cooper's political stance reaches an obvious impasse. Since he finds any form of government to be in some way an artificial harness on "natural" justice and virtue (as he remarks throughout *The American Democrat* and as the case of Natty Bumppo makes clear), Cooper's ideal government, as McWilliams points out, finally "contracts toward nonexistence."[35] Yet in the face of an intoxicated populace, a narrowly restricted government leads to anarchy and becomes impotent itself. This is the crude irony of the incestuous Effinghams—that their effort at protection by virtual self-enclosure and inbreeding threatens to evaporate or issue in deformity: the most rigidly ordered plan may produce the grimmest of "accidents" or completely fail to perpetuate itself. It would be straining reason to suggest that Cooper set out to accomplish an incestuous destruction of the Effingham line like that which befalls the Glendinnings in *Pierre,* that he had in mind a sort of familial suicide, a deliberate last hurrah in the midst of what was found to be a crumbling aristocratic fortress. But the effect—given Cooper's highly self-conscious staging of the marriage chapters and especially in light of the ridiculously blatant fairy-tale ending, where Nanny pronounces the marriage a fulfillment of a dream she had four years prior in which Eve marries a prince and all live happily ever after (446–47)—is both comic and grotesque.

Still more intriguing, though, is the fact that the prince Nanny has Eve married to is a "Denmarker." Has Eve married Hamlet? But Cooper is Hamlet. Has she, then, married Cooper? Before the reader objects to this seemingly rash invention, it will be well to remember that Cooper was often accused of rendering his elder sister Hannah, who was killed in a fall from a

horse in 1800, in the character of Elizabeth Temple in *The Pioneers.*
Though Cooper's own footnote to the scene in which Elizabeth nearly falls
from her horse ambiguously confirms the identification and even describes
the dead sister as a "second mother,"[36] he was thrown into an uncomfort-
able position after the publication of *Home as Found.* Since the Whig
newspapers crucified Cooper for presuming to draw his own portrait in the
character of the just and noble Edward Effingham, Cooper (even though the
portrait *is* self-flattering) needed a convincing rebuttal. The tack he chose is
hardly convincing, but it explodes his motives and desires before our eyes:
"I have an interest in clearing up this matter, since, if Elizabeth was Miss
[Hannah] Cooper, and I am Edward Effingham, the latter being distinctly
stated to be descended from the former, I am left in the awkward predicament of being the son, or grandson, of my own sister!"[37] Cooper's additional disclaimer that "the image [Hannah] has left on my mind is anything
but that which would create a desire to disturb her ashes to form a heroine of
a novel. A lapse of forty years has not removed the pain with which I allude
to this subject at all,"[38] is certainly more moving, but no more convincing; if
anything, Cooper's inability to come to terms after forty years with the loss
of his motherly sister is in itself enough to require us to plumb more deeply
the Effingham dynasty and particularly the union of Paul and Eve. And
since Cooper's father is undeniably represented by the testator of the Effingham will, it is not farfetched to suppose that Cooper displaced his own
devotion to his sister to the equally dangerous and fantastic affair of the two
cousins. That is as close to a representation of incest as Cooper could
reasonably come; it is left only for Mrs. Abbott to exclaim that "in a country
of laws" this kind of union—whether between Eve and John, whom she first
thinks are to be married, or, as it turns out, between Eve and Paul—ought
not to be permitted (234, 413). Cooper permits it, but his raising it as a legal
issue only accentuates his alertness to its full implications, whether cultural
or autobiographical. It is of course the final irony, though, that those who
invoke the illegality of the violation of taboo are otherwise the ones most unlikely to respect the letter of the law; and one might almost read Mrs. Abbott as Cooper's *alter ego,* as the corrective voice lurking behind his most
staunchly pronounced convictions of social right.

The garden scene, then, is a kind of spectacle, a ritual action. It takes its
place in the long line of representations of the garden which pervade American writing from the Puritans to the present. If Paul is not named Adam, it
is only because Eve's name carries enough force by itself. Yet there are
things rank and gross in the nature of this garden. It is still a type of the enclosed garden—almost perversely so an echo of that literary favorite in *Song
of Songs:* "A garden inclosed is my sister, my spouse: a spring shut up, a

fountaine sealed.''[39] But Cooper's aristocratic settlers are no longer exactly in a wilderness, and they must protect themselves not from satanic Indians but from their own mad countrymen. The risk they run, however, is of a suffocating inbreeding. In this respect, Cooper's American garden is perhaps most like the nightmarish Eden Hawthorne offers in "Rappaccini's Daughter," father and daughter conspiring to entrap the new Adam in a poisonous family web. To be sure, Cooper is hardly this blunt, but the implications of his family romance are no less startling.

In his study of Cooper's use of landscape, Blake Nevius has remarked how intensely Cooper anticipates Hawthorne's need, "for the purposes of psychological drama, to exploit the possibilities of the close circumscription of space."[40] The limitation of space may reach beyond the obvious clashes entailed by settlement to a more basic trauma acted out in the imposition of civilization on the wilderness. Cooper's use of the Glenn's Falls cavern in *The Last of the Mohicans,* which Annette Kolodny has analyzed as a womb-like enclosure whose protection is shattered by the futile explosion of Duncan Heyward's gun, comes immediately to mind.[41] The Effingham garden, a tilled and cultivated protective fortress of domesticity, performs a similar function. Cooper's vision of the American Eve in *Home as Found* still reflects the more optimistic attitude he entertained about his country when he wrote in the 1828 *Notions of the Americans* that America is a virtual "Paradise of woman," a place where she fulfills "the very station for which she was designed by nature. . . . Retired within the sacred precincts of her own abode, she is preserved from the destroying taint of excessive intercourse with the world. . . . She must be sought in the haunts of her domestic privacy, and not amid the wranglings, deceptions, and heart-burnings of keen and sordid traffic."[42] As clearly as Natty's lush and primitive wilderness, the virgin territory defiled by settlement, the Effingham garden stands for a nostalgic protection and a sentimental view of possession, not least because it contains an idealized version of the domestic partner which Adamic Natty could never allow himself to have.

Eve is Cooper's most poignant, if sometimes unbearable, voice of an aristocratic mixture of refinement and nostalgia—indeed, Nevius suggestively goes as far as to call her "Cooper in petticoats"[43]—and it is difficult not to sense on Cooper's part the same brotherly attachment for her that he projected toward Elizabeth Temple. She often speaks directly for him, even when telling John she hopes he has not heavily renovated the interior of the family home, since "nothing is more pleasant than the *cattism* of seeing objects that you remember in childhood. Pleasant I mean to those whom the mania of mutations has not affected" (130). Cooper's unbelievable neologism here is, one is tempted to say, unfortunate evidence of his ability to mutilate an important statement by outrageous ineptness. Or is it? *"Cattism"* harks back to the crucial scene in which Bragg, as we saw, praises the destruction of his house of birth and the sawing down of his tree; only a cat, Bragg had said, could "love a locality rather than its own interests" (25). No one would deny that Eve's use of *cattism* is a little thickheaded, and it is at moments like this in the book that one starts to agree with George Dekker that Eve is "easily the most loathsome of Cooper's heroines" and "reflect with grim irony that it was for this that the Indians were dispossessed of their lands and Natty Bumppo driven west."[44] Yet the word *cattism* is so wholly ridiculous that Cooper's parodic petticoats surely have begun to show. While Cooper's coinage yokes Eve in a patently sentimental way to his image of the unviolated home he should have found upon returning from Europe, it is no mistake that the scene is linked to what we have identified as Bragg's denial of paternal authority. Eve does speak for Cooper, but in a way he must have recognized as fantastic—literally so, since she at some level fulfills his fantasies of (re)union with his sister. *Cattism* is innocent enough on Eve's part, but not on Cooper's, so clearly is he both paying homage to and ridiculing his own melancholy.

Perhaps the most notable thing about Eve's role in the displacement of Natty, though, is that, however they seem to stand opposed, Eve belongs as well, in some touching corner of Cooper's psyche, to an irretrievable past which is half childhood, half mythology. Like Melville's Pierre, Cooper was haunted by the fact that "a sister had been omitted from the text"[45]; his recourse was to reinsert her at the center of a quirkily personal myth of the American paradise. The mazelike garden which encloses the Effinghams and structures the marriage pact of the next heirs, enacts geographically the circumscription that is occurring genealogically. Order and artifice are opposed to the surrounding moral chaos of Templeton, but the artifice is so severe as to be stunted by its own self-defeating imitation.

IV

Yet *Home as Found* is concerned precisely with the problem of imitation and concomitantly with the disappearance of the American garden, or at least its dream as represented by Natty Bumppo. Old Leatherstocking was on his way out in *The Pioneers;* in *Home as Found* he has become a virtual myth, the land on which his hut stood a spot to be pointed out during a tour of the countryside and his voice at best a mocking echo. Along with Washington he is one of the vanished fathers (200) who have taken with them the possibility of settlement based on natural virtue. The inland journey which the Effinghams make on their return to Templeton illustrates how different the topography of the American dream now is. The voyage up the Hudson reveals only one imitation Grecian temple after another; while the vulgar architecture of New York is bad enough, the farther inland the party proceeds, the more they find "imitation taking the place of instruction" (117). What distresses the Effinghams about their country, and what presumably distressed Cooper (though none of them seems able to maintain opinions which do not at some point contradict one another), is on the one hand the Americans' careless disregard of European cultivation, but on the other their servile imitation of its most superficial aspects. The journey to Templeton and the return home to the Effingham "Wigwam," ensconced in the middle of town, leads no longer to the wilderness garden of nature's paradise but to the very center of corrupt civilization; and the family drama of the Effinghams produces the sharp irony that they are themselves located geographically and maritally at the heart of the imitation they detest in their countrymen.

Perry Miller has claimed that the nineteenth-century American "appeal to Romantic Nature . . . served not so much for individual or artistic salvation as for an assuaging of national anxiety. The sublimity of our national backdrop . . . relieved us of having to apologize for a deficiency of picturesque ruins and hoary legends" and guaranteed that the country would "never be contaminated by artificiality."[46] While this applies accurately to a good deal of Cooper's work in landscape, it does not jibe with his feelings in *Home as Found*. Though Eve judges favorably the scenic bluffs along the Hudson, her standards are continually European (114–15); and her final pronouncement on Lake Otsego during the initial view from Mount Vision is as full of panting for antiquities as anything in James's *Hawthorne*: "'Fancy the shores of this lake lined with villas,' said Eve, 'church-towers raising their dark heads among these hills; each mountain crowned with a castle or a crumbling ruin, and all the other accessories of an old state of society, and what would then be the charms of the view!'" (136). Yet this view from the Vision, to which John Effingham cunningly leads the party on their way home, is as deliberately staged as the garden scene. When Cooper announces—after what at first seems a "void" becomes "a *coup d'oeil* that was almost Swiss in character and beauty"—that the "whole artifice of the surprise was exposed," the word "artifice" rings with a calculated irony (125). Cooper's chance to display the wild thrills of American landscape falters before both a changed terrain and the strictures of taste he has gained in the years abroad.

Cultivation in both senses has now forced the view to resemble "the scenery of a vast park or a royal pleasure-ground," teeming with "the fruits of human labor" and such "signs of life" as the network of roads which reproduces on a grand scale the mazed garden of the Wigwam. Templeton is now a "sober country town" which "offers a fair specimen of the more regular advancement of the whole nation in its progress towards civilization;" it is both "beautiful and map-like," crisscrossed by about a dozen streets (125–27). The houses of Templeton are predominantly the same as those the Effinghams have seen all along the river and which John says are "whited sepulchres" on the outside and wasted by "deformity within" (119); but the degree to which this in the long run applies to the Wigwam and the Effinghams is uncanny, for at the center of the family home—an odd hybrid of the "composite order" (13) which owes "its existence to the combined knowledge and taste, in the remoter ages of the region, of Mr. Richard Jones and Mr. Hiram Doolittle" (in *The Pioneers*) and the recent improvements of John Effingham (128)—is the sternest of deformity. It is Cooper's most interesting, if unconscious, ploy to set up a leveling drift toward the "center" as a gauge of America's democratic mediocrity and then provide a virtual *trompe-l'oeil* landscape successively turning inward through a web of country roads, village streets, and garden paths, and settling to a stagnant center in the Effinghams' own cage of incest, the most artificially ordered kind of crisscrossing possible.

Cooper's houses are almost always of symbolic importance, and the Effingham edifice is a particularly complex example of the anxiety infusing that symbolism. What is noteworthy about the "Wigwam" (which since it was a nickname of Tammany Hall,[47] not only stands as a pointed reminder of Natty Bumppo's displacement but also reverberates with the irony of its own corruption within) is that while the family takes comfort in the fact that it is only a Gothic "abortion" and not a Grecian or Roman one, as are most American dwellings (129), and is predictably astonished to find that Bragg could expect public distaste for the Wigwam might prevail over private right (14), the house is quite nearly a burlesque of what it purports to represent, not least because it is more or less a copy of Cooper's own house. Unlike the current gaudy fashion in American houses, John's revised Wigwam, a "nondescript-original" (172), has "not a column about it, whether Grecian, Roman, or Egyptian; no Venetian blinds, no veranda or piazza; no outside paint, no gay blending of colors" (151). But the interior has not been much changed. In *The Pioneers,* the particular objects of interest are a series of blacked plaster busts from Paris—a Homer, a Shakespeare, a Franklin, a Washington, an urn of Dido's ashes, and what might be a Julius Caesar or a Dr. Faustus—and a morbid wallpaper that represents Britannia weeping over Wolfe's tomb, but which has been put up so ineptly that in a number of panels the hero's right arm is clumsily amputated.[48] In *Home as Found* a. Gothic wallpaper has alleviated Wolfe's predicament, and the row of busts, which have died natural deaths or fallen victim to the housekeeper's cleaning, has been replaced by a new group of effigies purchased in New York. Washington and Franklin are now noticeably missing from a group comprised of Shakespeare, Milton, Dryden, Caesar, and Locke, around which "dust and neglect were already throwing...the tint of antiquity" (152). Like so many of the seemingly symbolic constructs in *Home as Found,* the collection of venerable heads teeters on the verge of the ridiculous without quite committing itself. One can easily enough imagine Cooper's admiration for the names in question, yet mutely lodged in an American home barely past the second stage of settlement, the figures rapidly approach the dimensions of travesty.

But absurd as the concoction of surrogate busts may seem, Cooper has taken what in *The Pioneers* is merely ostentatious and a little pathetic, and, by the very fact of requiring a new set of substitutions, dramatized symbolically the most stirring motives at work in *Home as Found.* If, as Cooper asserts, "taste, whether in the arts, literature, or anything else, is a natural impulse, like love" (79), the Wigwam's interior is as problematic as the match between Eve and Paul. The busts, like Cooper's insidiously placed epigraph from Hamlet's soliloquy, sharpen the focus on the book's artificiality to the point of self-parody, turning it into a virtual aping of Cooper's original intention, which was to vindicate his legal rights and social beliefs through the surrogate Effinghams. In a way that for Cooper must have been at once completely sincere yet pierced with irony, the busts offer a complex, even contradictory, array of Anglo-Roman cultural and political authority, the very standards America does not yet meet and cannot yet offer. Provincialism, Cooper keeps reasserting, is America's predominant fault—a combination of "narrow prejudices," the "disposition to set up mediocrity as perfection," and "an ignorance that unavoidably arises from a want of models" (375). Yet when Cooper's models are tawdry English busts bought in a New York shop and arranged in a house-turned-museum, the effective authority is at once asserted and mocked, and like Hamlet, Cooper is left at best in the midst of an anxious paradox.

According to John Effingham, the present architectural maladies in American are due to the tendency "to consult the books too rigidly, and to trust too little to invention" (113); Paul complains to Eve (during their garden courtship, ironically enough) that "the example of the rest of the world is before our own wealthy, and, *faute d'imagination,* they imitate because they cannot invent" (335); and John explains to Sir George the strange sophistication of the provincial guests at Mrs. Jarvis's party by the fact that "Americans are an imitative people, of necessity, and they are apt at this part of imitation [simplicity] in particular" (50). But the line Cooper is

walking is precarious indeed, for gross originality in manner and enterprise—an originality founded on the crowd's naive belief that a revolutionary repudiation of the past is not itself mimetic—proves his deadly foe in the
book. It is this side of Cooper's Jekyll-and-Hyde doctrine that gets voiced
when Mrs. Bloomfield remarks to Eve that "one must think a little originally, let it be ever so falsely, in order to get up a fashion" (54), or when Eve
herself rebukes John for the sins of his architectural hybrid by saying that
"nothing that is out of rule ought to strike one in a country where imitation
governs in all things immaterial, and originality unsettles all things sacred
and dear" (149).

But what Eve holds sacred and dear is represented by a row of tacky
busts, near shams of authority which, if they are not as uncanny as those
which stock Hawthorne's "Hall of Fantasy," nonetheless provide an ironic
commentary on the incestuous trap of imitation Cooper's home has become
in attempting to mime the interior of the first Wigwam and the days of
Judge Cooper. That the tribute Cooper pays by means of the busts is both
honest and parodic is a perfect index of his own ambivalence about the question of imitation. He is at once violently startled by the disrespect for authority revealed in the affair of Three-Mile Point, for example, yet irritatingly aware that within the unruly Templeton mob there stands the right,
the one America was founded upon, to expose any authority as a mere husk.
Almost by instinct Cooper finds originality to be a falsification of value, an
unsettling if not legal mutation represented by the birds of passage and by
Bragg and Dodge; but the alternative appears to be rank imitation, which in
the American fashionmongers is cloying and in his own family and work
frighteningly, even perversely, inbred.

Since so much of *Home as Found* is concerned with the ferreting out of
fathers or their vindication, the case of the busts is a particularly interesting
one. Yet no matter how parodic the scene seems, an unnerving sense of indecision remains, a sense that Cooper could not in fact make up his mind
whether to burlesque the Effinghams, along with his whole enterprise, or
take it and them as serious representations of moral responsibility. The rank
contradiction which tears the book in half is founded on Cooper's partial
awareness of the fact that when he first rebukes his countrymen for their addiction to change and replacement, and then turns right around to attack
their servile adoption of imitative forms, he is in fact turning upon himself.
Cooper knows better than most readers have been willing to admit that his
models have started to look like clowns and that his succumbing to imitation
as an explicit ideological issue cannot help but spoil his own hand. The result is a stylistic menagerie, half intentional, half surely not, which illustrates with eloquent suspension Lewis's insight into the fact that "it is
always hard to locate the source of Cooper's power," since "the most illumi-

nating clashes and insights occur on the margins of his plots.''[49] Cooper's
power in *Home as Found* lies in the way he continually calls attention to
his plot as a device that merely sets in motion an array of speculations about
the place of imitation in the American experiment, speculations which have
no clear resolution.

That power comes too from the fact that Cooper was writing at a time
when the choice was bleak for one who clung to faltering aristocratic forms,
or who dared assert too strongly the rights of inherited property in a New
York where the Dutch patroon system was breaking up on the verge of the
Anti-Rent Wars, which Stephen Van Rensselaer's death in 1839 would pre-
cipitate (events, of course, whose history Cooper would chronicle in defense
of the New York landlords in the Littlepage trilogy of 1845–46). This is why
Home as Found must be read as a sequel to *The Pioneers,* one in which the
questions of dynasty and authority have taken a marked turn. At stake in the
first Templeton book is Natty's refusal to abide by the letter of the law; but
whatever the virtues of the wilderness romanticism Natty stands for, Cooper
recognizes him even there as an antique, an outmoded if tragic figure whose
way of life must necessarily be supplanted by the civic law of Marmaduke
Temple. The letter of the law, that is, the written and codified law, is for
Natty and his sympathizers opposed to the natural right of the spirit; by
Home as Found, however, the power of the letter, the *written* word, has become central, and there is an array of texts which function variously in the
novel and which almost always attempt to supply a missing basis for conduct. Since what is in question is the nature of authority in America, written
documents perform a number of roles for Cooper, but all reflect in some
fashion his veneration of his own father's will and of the Constitution,
which he believed in danger at the hands of both the people and the Congress. In *Home as Found* the Effingham will has an obvious importance as
a way of keeping the land in the family and, as it turns out, the family in the
land; Monday's letters, which reveal the truth of Paul's identity, the family
prayerbook, and John's character sketchbook all indicate that stability and
order depend on the authority of the written word.

But the matter is hardly that simple, as Cooper clearly recognized. He is
at great pains throughout the book to prove that since the American press
seizes avidly on anything that will create a stir and fill its columns, without
bothering ''to inquire into the truth of the account, or after the character of
the original authority'' (238), what passes for printed truth in the public eye
is as much a sham as the public's claim to the Point. More curious, however,
is Cooper's attitude towards the authority of his own work and that of American writing in general. America, Cooper complains in his preface, as James
would more eloquently in his study of Hawthorne, ''probably presents as
barren a field to the writer of fiction, and to the dramatist, as any other on

earth; we are not certain that we might not say the most barren. . . . It would indeed be a desperate undertaking, to think of making anything interesting in the way of a *Roman de Société* in this country" (xxvii–xxviii). Many would agree that *Home as Found* is no proof against Cooper's complaint, and it is certainly marked by a desperate quality; yet it is exactly because a novel of manners in the America of 1838 is both desperate and foolish that *Home as Found* compels by the very act of verging on catastrophe. Its near failure says as much about the climate into which it had to be received as it does about Cooper's abilities as a writer.

The self-consciousness on Cooper's part that I have called attention to— the proposal scenes, the fairy-tale ending, the Wigwam busts, the *Hamlet* influence, and so forth—keeps the novel woodenly stilted to a purpose: it provides Cooper his only defense in an America whose morals he finds a shambles and whose tastes unformed. But it also mocks his own dependence on the forms and conventions of the novel that are necessarily European. Cooper is not likely to have forgotten that his first novel, *Precaution,* was modeled on Austen's *Persuasion,* nor that he had borrowed heavily from Scott, for example; this is no criticism, surely, but the question of literary authority seems to have become especially acute for Cooper by the time of *Home as Found.* The primarily European epigraphs which stud nearly all his novels are often somewhat buffoonish, particularly in the Leatherstocking Tales, where one would suppose a completely original American myth was being generated. But in *Home as Found,* at least, the epigraphs seem more clearly an integral part of Cooper's last defense of all he holds sacred and dear. Like the busts, they are a strange flourish of classicism in what for Cooper was worse than a wilderness. Yet their authority is often equally ironic: the sudden self-flagellation of Hamlet's speech, right at the moment the plot throws up its grandest wall of artifice, exposes Cooper's most ardent anxieties not only about familial incest but also about fictional incest; it turns the realistic illusion of Cooper's drama into a mock show, unmistakably linking together the revered father and the literary tradition as objects of imitation.

Cooper is running a risk with his epigraphic quotations, however, for in the 1834 *Letter to His Countrymen,* an attack on the corrosion which the Constitution was suffering through American subservience to and imitation of European handling of governmental affairs, Cooper severely criticized his fellow Americans for looking to European writers, particularly journalists, for their opinions:

> The practice of quoting the opinions of foreign nations, by way of helping to make up its own estimate of the degree of merit that belongs to its public men, is, I believe, a custom peculiar to America. That our colonial origin and provin-

cial habits should have given rise to such a usage is sufficiently natural; that journals which have a poverty of original matter should have recourse to that which
can be obtained not only gratuitously but, by an extraordinary convention,
without loss of reputation, and without even the necessity of a translation, need
be no mystery; but the readiness with which the practice can be accounted for
will not, I think, prove its justification, if it can be shown that it is destructive of
those sentiments of self-respect, and of that manliness and independence of
thought, that are necessary to render a people great, or a nation respectable.[50]

It may be that Cooper spoke so eloquently against quotation because he had
repressed and internalized his own practice so thoroughly. Of course the
point can be made that in the *Letter* Cooper is speaking to a specific issue in
political journalism; yet it is hard to imagine a more political book, within
the guidelines posed in the *Letter,* than *Home as Found,* and it is surely subject to Cooper's own criticism. As a summons of authority, the epigraphs
take on a paternal role equal to that of Judge Cooper's will; they are not
mere decoration, but as a particular kind of *naming* they provide model and
form for a tradition that does not yet fully exist. As much as the journalism
of the day they indicate subservience to European thought, and since
Cooper's overwhelming concern in *Home as Found* is imitation, they reveal
his ambivalence as certainly as the Effingham marriage.

Cooper's epigraphs are in part an exquisite illustration of Edward Said's
contention that "quotation is a constant reminder that writing is a form of
displacement," that it "symbolizes other writing as encroachment, as a disturbing force moving potentially to take over what is presently being written."[51] But even if this is the case in *Home as Found,* it is only half the case,
for the epigraphs are also a form of protection, of control and homage: they
authorize Cooper's book by their very presence at the same time that they
reveal his own activity as one of displacement and encroachment. The awkward position he lands in here is similar to almost every other theoretical
bind in the novel. Cooper is more than half-dedicated to producing an original form of American fiction, to founding a native literary tradition—and
the Leatherstocking Tales are in this regard an indisputably major achievement—but since what Cooper is fighting ideologically in *Home as Found* is
the kind of radical originality and displacement represented by the Templeton populace, his falling back on quotation is more than a literary convention. It is also the signature of his anxious bid for the paternal security of
tradition, if not a stubbornly visible reminder of that remark by Emerson
that broods unquietly over countless attempts, like that of Cooper, to settle
the issue of American authority: "every book is a quotation; and every
house is a quotation out of all forests, and mines, and stone-quarries; and
every man is a quotation from all his ancestors."[52] The name of Shakespeare

on Cooper's page is as talismanic in one sense as Judge Cooper's is in another.

Cooper puts the question in a way which bears more closely on his novel when he points out that in America "the arts of life, like Minerva, who was struck out of the intellectual being of her father at a blow, have started full-grown into existence, as the legitimate inheritance of the colonists" (150). The implication is that the arts are a legitimate right granted by the revolution; but if the arts are defined as the product of cultivation and tradition, a paradox is at hand. That the arts have been struck at a blow out of the "father" raises the stakes significantly (and we might recall that Cooper's inquiry into the place of "accident" in revolution and paternity calls into question not only America's "legitimacy" but Paul's as well). The problems of tradition and the origin of American arts on the one hand, and of imitation and authority on the other, come together in Cooper's treatment of his hero, Paul Blunt-Powis-Assheton-Effingham. That Paul, the revelation of whose mysterious identity welds shut the Effingham dynasty, appears first as a poet, so identified on the basis of the singular fact that he has *no name,* is no more an accident than the Fourth of July proposal. He is verified as a poet in the eyes of Templeton when he copies the opening couplet of Pope's *Essay on Man* and drops it where it is sure to be found by Bragg. As Paul admits to the Effinghams, though, he is no poet at all, merely a "rank plagiarist" (143). But while Pope's allusion to the "pride of kings" guarantees, as Cooper sarcastically notes, that the verse will pass for an American original, the unquoted lines which follow in the *Essay,* describing the universe as

> A mighty maze! but not without a plan;
> A Wild, where weeds and flow'rs promiscuous shoot,
> Or garden, tempting with forbidden fruit,

render Paul's imitation more than slightly problematic by turning the Effinghams' mazelike garden into an echo of the mazed, and hence fallen, Eden of *Paradise Lost.*[53] The episode concisely indicates Cooper's worry about both his country and his craft; yet since the uncovering of Paul's true *name* is of crucial importance to Cooper's vision of authority, the gross irony of Paul's feigned career is made clear only when he turns out to be but a *ficelle* for the Effingham family's own "rank plagiarism" of itself.

V

The Effinghams' incest keeps the family secure in name and blood by erecting a copy, by in effect quoting and repeating its own authority. Paul's role points up the extreme tenuousness not only of authority in America but concurrently of Cooper's desperate groping after it. Especially significant is the fact that *Home as Found* to a certain extent repeats and copies *The Pioneers*; but it does so by way of proving that in fact *The Pioneers* cannot be repeated, that the first imitation of Cooper's home town, presided over by the figure of his father in the guise of Judge Temple, has been trampled down by a herd of fortune-seekers and demagogues. The scene that could not accommodate Natty Bumppo, but shuttled him deeper into the West, is now threatened itself; the Effinghams' natural aristocracy has contracted into an enclosed camp. Cooper's most effective extension of the problem of imitation thus shows up in the dialogue between the two books, for his testimony to the vanished past of Natty takes the form of an echo that derides at the same time it honors. The references to Natty in *Home as Found* situate him as the representative of an heroic age past, his voice that of a vanished god; but Cooper's invocations of the venerable spirit are answered not by sage advice but by grotesque repetition. The echoes that the Effingham party delights in at the Speaking Rocks are thought to "come from the spirit of the Leatherstocking, which keeps about its old haunts, and repeats everything we say, in mockery of the invasion of the woods" (200). The mocking echoes reveal that settlement itself is repetition, a fact that it is Natty's horror continually to realize, since he acts as the harbinger of a process that repeats itself westward across the continent. Natty's echoes are especially cutting in that Cooper has become brilliantly schizophrenic on the subject of imitation, on the one hand denouncing the American aping of culture, on the other recoiling from originality into his own mimetic shell. Natty's voice copies that of John Effingham with "mocking sounds... thrown back again with a closeness of resemblance that actually startled the novice. Then followed other calls and other repetitions of the echoes, which did not lose the minutest intonation of the voice" (203). Cooper could not have found a more chilling way to frame the Effinghams' dynasty than by deriding them with the voice of the very dream their ancestors drove away in the original act of settlement.

As though to make perfectly clear the power that has swept aside the romantic wilderness of Natty and opened the way for westward expansion, Cooper allows the Effinghams to entertain themselves by firing the field artillery stored at Lake Otsego. The event recalls the kind of military spectacle in which Richard Jones loved to indulge in *The Pioneers*; but like the patriotic Concord guns that "echo like popguns" to Thoreau's woods and rouse him to the point where he feels as though he "could spit a Mexican with a good relish,"[54] these weapons reverberate with pointed irony. While the gun-house purports to be a "speaking picture of the entire security of the country, from foes within as well as from foes without" (204), it is only one page later that the Effinghams' security begins to disintegrate, as John reveals that the "public—the all-powerful, omnipotent, overruling, lawmaking, law-breaking public—has a passing caprice to possess itself of [the] beloved Point" (205). Inserted between these two passages is the firing of the gun; three times repeated, the reverberations roll down the valley "always with the same magnificent effect, the western hills actually echoing the echoes of the eastern mountains, like the dying strains of some falling music" (204). The progress of the repeated echoes from east to west may be incidental, but the show of power built on copy is an impressive display— until, that is, the allusion to *Twelfth Night* underlines the military echoes with a literary one and calls ironic attention to their fading force. Paul ensures our recognition that the firing of the guns is a show designed to exhibit mock potency when, prompted by the echoes, he remarks that "such a locality would be a treasure in the vicinity of a melodramatic theatre...for certainly no artificial thunder I have ever heard has equalled this. This sheet of water might even receive a gondola" (205).

Yet the questions of melodrama and artifice have become very real ones for Cooper. The allusion to the opening speech by the Duke in *Twelfth Night*—

> If music be the food of love, play on;
> Give me excess of it, that, surfeiting,
> The appetite may sicken, and so die.
> That strain again! it had a dying fall[55]

—suggests that Cooper's own appetite for imitation has been surfeited, even to excess. The "dying strains" of the cannon lead us to suspect, moreover, that Cooper's use of speeches from *Twelfth Night* as chapter epigraphs (e.g., 150, 162) has more than passing significance; for not only are Bragg and Dodge set up as foolish figures of Toby Belch and Andrew Aguecheek, but more importantly Eve and Paul, as the perfectly matched couple, strangely correspond to the doubled character passing in Shakespeare's play for both Viola and her look-alike brother Sebastian, until at the end both appear on stage together, confronting the Duke with "One face, one voice, one habit, and two persons;/A natural perspective, that is, and is not!" (v,i). It is Antonio, however, who most interestingly characterizes the matching pair. His remark that "An apple cleft in two is not more twin/ Than these two creatures" explicitly invokes Aristophanes' mythical hermaphrodites in Plato's *Symposium* (189e–191d), figures which Zeus chopped in half like "sorb apples for pickling" to create the separate sexes of man and woman. According to Aristophanes, love between the sexes is thus an attempt "to reintegrate our former nature, to make two into one";[56] and according to Freud's *Beyond the Pleasure Principle,* Aristophanes' myth corroborates his tracing of sexual instincts to "*a need to restore an earlier state of things,*" a need in which an attempted return to the womb reveals and constantly repeats itself both in a drive toward death and in the desire for incestuous sexual relations.[57] Certainly we must doubt that the union of Cooper's perfect couple involved such intricacies on his part, but the incest of Eve and Paul, the matched "natural heirs" of one another, *is* an attempt to retain a shaky unity, if not to restore a lost one, and the affair of the cousins does indeed have its place in Cooper's own fantasies and his compulsion to repeat and imitate.

The echoes of Cooper's guns contain more than one ironic echo of their own, however, for Cooper borrows the phrase "speaking picture" from a striking passage in Sidney's *Apology:* "Poesy therefore is an art of imitation, for so Aristotle termeth it in this word *mimesis,* that is to say, a representing, counterfeiting, a figuring forth—to speak metaphorically, a speaking picture—with this end, to teach and delight."[58] The tension in Sidney's statement between "representation" and "counterfeit" is as troubling as the ambivalence in Cooper's own dealings with imitation; but by locating the crumbling authority figured by his field guns in so complex a tradition of mimesis, Cooper further accents the immense problems surrounding his attempt to unravel the question of mimetic power, whether political, cultural, or autobiographical. Like the allusions to Pope and Shakespeare, the allusion to Sidney is an invocation of the security of tradition whose honesty is in the end radically ironic. The artillery echoes, which began as a demonstration of security and power, have created an enclosure of theatrical artifice that measures the attainment of the Effinghams as accurately as do the mocking echoes of Natty's voice. The very center of artifice and convention, it is the Effinghams who are on stage; it is they who are fading echoes. If Natty's Killdeer is the weapon of chastity, the Effinghams' field guns have become the equipment of failed power and faltering imitation. Even more pointedly than the Speaking Rocks, where, as the commodore jokes, women who "are not satisfied with what they have once said, but . . . like to hear it again" can go "to have a chat with [themselves]" (200), the echoing guns mark Cooper's narcissistic indulgence in a form of mimesis whose authority has turned back on itself and nearly collapsed into self-mockery.

But if on the one hand Natty's echoes are derision, Cooper's on the other are homage—indeed, the party is said to be holding "communion with the spirit of the Leather-Stocking" (203). To this extent, *Home as Found* elegizes the passing of Natty and of the old Templeton; and an elegy

is only possible, one presumes, when something has passed, when there *is* a
past, a fact Cooper proudly calls attention to in one of the letters defending
the book: "In the Pioneers I had attempted to pourtray [sic] a peculiar state
of society in its commencement, and by preserving this connection, it saved
much preliminary explanation, and enabled me to give a picture of the same
again half a century later, and of obtaining some reflected interest for my
scenes; a point of some moment in a country almost without a history."[59]
Against the original model, Cooper can truly measure the lapse of time and
conjure up an American past; yet when, in the initial view of home the Effinghams have from Mount Vision, Cooper refers to the town in sight as
"the Templeton of 'The Pioneers'" (126), he is in effect laying open whatever illusion of historical portraiture has been generated and showing it as a
fiction. Since we know all along, though, that Templeton is modeled on
Cooperstown, the satire that accompanies Cooper's treatment of the fictional family and his own doubles back on itself with a vengeance. Cooper's
involvement in a mimetic mire is thickened not only by acting out his own
personal predicament in the novel but also by taking part of his authority
from a previous work of fiction.

The problem of fiction's claim to authority haunted Cooper; the letters
in which he is particularly concerned, as we have seen, with disproving any
link between Elizabeth Temple and his dead sister or Edward Effingham
and himself, are filled with more abstract (though not strikingly interesting)
broodings about the degree to which fictional characters can or should be
based on real ones.[60] Yet what must have stung him most is that, precisely
by denying the novel's intimate connection with his life, Cooper was undermining his own authority and the very point he was trying to make. Indeed,
Home as Found mocks by echo as much as Natty does. By importing Natty
as a mythical totem figure who, for example, is reputed to have "talk[ed] for
hours at a time with the animals of the forest" (199), *Home as Found* turns
The Pioneers into a fading myth that lives by way of echo and repetition,
ironically severed from the chaotic present, and it turns the Effinghams
themselves into a fictive chain of names precariously yoked by something
that may prove to be no more substantial. *The Pioneers* takes its place
among the written documents so important to *Home as Found,* but in a
way startlingly different from the others: more than any it marks Cooper's
recognition that the very work he intends to bolster his authority is founded
on a previous fiction. Yet such an act invokes its own kind of *authority,* and
in this respect one might well compare it to the self-conscious invocation of
bibliography which Huck Finn employs when he begins his own story by
telling the reader, "You don't know about me without you have read a
book by the name of 'The Adventures of Tom Sawyer,' but that ain't no

matter.''[61] Of course it *is* a matter for concern to Twain, quite a serious one. It matters also to Cooper, for the result of his continual return to the problem of echo and repetition is that the whole book circles around but backs away from the truth Cooper lets slip when Captain Truck inadvertently undoes the customary ban on smoking in drawing-room society: the ladies' agreement that smoking be allowed in America since it apparently is in England, Cooper remarks, is "simply to make one fiction authority for another" (93). Yet this is exactly what Cooper does with *The Pioneers*. For even while the first Templeton book performs its own kind of incestuous function and prevents, in the realm of fiction, that indebtedness and economic disorder which Cooper lamented in the American obsession with "transfer of title," it also speaks against complete originality and in favor of the establishment of a new tradition to which debt will be owed. Making one fiction the authority for another is Cooper's quickest way to found a literary home and "father" American fiction. What unnerved him, though, was his recognition of the degree to which such an action applied to his whole book, perhaps, in fact, to all he held sacred and dear. His echoes, whether of Natty or of his own work, fluctuate between affirmation and dissolution, between authority and mockery, and bring us back again to the question of *names*.

VI

In haunting contrast to the echoing rocks stands the "Silent Pine," rising "in solitary glory, a memorial of what the mountains which were yet so rich in vegetation had really been in their days of nature and pride." This "tall, column-like tree," reputed to have a catalytic effect on those of poetic persuasion, is a true "American antiquity." But its age and grandeur alone are not what makes it particularly American; what sets it off as an authentic native is the fact, as poet-plagiarist Paul recognizes, that "its silence is, after all, its eloquence" (201–3). This silence can be read several ways, though, as can the highly symbolic tree itself. Given the autobiographical fact of the tree lopped off at Three-Mile Point which Cooper intimately connected with his father (a detail we have seen displaced into Bragg's pride in his lack of sentimental ties to home and history), the Silent Pine takes on a mythically phallic stature, like an emblem of natural authority lording it over the land. Yet what of its silence? What too of the fact that toward the close of the book, Captain Truck, finding himself surrounded by a "marrying mania," remarks that he is now in "a solitary category," having been left, "like a single dead pine in one of your clearings" (437). The Pine now becomes recognizable as a figure of the chaste frontiersman—like Natty himself, a patriarch who is not truly a *father*. To this extent the Silent Pine is one more representative of the mythical past, which is barely alive in memory and which, like Bragg's tree and that of Judge Cooper, will soon be threatened with wanton severance. Its silence is split between proud defiance and stifled potency, a failing force that has lost its voice. In contrast to the mocking echoes of the Speaking Rocks which ridicule both the settlement of the land and the Effinghams' mimetic dynasty, the Pine stands still, unconsumed by the passion for repetition that settlement entails. But whether it represents the virile bachelor, nakedly isolated in his mistress woods, or the lapsed paternal voice of Judge Cooper, the consequence is the same: the patriarchal authority is stymied and the echo of generation closed off into either faltering myth or the desperate self-parody of incest.

If we had only the Silent Pine in *Home as Found,* we would have sufficient evidence to support Bewley's refutation of the usual critical notion "that Cooper was not interested in symbols and that the writers who came later were not interested in anything else."[62] The Pine effectively yokes ecology and paternity, settlement and mythology. Its silence also stands in marked contrast to the various documents, from Judge Cooper's will to the Shakespearian epigraphs, that "speak" with historical authority throughout the book; it is a true form of American eloquence because it has no voice, no past at all. Cooper's Pine stands in this respect for the untainted wilds, the silent Nature not yet penetrated by a disruptive language which Thoreau would make his sequestered lover in the *Week*: "All sounds are her servants, and purveyors, proclaiming not only that their mistress is, but is a rare mistress, and earnestly to be sought after....Silence is the universal refuge...our inviolable asylum, where no indignity can assail, no personality disturb us."[63] But it stands as well for the horrifying lacuna of authority in America that Melville uncovered in his assault on paternity in *Pierre*: "Silence is at once the most harmless and most awful thing in all nature. It speaks of the Reserved Forces of Fate. Silence is the only Voice of our God."[64] Melville finds an empty sarcophagus when he delves into authority; Cooper is anxiously determined not to, but to find instead the happy vision signified by a fulfillment of the text of his father's will. The Silent Pine speaks for the freedom granted a country set loose from authority, a beautiful dream of absence; but it speaks too for how quickly the dream becomes a nightmare. The irony of the fact that it is Paul who names the pine's eloquence lies in Cooper's need to vocalize the silence of Paul's past by giving him the Effingham name, by giving him a history that will allow him to found an American home by incest and repetition.

Yet might not Judge Cooper's will be as much a myth as the Silent Pine or Natty Bumppo, one fiction made the authority for another? Is it not the

mission of America to eradicate hereditary authority? We have observed a
number of ways Cooper keeps cunningly reconsidering this issue, but one
particular scene—that in which Captain Truck and the commodore float
lazily on the lake, discussing the mythical "sogdollager"—stands out with
enchanting clarity. Leary may be right when he says that this scene is "the
effective center of the book,"[65] but it is so only by way of violent contrast to
the concentered and strangling garden of the Effinghams, and only because
it reveals symbolically the underlying structure of their family dynasty. The
sogdollager is introduced earlier, in the scene concerned with the mythical
wonders of the Speaking Rocks and the Silent Pine, where it is defined by
the commodore as "the perfection of a thing," a "patriarch of the lake"
whose name is one of the "many words that ought to be in dictionaries [but]
that have been forgotten by the printers" (198). This first glimpse of the
sogdollager comes virtually on the heels of a discussion among the party of
the cross as a religious symbol, in which it is shown that while the American
forefathers, "in their horror of idolatry," aimed "at a sublimation that
peculiarly favors spiritual pride and a pious conceit" rather than fawning
over the display of symbols, they paradoxically emblazoned every door with
"a sign of the beast" yet recoiled from it in church (193–94). The "beast"
here is of course the Catholic or Anglican church, but Cooper subtly introduces the term to prepare his ground for the sogdollager and to recall the
earlier mockery of poet Paul as one among the "caravans of wild beasts"
that are now "brought in as curiosities" to Templeton (132). The satire
Cooper sets in motion is keen and complex: not only have the real beasts of
the landscape been replaced by a traveling circus which must visit
Templeton in order to show the townspeople what, in effect, they have
destroyed, but the poet—the one who, like Cooper, will elegize the passing
of the wilderness but plagiarize Pope (perhaps another pun) at the same
time—is himself deemed one of the specimens on show and, moreover,
someone as addicted to idolatry as a papist.

Both of these scenes are behind Cooper's figure of the sogdollager. Particularly because the wilderness and its beasts have succumbed to the settlement of the pioneers does a mythical beast like the sogdollager, an
American totem, become part of the vocabulary. Like Melville's whale,
Natty's deer, or Faulkner's bear, the sogdollager is one more American
totem to be married and murdered at the same time. It represents nostal-
gically both the disappearance of the wilderness and civilization's guilt in
its vanquishing. Because it is simultaneously revered and pursued or
destroyed, the totem animal is frequently a paternal surrogate, though in
Home as Found it thus has a peculiarly ironic force. Against the Puritan
desire to eradicate the trappings of symbol, the totem reasserts itself as a

pure and potent American spiritual emblem, a sign of the beast as Father. This is a familiar enough theme; what Cooper's treatment brings to the fore, however, is the sheerly mythical character of the totem as a thing that has either receded so far into history or been so carefully veiled as to be only a *name*—one that is in no dictionary. The sogdollager would seem to be purely an American *original*; yet while it may as well have been invented by the commodore as by anybody, it is precisely the point that the origin of its name lies folded in secrecy and that the one chosen is intrinsically no more appropriate than another. The same unfounded speculation which Cooper condemns as an abuse of the English language ironically produces his most revered symbol of the romantic wilderness and the nostalgic good life.

The legend of the sogdollager is the archetypal fish story, the tale of the one that got away, and because Cooper's totem figure is deceptively simple, we may not notice at first its important function in *Home as Found*. The leisure drifting of Captain Truck and the commodore on the lake is closer to Isaak Walton than to Melville, but its message is thoroughly American. It is both comic and touching, for buried beneath the two sailors' finicky arguing over lake versus ocean, their jokes about the devil, their philosophical specula- tions about the equation of west and east, and their tautological inquiries into the purposes of liquor, is a haunting elegy. Just as the real beasts of America have been replaced by a traveling circus, so the real struggles of Natty with the wilds have been replaced by two old salts drinking themselves silly and spinning out yarns to entangle one another on a lazy summer day. It is the American hunt turned vacation, a hotbed of tall tales and indulgent bachelorhood. Yet even in this highly Thoreauvian moment, the com- modore's sogdollager—which he calls here ''a sort of father to all the salmon-trout in this part of the world; a scaly patriarch'' (280)—persistently turns the relaxed, contemplative mood back toward the question of paternal authority which presides over Cooper's novel. The more accurate reason one is tempted to call the sogdollager chapter the center of the book is that it emblematizes what the Leatherstocking Tales represent in the American ex- perience, while at the same time reflecting ironically the disintegration of patriarchal authority figured in the Effingham drama. The names ''Effing- ham'' and ''sogdollager'' stand finally in strange contrast and kinship in *Home as Found*. One is loaded with a history of respect and authority, while the other is completely mythical, an unlegislated name. Set alongside the totem animal is the ancestral father; both live by repetition and imitation, the totem by tale and worship, the father by the regeneration of his name and blood. The sogdollager and the authority of the father, whether Cooper or Effingham, are two sides of the same coin for Cooper, both threatened by the horde that would repudiate them through ignorance or lust. Yet the mythical name cannot help but expose the family name as an equally precarious, if powerful, invention.

We noted before, in the discussion of Natty's names and Paul's courtship, that the hunt as marriage is replaced by the marriage as hunt and that the name of the "prey" is ironically mirrored by the hunter's own, a mocking echo. One of the effects of the tale of the sogdollager is to measure the distance between the hunt as sacred marriage to the totem and the actual Effingham marriage, which in effect totemizes the name of the father and breaks the taboo of exogamy to ensure the name's perpetuation. The marriage hunt takes place not in the wilderness but in the formally enclosed garden, and the father himself presides over and completes the ritual. His name, and his father's name before him, and so forth, is repeated by inbreeding; the hunt has ceased to be sport and has become a desperate ruse. And paradoxically enough, as we have seen, the very imitation that the Effinghams despise in their own countrymen is carried out with a vengeance in their own clan. But the other side of the issue is equally forceful; for when Cooper has Mrs. Abbott protest the legality of the Effingham marriage, he exposes his own hidden fears over the possibility that, in their violation of the incest taboo, the family will indeed swallow up the interests necessary to the development of the community as a whole, even if in their eyes that violation is of vital necessity to the maintenance of authority in the community. When Mrs. Abbott replies to Captain Truck's light-hearted rebuke of her daughter's rope-skipping by remarking that "there are 'vain repetitions' in doing the same thing over and over so often" (419), she strikes not only at the Effinghams' prayer-reading and cardplaying but also acutely close to the very heart of their family home. The Effinghams' repetition, their echoing and plagiarizing, at once constitutes an inviolable authority and threatens to collapse into itself.

Cooper wrote in his preface to *Notions of the Americans* that he was "not without some of the yearnings of paternity in committing the offspring of his brain to the world."[66] American authors have, of course, been particularly obsessed with *fathering* a tradition which will stand alone, and in this respect we must allow that Cooper laid the solidest of foundations, particularly with the Leatherstocking Tales. What he also did in *Home as Found* was call into question the possibility and desirability of complete originality. The last Effingham novel is not only Cooper's defense of himself and an attack on his countrymen, it is also a terse exposure of his own precarious position—as a democrat and as a writer. For though he stingingly burlesques America's indulgence in servile social imitation, Cooper's own embracing of incest, his inquiry into the mystery of names, the many self-consciously parodic moments in his narrative, and not least his use of the setting and events of his own life—all reveal his anxiety about both authorial and cultural paternity. *Home as Found* acts out a crucial chapter in the history of American society, but it does so in an arcanely autobiographical and artificial fashion. Precisely because Cooper pursued his revenge on Cooperstown in the public forum of fiction, however, the book's stylized rituals do not flounder in excess or decay into absurd sentimentality. His indulgence in romance, indeed in family romance, both honors and mocks its own commitment, which is to found a home. If the home Cooper found(ed) is surprisingly uncanny, *unheimlich,* and one whose perpetuation is ensured by an unnerving imitation in the marriage home of what Eve, speaking transparently for Cooper, called "the home of my childhood," it is because his one sure locus of authority lay in a sullied name which could be redeemed only by the power of echo.

TWO

"Plowing homeward"

Cultivation and Grafting in Thoreau and the *Week*

A person to spend all his life and splendid talents in trying to achieve something naturally impossible,—as to make a conquest over Nature.

—Hawthorne, *The American Notebooks*

As we drew near to Oldtown I asked Polis if he was not glad to get home again; but there was no relenting to his wildness, and he said, "It makes no difference to me where I am." Such is the Indian's pretence always.

—Thoreau, *The Maine Woods*

When the roof of Marmaduke Temple's new house is found to protrude unnaturally into the landscape in *The Pioneers,* Richard Jones tests three colors of paint—"sky blue," "cloud," and "invisible green"—in his attempt to cover up civilization's incursion into the wilderness; all fail, of course, and renouncing concealment, Richard decides instead to "ornament the offensive shingles" with a gaudy "sunshine" paint, as though to blaze the way for further waste under the guise of enlightenment.[1] The boat in which Thoreau and his brother John sail up and down the Concord and Merrimack Rivers is painted half blue, half green (1:12),[2] at best a rather half-hearted attempt to hide, if only symbolically, the fact that the trip they are on is a suspicious enterprise—suspicious not because they have a criminally ulterior motive, but because, as Thoreau recognizes, they are unavoidably civilization's agents. The two-week voyage is ostensibly a return to "Nature," a rooting out of the primitive and an engagement with the uncertain origins

41

of American history. What *A Week on the Concord and Merrimack Rivers* records, though, is the unrelenting difficulty Thoreau has in finding Nature, that is, in uncovering something which is sufficiently far removed from his own defilement to qualify as that American garden at once primitive and Edenic. When Thoreau's tools themselves—his faculties of observation, his speech, and his writing—are brought to test and found lacking, he is forced to reevaluate the categories of Nature and the primitive with dramatic urgency. Unlike the river itself, which "steals into the scenery it traverses without intrusions" (1:249), Thoreau cannot quite sneak into Nature without leaving behind the scars of his entrance. Although the *Week*'s trip for a good part of the time is veiled as a leisure charade "on the placid current of our dreams, floating from past to future" (1:13), it is frequently rifled by Thoreau's disturbing recognition that his every encampment, if not the river journey itself, marks "the first encroachment of commerce on this land" (1:39).

A brief remark from Thoreau's journals may be one of the more incisive critiques of, if not all of his writings, at least of the *Week*: "It is vain to dream of a wilderness distant from ourselves. There is none such. It is the bog in our brain and bowels, the primitive vigor of Nature in us, that inspires that dream. I shall never find in the wilds of Labrador any greater wilderness than in some recess in Concord, *i.e.* than I import into it" (15:43). What this fierce circularity—that an interior wilderness inspires the dream of its own exterior distance—underlines, is an intricate awareness on Thoreau's part that his hunt for unravished and "original" American frontiers, so much his pervasive concern, especially in the *Week*, is necessarily one in which the pioneer is constantly frustrated by the elusiveness of that which he would possess. Thoreau is again and again overly conscious of the fact that his *essays* out of Concord do not quite allow him to escape its civilized encumbrances, but only leave him torn between two worlds—one which he seemingly wants to repudiate, but which trails naggingly behind as soon as he shoves off in search of that other one he can never have. Like Natty Bumppo, Thoreau might well be called the archetypal "man without a home." But in the long run it may be no different to say, as he does in "Walking," that Thoreau has "no particular home, but [is] equally at home everywhere" (5:205). Yet it is only a short step then to Thoreau's admission in *The Maine Woods* that whatever place you select "for your camp... begins at once to have its attractions, and becomes a very centre of civilization, to you: 'Home is home, be it never so homely' " (3:310).

Cooper's home in *Home as Found* is literally *found*; it is that which he returned to, though as we have discovered, Cooper goes to an extravagant length to *found* that home in another sense. Thoreau's case is equally ambiguous when scrutinized under the vocabulary of *finding* and *founding*. *Walden* has often been taken to be the primary text on the American way of taking up residence, of founding a home in the most basic sense, though it is again and again unsettled by civilized doubts and savage eruptions that threaten to tear its elegantly labored edifice apart at the seams. What is most unnerving about the book, however, is that despite Thoreau's constant parading of simplicity and economy, a more rhetorically ornate volume is hard to imagine. *Walden* recounts an experiment in settlement, one that strips itself down to essentials of a sort, but the record finally contains far more showmanship than primitivism. In this respect, Thoreau's *Week* may be a more forceful account of his head-on encounter with the frontier that America itself is; and the book's very power lies in the fact that it is less refined than *Walden*, as though the very wildness Thoreau is after has entered into the written record of the journey. The *Week*, as Thoreau wrote of it in his journal of 1851, is a much more "hypaethral or unroofed book, lying open under the ether and permeated by it, open to all weathers, not easy to be kept on a shelf" (8:274–75).

But if Thoreau did not "cultivate" or "domesticate" the *Week* as carefully as he did *Walden*, it is not because these actions do not inform and qualify the motives of his exploration. Rather, the domestication of the wilderness is what the *Week* is so anxiously about: it is to be avoided if the wilderness is to be preserved, but is inevitable in the labor Thoreau himself undertakes, not least the labor which forms the book. The same writing which produces his account is inextricably bound up with the incursion into a unprofaned terrain that eludes his grasp and leaves him stranded on the frontier, then returns him "home" to elegize the fall recapitulated by his own adventure. "Men plow and sail for [the Wild]," writes Thoreau in "Walking" (5:224); he does both in the *Week*, but as the term plowing suggests, it may be that the very act of searching for the wild undermines all hope of its attainment, renders its existence suspect, or even destroys it. Before elaborating the melodrama of circularity that his notions about traveling and writing produce, however, it is worth determining what, in fact, Thoreau goes in search of.

I

When he notes early on in the *Week* that "it is worth the while to make a voyage up this stream...only to see how much country there is in the rear of us" (1:5) and much later that "facts are being so rapidly added to the sum of human experience, that it appears as if the theorizer would always be in arrears, and were doomed forever to arrive at imperfect conclusions"

(1:389), Thoreau is being crucially, if paradoxically, exact about both the journey and his written record of it. The ambiguity of the "rear" in the first remark—is the rear upstream or is it downstream?—is one we will find Thoreau playing with continually in his contemplation of the ratio between the natural and the historical; and as the second remark suggests, the completion of the journey issues not in a settled account of that which is "in the rear" but rather in its circular displacement. The recovery of that which is "in the rear" can but add to the journey, driving a final conclusion always into a deeper recess. But since what is "in the rear"—the origins of American history, the primitive Indian language, the pure wilderness—is almost by definition unavailable to recovery, Thoreau's search becomes an exercise in evasion which perhaps succeeds theoretically, but, because it is only theoretical, fails. Thoreau is doomed always to be "in arrears," and his debt is an exact measure of his nervousness not just about civilization's destruction of "Nature," but also about America's relative lack of a documentary history.

Thoreau's vocabulary of debt is hardly peculiar to him, no more than his ambivalence about the contending benefits and deficiencies which accrue from an act of revolution and the foundation of a new society. Cooper had already lamented in *Home as Found* that "the American nation," despite its brief tenure, was already "lamentably in arrears to its own avowed principles."[3] The advance of Cooper's career found him less and less optimistic about the possibility of recouping the debt to a Jeffersonian dream, a debt which only became magnified as the dream played itself out in the westward expansion it had sanctioned. And some seventy years later, one of James's bizarre ventriloquistic voices in *The American Scene,* presumably that of "one of the painted savages" America has "dispossessed," complains that the "pretended message of civilization is but a colossal recipe for the *creation* of arrears, and of such as can but remain forever out of hand."[4] James is no Thoreauvian lover of the wilds, but his sentiment is not far from that of the beleaguered Concord explorer; the American act of settlement, ruthlessly imperialistic and wantonly regardless of tradition, remains in debt to an ideal which is as yet unfulfilled but which began itself with an erasure of debt, a revolutionary denial of America's dependence on the models of history in its "rear." The American position has been marked by this paradox: while its disavowal of the past portended a clean slate, a new social and political Eden, the pressure to enact the fantasy of a new beginning at once disfigured the dream and fell short, in the eyes of both foreign and native observers, of those conventions and institutions which had initially been repudiated. While James makes America's blank past his constant whipping boy, Thoreau desires on the one hand to search out a justification for the blankness, and on the other to fill it in with authentic native lore. But as he keeps realizing, once the blank is filled, it no longer functions as the lost innocence avidly pined after; paying up the debt merely displaces, or in fact augments, its demand. What is striking, though, is Thoreau's subtle alertness to the fact that the very figures with which he fills the blank of America, the figures of his own writing, perpetuate both the dream and the debt, and turn him into an entrepreneur who corrupts his Edenic property at the same time he advertises its value.

Thoreau's position is precarious, and combined with his allegiance to the American Indian, its playful and tricky logic-chopping often quickly turns remorseful. Since the *Week* is not so formidably braced with paradox and pun as *Walden,* its melancholy undercurrent is much plainer, its regret more forthright. Thoreau seeks to recover the lost state of Nature, the simple life of the Indian; that much is a common enough way of putting it. Like Rousseau, however, Thoreau recognizes that "it is no light undertaking to separate what is original from what is artificial in the present nature of man, and to know correctly a state which no longer exists, which perhaps never existed, which probably never will exist, [but] about which it is nevertheless necessary to have precise notions in order to judge our present state correctly."[5] The confusing use of the terms "nature" and "state" in Rousseau's statement is indicative of the thinness of the line separating "original" and "artificial," and the state of Nature finally remains as much a hypothesis for him as it does for Thoreau. What distinguishes the American position, though, and makes Thoreau's a more exacting and acrobatic undertaking, is that going *back* and going *forth* are the same: the primitive is Past, but it is also West, and West is Future. As a result, Thoreau's pioneer must walk a line which goes both ways at once, and to this extent, the Rousseauvian state which "probably never will exist" is a much more emphatic vector on Thoreau's map and a more forceful index of the debt which cannot be paid up. The *Week* is marked throughout by the torque of this paradox, for not only is it a haunting elegy for the passing of the American Indian and an unspoiled state of Nature, but it also must account for its own implication in the act of violation, one that goes nearly under its auspices.

Two passages in particular from the *Week* point up a telling ambivalence in Thoreau's attitude toward the Indian's uprooting and displacement, and moreover toward his own uprooting of a narrative about this part of America's story:

> The honey-bee hummed through the Massachusetts woods, and sipped the wild-flowers round the Indian's wigwam, perchance unnoticed, when, with prophetic warning, it stung the Red child's hand, forerunner of that industrious

tribe that was to come and pluck the wildflower of his race up by the root.

The white man comes, pale as dawn, with a load of thought, with a slumbering intelligence as a fire raked up, knowing well what he knows, not guessing but calculating . . . a laboring man, despising game and sport; building a house that endures, a framed house. He buys the Indian's moccasins and baskets, then buys his hunting-grounds, and at length forgets where he is buried and plows up his bones. And here town records, old, tattered, time-worn, weather-stained chronicles, contain the Indian sachem's mark perchance, an arrow or a beaver, and the few fatal words by which he deeded his hunting-grounds away. (1:52–53)

> Such is Commerce, which shakes the cocoa-nut and bread-fruit tree in the remotest isle, and sooner or later dawns on the duskiest and most simpleminded savage. If we may be pardoned the digression, who can help being affected by the thought of the very fine and slight, but positive relation, in which the savage inhabitants of some remote isle stand to the mysterious white mariner, the child of the sun?—as if *we* were to have dealings with an animal higher in the scale of being than ourselves. It is a barely recognized fact to the native that he exists, and has his home far away somewhere, and is glad to buy their fresh fruits with his superfluous commodities. (1:224)

We will return to these passages in several other contexts, since as well as any in the book they disturbingly yoke Thoreau's archeology with his imperialism. For now it is enough to note the way in which the white man's "load of thought," which strikingly plays off his "superfluous commodities" and underscores the position of the theorizer always in arrears, is subtly transfigured into the capital for a laborious and ruinous purchase of the primitive hunting-grounds. The second passage, however, is less decisive in its bargaining. With characteristic syntactical ambiguity, Thoreau leaves the reference of "animal" unsettled. It can refer to the "white mariner," leaving "*we*" to be fused with the savages, a possibility certainly germane to Thoreau's playful enterprise; or in an equally paradoxical trap it can refer to those savages "higher in the scale of being" with whom the "white mariner"—for example, Thoreau himself in the *Week*— has dealings, getting in trade for his commodities the savage's "fresh fruits."

But of course once the white mariner lays hold of the fresh fruits, they will wither in his grasp. Thoreau's various relics of wildness unendingly coax and wheedle his attention only to slip out of reach at the last instant, and in so doing leave him still further in arrears, as though the price of the primitive rises as a correlative function of Thoreau's willingness to involve himself in the negotiations of its surrender. That Thoreau found the very act of writing to be concurrent with the frustrated attempt to recover the fresh fruits of an innocent, primitive state raises the stakes of his game precipitously. He intimates the violence of his seemingly routine act when he remarks that the writer must "grasp the pen firmly so, and wield it gracefully and effectively, as an axe or a sword"; but the more devious and accurate figure for Thoreau's craft is exposed in his further claim that "a sentence should read as if its author, had he held a plow instead of a pen, could have drawn a furrow deep and straight to the end" (1:110). Writing, like the commerce of agriculture, is figured as a violent scarring of the land, and the two are made to form a mutually despoiling force that perpetuates itself by adding continually to the profane load of both thought and commodities with which a presumably once virgin land is encumbered: "what have [settlers] not written on the face of the earth already, clearing, and burning, and scratching, and harrowing, and plowing, and subsoiling, in and in, and out and out, and over and over, again and again, erasing what they had already written for want of parchment" (1:6). In Thoreau's case, the term *cultivation* could not be more appropriate. His traveling and his writing, both endorsed figuratively by the literal plowing he also did, are acts inflicted on a pristine landscape that at once violate its soil and instigate production.

Thoreau's plowing prepares the ground for seeding, for the insemination and grafting of his craft; but it also performs a preliminary function that obsesses him throughout his writings—it turns up arrowheads, almost magically. Hawthorne, among others, remarked with some astonishment the way in which arrowheads seemed to gravitate about Thoreau, as though Indian "spirits [had] willed him to be the inheritor of their simple wealth."[6] Be this as it may, Thoreau's Indian relics are his pervasive signs of originality and primitivism, though it cannot be ignored that they are most often turned up by the violence of the plow, that, as Thoreau notes in his journal of 1842, "in planting my corn in the same furrow which yielded its increase to [the Indian's] support so long, I displace some memorial of him" (7:337). An 1859 journal entry, late enough perhaps to be taken as Thoreau's definitive statement on arrowheads, clarifies the problem he encountered in his attempt to uncover an American foundation. The arrowheads, "sown like a grain that is slow to germinate...bear crops of philosophers and poets," says Thoreau, "and the same seed is just as good to plant again. It is a stone fruit." These seedy relics are guaranteed to be planted again and again, because those collected a hundred years ago "have been dispersed again" and one "cannot tell the third-hand ones (for they are all second-hand) from the others." Indeed, "they were chiefly made to be lost." Thoreau's Indian pun is rather pathetic, but he is exact about the archeology of arrowheads. It is precisely because the arrowhead is always "second-hand" that it does not matter how often it has been retrieved: it is never original, never the first, for when "you do plow and hoe amid them...[and] turn up one layer you bury another so much the more securely." Thoreau's integration of the cultural artifact with nature—the arrowhead as "seed" and "fruit"—accentuates the limitless regression in which the sign of the primitive becomes involved. Making the arrowhead *natural* ensures that it will always remain the ghost of an artifact that can never be properly measured or understood. The degree to which Thoreau was played upon by this paradox of domestication and evidence shows up clearly when he finally can revolve the issue no further and lets the arrowhead speak for itself: "Eh, you think you have got me, do you? But I shall wear a hole in your pocket at last, or if you put me in your cabinet, your heir or great-grandson will forget me or throw me out the window directly, or when the house falls I shall drop into the cellar, and there I shall be quite at home again. Ready to be *found* again, eh?" (18:90–93).

Like Thoreau himself, the arrowhead is most at home when lost; or more accurately, it "cannot be said to be lost or found" (18:92). Because what is uncovered is certainly never first-hand and not even demonstrably second-hand, it can never be identified as part of the original foundation. Edwin Fussell has remarked that the plowing up of relics and bones provided Thoreau "the necessary reassurance that he was currently at home where other men had made themselves at home."[7] This is no doubt the case, but what disturbed Thoreau at first, though in the end probably just bemused him, was that he could not get to the bottom of his search for the Indian, and "Indian" itself came finally to be almost an empty label for whatever phenomena, artifactual or fantastic, were presently missing from the landscape. Although James would still complain in 1879 that history "has left in the United States but so thin and impalpable a deposit that we very soon touch the hard substratum of nature; and nature herself, in the Western World, has the peculiarity of seeming rather crude and immature,"[8] Thoreau found that the ease with which the substratum of nature could be reached was a monumental deception, an American con game played on native grounds. "Let us settle ourselves," he advises in *Walden*, "and work and wedge our feet downward through the mud and slush of opinion, and prejudice, and tradition, and delusion, and appearance, that alluvion which covers the globe. . . till we come to a hard bottom and rocks in place, which we call *reality*, and say, This is, and no mistake; and then begin, having a *point d'appui*. . .a place where you might found a wall or a state. . ." (2:108–9). But that wall or state can be no more securely *founded* than the arrowhead of primitive America can be *found*. For Thoreau, the act of locating a foundation is like the first chapter of *Walden* on "Economy"—a ritual of stripping down to the bare minimum; yet as he discovers in that chapter's shifting miasma of clothes metaphors, the bare minimum is always hidden under one more layer of convention's garments. The *point d'appui* would ideally be stripped bare, a ground prepared for building, whether the edifice stands on the edge of a pond or at the edge of the mind. The "bottom," like the first arrowhead, is a projection which acts as a hypothetical gauge, the very foundation of culture; but once the Indian is granted a culture of his own, the bottom of Nature drops out once more. The inherent conflict of this situation is what leads Thoreau to say that the arrowhead is a "stone fruit" and that it "cannot be lost or found." Like Rousseau's hypothetical "state of Nature," in which the very phrase embodies the contradiction, Thoreau's un*found* arrowheads come in and out of focus like Walden Pond's alternately solid and limitless bottom; the *point d'appui* remains finally unfathomed.[9]

Still, as Thoreau asks in *Cape Cod,* "of what use is a bottom if it is out of sight, if it is two or three miles from the surface, and you are to be drowned so long before you get to it, though it were made of the same stuff with your native soil?" (4:123). There is a practical value to instituting such terms as "bottom," "foundation," and "Nature"; like Rousseau's state that may never have existed or never will exist, Thoreau's Nature makes measurement possible at the same time it clouds its accuracy, or rather, at the same time it makes questionable what accuracy might mean in what is an abstrusely theoretical kind of archeology. As a label for that which seems to recede along with the edge of the frontier, or which is signified always by the next, deeper layer of arrowheads, Thoreau's Nature is a self-emptying term that works as a constant in his unending attempt to balance the equation of wilderness and civilization. The theorizer always in arrears because of the constant addition to the facts of human knowledge is thus in a doubly bound position when he purports to be sifting through the strata of the past: the very act of shedding the impediments of antiquity may only restrengthen their power to elude, so that the further one seeks the foundation, the home of Nature, the further away it is.

The swirl of terms in which Thoreau becomes trapped is as baffling as Cooper's quagmire of imitation, and one can easily sympathize with John Seelye's conclusion that for Thoreau, "The Maine Woods, the Indian, the Primitive Past, all seem to have proved nothing more than a *pokelogan,* a cul-de-sac, ending at the blank wall of Ktaadn."[10] To a certain extent this is necessarily the case; for as Thoreau continues in the passage cited above, the arrowhead is "no disgusting mummy, but a clean stone, the best symbol or letter that could have been transmitted to me. . . It is no single inscription on a particular rock, but a footprint—rather a mindprint—left everywhere, and altogether illegible" (18:91). The statement is telling: that the arrowhead can pass at all for part of Nature, for part of what is truly primitive, depends on its being illegible, in effect unable to be correctly interpreted.

Thoreau is reduced in his account to simply presenting the fact of the arrowhead by illustration, thus:

The Red Man, his mark

Thoreau's suspicion of the mediatory negotiations that attach to trade and economic bargaining is evident throughout his career, even if his stance is often more a rhetorical pose than a staunch conviction. But the question of commercial mediation has a deeper vein than is first evident, one that runs at the base of his theories of language. In an 1841 journal entry Thoreau remarks, "we should communicate our wealth, and not purchase that which does not belong to us for a sign. Why give each other a sign to keep? If we gave the thing itself, there would be no need of a sign" (7:202). The outcome of such a theory is, of course, something akin to Swift's Grand Academy of Lagado, where the abolition of all words is "urged as a great advantage in point of health as well as brevity," and where it is thus determined "that since words are only names for *things,* it would be more convenient for all men to carry about them such *things* as were necessary to express the particular business they are to discourse on."[11]

Thoreau's desire to eliminate the mediating symbol of money is closely aligned with his desire to denude language of similar encumbrances, though both end at similarly embarrassing impasses. His need to define the arrowhead simply by reproducing it in a picture springs from a desire, however often or drastically qualified, to locate the point at which language stops being multiplicitous and slippery, the *point d'appui* where word and thing are yoked. Yet that desire has all the trappings of an impossible Swiftian fantasy, for when Thoreau complains in *Walden* that "the very language of our parlors" threatens to "lose all its nerve and degenerate into *parlaver*" because "our lives pass at such remoteness from its symbols, and its metaphors and tropes are necessarily far fetched, through slides and dumbwaiters," as though "only the savage dwelt near enough to Nature and Truth to borrow a trope from them" (2:270), he not only fetches his own metaphors from afar but also undermines the hypothetical proximity of savage life and symbol by turning Nature itself into a "trope" which must be "borrowed." Like the "fresh fruits" of the savage, yet another trope, Nature is transformed into a *figure* by the mediating process of trade which seeks it out; and as figure, the prized conjunction of word and thing splinters. If Thoreau, as it seems, is leaning on Emerson when he addresses this problem, it is no wonder he can reach only a paradoxical conclusion, since Emerson's essay on language in *Nature* (1836) veers off into a similar cul-de-sac. In a state where "the corruption of man is followed by the corruption of language" and "a paper currency is employed, when there is no bullion in the vaults," Emerson advises "wise men [to] pierce this rotten diction and fasten words again to visible things"; yet this reversion toward an historical moment when "language becomes more picturesque, until its infancy, when it is all poetry," also finds its Eden among "savages, who have only what is necessary, [and thus] converse in figures."[12] Emerson's *figure*, even more pointedly than Thoreau's *trope*, accentuates the paradox of their desire to regain the infancy of language: *figure* is at once a picture, an emblem of one-to-one correspondence like Thoreau's arrowhead; yet as figure, as metaphor, it thrusts the projected correspondence into indirection and displacement, turning representation into re-presentation. The tension in the term between illustration and *re*presentation, between transparency and trope, leaves its status finally unsettled; Emerson's *figure* must also be "borrowed," even at the risk of that overextension of credit it hopes to avoid.

Thoreau's view of Indian language is thus no simple one, though in its hypothetical moment it is similar to the ritualistic theory held by Natty Bumppo: names and thing should have a necessary relation—"Deer-slayer," for example. Yet the illustration of the arrowhead indicates that Thoreau spotted the absurd limitations of such a theory. Word and thing, if not irremediably divorced by the introduction of the term *figure*, eventually come so close that "word" vanishes into "thing," or vice versa; the word becomes unintelligible, and the thing can be conveyed only by its own repetition. Thus Thoreau, unable to say what the arrowhead means, merely *re*presents it, partly as though that act were sufficient, but partly in despair too. He can no more successfully define the arrowhead than he can be sure he has found the earliest American one; like the currency of any system of exchange, linguistic or monetary, the arrowhead is "illegible" outside its system, while inside it, it is destined to remain a *figure* in an un-fathomable account. Moreover, the system itself, if it masks itself as part of Nature, is likewise illegible. In this regard, the Red Man and his mark *are* virtually the same, mere signs of one another. The choice is between the instability and frustration of mediation, upon which the act of definition depends, and that sure stasis which resides only in a Swiftian utopia. No more, Thoreau laments in an important journal passage of 1838, "do we live a quiet, free life, such as Adam's, but are enveloped in an invisible network of speculations....Could we for a moment drop this by-play, and simply wonder, without reference or inference" (7:61). But "simply wonder" is exactly right; the absence of reference or inference would issue in a dumb, blank stare, a thoroughly "natural" state. While Thoreau remarks in *The Maine Woods* that Indian language is a "wild and primitive American sound," he is quick to add that "we may suspect change and deteriorization in almost every other particular but the language which is so wholly unintelligible to us" (3:151). The qualification is hardly too fine: lack of deterioration is consequent only upon unintelligibility; that is, only a language which renders nothing intelligible is undefiled by the speculations of reference. Any intelligibility drawn from that *ur*-language involves a necessary falling away from a pure "sound," which in its concurrent desirability and impracticality corresponds to the pure figure of the arrowhead, both presumably free from the commerce of mediation.

"Pure sound" and "pure figure," since they are tropes of a fantasized moment, an Eden at the outset of the history of rhetoric, name a condition which is ultimately mystical or totemic in dimension, one which *must not,* yet *can only,* be figurative, like the speech of a lost god. The unintelligibility of the arrowhead and the sound of savage language endow them with magical resonance, with what Lévi-Strauss has called *mana,* an overabundance of signifier in relation to what is signified: they mean more than can be known. As symbols "in the pure state," they inhabit and define an Eden of signification verging on the mystical and, since they can be filled with whatever content is desired, possess "symbolic value zero."[13] The zero value of the arrowhead suggests not that it is worthless, but rather that it performs a function that cannot be accurately defined and hence cannot be assigned a specific *value* in a linguistic economy: its worth is at once null and limitless. Thoreau provides an acute explication of the coincidence of forces both sacred and psychological that are at play in the drama of the pure figure, when he remarks at one point in the *Week* that "poetry is the mysticism of mankind," that "if you can speak what you will never hear, if you can write what you will never read, you have done rare things," for "the unconsciousness of man is the consciousness of God." He then sets down an example of such poetry that amounts to a kind of primitive Rorschach test and illuminates the power latent in the pure figure of the arrowhead: "What is produced by a free stroke charms us.... Draw a blunt quill filled with ink over a sheet of paper, and fold the paper before the ink is dry, transversely to this line, and a delicately shaded and regular figure will be produced, in some respects more pleasing than an elaborate drawing" (1:350–51). I will want to return to the question of the violence implicit in Thoreau's "free stroke" (for he goes on to compare it to the taking of a scalp), but want now only to point out that there is an economic rhetoric at work here, that it is a "free" stroke that is required to produce the pure figure, the figure which virtually represents nothing and hence has zero value, but which nonetheless contains limitless meaning by the very token of its ambiguous purity. Such a figure, then, belongs at once to the unconscious and to the mystical realm of the primitive, and Thoreau's whole project is directed at working out the conjunction of the two.

Yet this project is no simple one, for if the freedom and purity of the primitive figure depend upon its unintelligibility, Thoreau's penetration of the sacred abode must risk turning the treasure into plunder and profaning the very Eden he would investigate. Thoreau's paradoxical burden corresponds to that voiced by Lévi-Strauss in *Tristes Tropiques*—that since "man is inseparable from language and language implies society," the privileged state of Nature is destined to remain but a fantasy, an alluring cul-de-sac. Lévi-Strauss records that his search for specimens of the nonexistent Rousseauvian state led him finally, at the "extreme limits of the savage," to a tribe, the Munde, who were totally unintelligible to him, a circumstance that thwarts the very foundation of his professional interests and prompts an outcry worthy of Thoreau's sense of predicament:

> There they were, all ready to teach me their customs and beliefs, and I did not know their language. They were as close to me as a reflection in a mirror; I could touch them, but I could not understand them. I had been given, at one and the same time, my reward and my punishment. . . . I had only to succeed in guessing what they were like for them to be deprived of their strangeness: in which case, I might just as well have stayed in my village. Or if, as was the case here, they retained their strangeness, I could make no use of it, since I was incapable of even grasping what it consisted of. Between these two extremes, what ambiguous instances provide us with the excuses by which we live? Who, in the last resort, is the real dupe of the confusion created in the reader's mind by observations which are carried just far enough to be intelligible and then are stopped in mid-career, because they cause surprise in human beings so similar to those who take such customs as a matter of course? Is it the reader who believes in us, or we ourselves who have no right to be satisfied until we have succeeded in dissipating a residue which serves as a pretext for our vanity?[14]

Thoreau rarely took so dark a view of his own activities, but that can perhaps be ascribed to the fact that he hardly ever dealt with "real" Indians, or at least with any which could even tentatively have been called "savage." Yet his awareness of the paradoxical hinge upon which anthropology turns is just as pressing. To discover a state of Nature and its inhabitants would mean to find something that was, in effect, incommunicable. Lévi-Strauss's figuring of the savage as an ungraspable "reflection in a mirror" summons up a narcissistic stupefaction like that Thoreau indulges in when he lies on his belly and stares into Walden Pond, searching in vain for its true bottom. Completely savage language would for all practical purposes be mute, and the explorer (like Adam, one guesses) could but "simply wonder."

Thoreau's admission that the arrowhead can only be known by the mark of its outline or that the only Indian language that is pure is the one that is unintelligible, points up his blunt recognition that his own enterprise fails sooner or later, almost by definition. Such an admission dissipates the residue of the "natural"; what it does for Thoreau's vanity is unclear, though it seems unlikely to have decreased it.

II

Since man, language, and society are inseparable, the only avenue to Nature lies in a merciless retreat away from the speculative web of reference and inference. This is why late in the *Week* Thoreau must take the position that "the most excellent speech falls finally into Silence.... Creation has not displaced her, but is her visible framework and foil. All sounds are her servants, and purveyors, proclaiming not only that their mistress is, but is a rare mistress, and earnestly to be sought after.... Silence is the universal refuge... ever our inviolable asylum, where no indignity can assail, no personality disturb us" (1:418–19). Thoreau's Silence is an Adamic state, a sacred enclosure cut free from the commerce of language, yet teasingly purveyed by every sound. Silence is *figure* in its purest state—the virtual absence of figure, the true symbolic value zero; yet Thoreau's sexual rhetoric again impinges upon the commercial, and his mistress becomes a seductress on whose behalf mere sounds, not to mention speech, engage in a bargaining which at once flaunts her charms and denies her possession. Because "speech is fractional, [and] silence is integral."[15] as Thoreau notes in his journal of 1840, the encroachment of language can only disfigure the integrity and purity of Silence. If Silence is the inviting refuge, the metaphysical equivalent of the pure primitive, it is nevertheless at the constant mercy of language, the equivalent of the cultural. A journal entry of 1853 invokes some familiar terms and makes clear the role of Thoreau's purest figure: "Silence is of various depth and fertility, like soil. Now it is a mere Sahara, where men perish of hunger and thirst, now a fertile bottom, or prairie of the West" (10:472). But like Walden's curious bottom, the bottom of Silence may be a trap, an insidious enticement. "I have been breaking silence these twenty-three years," Thoreau writes in his 1841 journal, "and have hardly made a rent in it. Silence has no end; speech is but the beginning of it" (7:210). The rhetorics of ownership and violence contained in the word "rent" further link the figure of Silence with the fertile soil of Nature, the unspoiled virgin who "by one bait or another... allures inhabitants into all her recesses" (1:21). That Silence and Nature are West is relatively clear, but another passage in the *Week* confirms the association.

After recording a Hindu proverb which runs "As a dancer, having exhibited herself to the spectator, desists from the dance, so does Nature desist, having manifested herself to soul," Thoreau continues:

> It is easier to discover another such world as Columbus did, than to go within one fold of this which we appear to know so well; the land is lost sight of, the compass varies, and mankind mutiny; and still history accumulates like rubbish before the portals of nature. But there is only necessary a moment's sanity and sound senses, to teach us that there is a nature behind the ordinary, in which we have only some vague pre-emption right and western reserve as yet. We live on the outskirts of that region. . . . Let us wait a little, and not purchase any clearing here, trusting that richer bottoms will soon be put up. (1:409)

Nature, Silence, and West are Thoreau's baits; yet as the passage suggests, and as Thoreau often insists, West is a state of mind, rather than a geographical location. West is a remote region buried within the mind, an unconscious region captured only by a "free stroke"; the language of history is denied entrance to that region and accumulates like rubbish at its portals. Purer than language is sheer sound or music, "the flower of language, thought colored and curved, fluent and flexible," which to the senses is "farthest from us" because it "addresses the greatest depth within us" (1:182–83). Yet deeper still and more pure, virginally pure, must be perfect Silence, for "our finest relations are not simply kept silent about, but buried under a positive depth of silence never to be revealed" (1:295). That Thoreau's Silence also corresponds to the source of the river as a sanctuary of purity and originality is suggested in a journal passage of 1842, where he notes that "the best intercourse and communion [men] would have is in silence above and behind their speech" (7:355).

Despite Thoreau's persistent attempts to remain *outside* of something—town, society, commerce, and so forth—there is an overwhelming counter-sense of his need to get *inside* a shelter of one kind or another. This can, as in *Walden,* take the form of indulging in that "pleasure of construction" (2:51) Thoreau enjoys when building his house about himself with boards or with words; or it can appear as a more primeval urge to crawl into the womb of nature, that mysterious region that is both interior and exterior. Thoreau's belief that his solitude weaves about him "a silken web or *chrysalis,*" from which he, "nymph-like, shall ere long burst forth a more perfect creature" (15:246), yokes together his reverence for the mind as a kind of "*sanctum sanctorum*" (8:290) with a similar description in "Walking" of his restorative pilgrimage into nature: "When I would recreate myself, I seek the darkest wood, the thickest and most interminable and, to the citizen, most dismal swamp. I enter a swamp as a sacred place, a *sanctum sanctorum*. There is the strength, the marrow of Nature" (5:228). Yet it would seem that the kind of blessedness offered here could turn quickly into another *pokelogan.* Since what Thoreau would like to be or become is always over the western horizon—"Let us migrate interiorly with intermission, and pitch our tent each day nearer the western horizon," he records in his journal of 1840 (7:131)—it is nearly useless to define it in terms that always fracture as soon as they are invoked or which lead only to Ktaadn's blank wall of Silence. Thoreau's respect for the immobilization induced by the metaphysics of wilderness sublimity is certainly not so highly charged as, say, that in Poe's *Narrative of A. Gordon Pym,* where at the edge of a frontier nightmare the story's namesake careens off into a chasm guarded by a monstrous white figure, or even in *Pierre,* in which Melville warns "that it is not for man to follow the trail of truth too far, since by doing so he entirely loses the directing compass of his mind; for arrived at the Pole, to whose barrenness only it points, there, the needle indifferently respects all points of the horizon alike."[16] Yet more than anything else, Thoreau's West is "our own interior white on the chart," as he puts it in *Walden* (2:353); but to fully enter such a region, the chamber of the pure figure of Silence, would mean reaching a place where one's compass ceases to function and all modes of reference blow apart.

Going West for Thoreau entails entering a spiritual domain in which he tracks himself like an animal in deep brush. His fascination with the raw violence and strategies of the hunt energizes his writing, for thought itself is a kind of game to be raised and captured. To succeed in the hunt one must live as though in constant preparation for it, for the hunter, of whatever kind, "will not bag any [game] if he does not already know its seasons and haunts and the color of its wing,—if he has not dreamed of it, so that he can *anticipate* it" (17:286). Thoreau's spiritual exercises in the woods confirm Kenneth Burke's observation that "mystic *silence* has its roots" in the hunt, since "in the quest one is naturally silent, be it as the animal stalking its quarry or as the thinker meditating upon an idea. Thus, even the utterance of the question begins in the silence of the quest."[17] Burke would even seem to have been reading Thoreau, who records in his 1851 journal, "the longest silence is the most pertinent question most pertinently put. Emphatically silent" (8:137). The silent cavern entered by Thoreau is the wilderness of himself and of America, both pertinent and emphatic questions. For Cooper, as we noted, only *Home as Found*'s haunting Silent Pine, symbol of a paternity whose voice is wholly in question, is a true "American antiquity"; and for Melville's Pierre, silence is the very voice of god and of the literary craft, which in the end are for him very much the same. Thoreau's silence also reverberates with the question of American authority, but for him the quarry is an object of search like *Walden*'s raw woodchuck, whose attributes he takes in by devouring (2:232), a feast which John Seelye finds to symbolize Thoreau's appropriation of "the spiritual landscape by turning it inside out, putting the furside inside and the skinside out, by internalizing the wildness."[18] For Thoreau the hunter, the earth "spread out like a map around [him] is but the lining of [his] inmost soul exposed" (12:294), much as in *Moby-Dick* Ahab's wrinkles finally come into enigmatic correspondence with the map by which he plans his revenge, "as if some invisible pencil was also tracing lines and courses upon the deeply marked chart of his forehead."[19]

Thoreau enacts both roles in Ortega's apt hunting analogy: "Like the hunter in the absolute *outside* of the countryside, the philosopher is the alert man in the absolute *inside* of ideas, which are also an unconquerable and dangerous jungle." Yet Ortega points out another aspect of the hunt that is perhaps even more relevant for Thoreau, who is always on guard against snares in his path, a soft-bottomed bog in Nature's sanctuary, or an unintelligible Indian relic. "*It is not essential to the hunt that it be success-ful,*" says Ortega. "On the contrary were the hunter's efforts always and inevitably successful it would not be the effort we call hunting, it would be something else. Corresponding to the eventuality or chance of the prey's escaping is the eventuality of the hunter's *rentrer bredouille* [going home empty-handed]. The beauty of hunting lies in the fact that it is always problematic." Likewise, of course, "meditation always runs the risk of returning home empty-handed."[20] This is the risk Thoreau continually runs; but to repeat, there would be no hunt without the risk, and one could almost push as far in Thoreau's case as to say there would be no hunt if he did not *always* go home empty-handed, or nearly so. Indeed it is hard to guess what it might mean for Thoreau to succeed, to snag his prey, which is so vaporous and flees on so many fronts at once. Thoreau remarks in his journal entry concerning his search for arrowheads, "I would fain know that I am treading in the tracks of human game,—that I am on the trail of mind" (18:91). The reason his tracking never ceases is that the trail of mind he is on is his own. But if it is also the case that the talent of composition is comparable to the taking of a scalp, Thoreau may, failing other game, at least go home with his head in his hands.

Nietzsche writes in *Beyond Good and Evil* that "in the writings of a hermit one always hears something of the echo of the desolate regions, something of the whispered tones and the furtive look of solitude; in his strongest words, even in his cry, there still vibrates a new and dangerous kind of silence—of burying something in silence." Consequently, the hermit will be suspicious of the writings of any philosopher, will doubt "whether behind every one of his caves there is not, must not be, another deeper cave—a more comprehensive, stranger, richer world beyond the surface, an abysmally deep ground behind every ground, under every attempt to furnish 'grounds.' " The hermit will claim that "there is something arbitrary in [the philosopher's] stopping *here* to look back and look around, in his not digging deeper *here* but laying his spade aside."[21] Thoreau, of course, is both hermit and philosopher, and his writings continually scrutinize themselves with the suspicious eye of the hermit, one which finds its finest relations buried beneath a positive depth of silence and its richest bottoms yet outstanding. Thoreau keeps his West—that place which would furnish a true American *ground*—forever in abeyance, since to achieve it would mean to obliterate it. Yet such frustrating self-awareness does not prevent him from setting up shop and declaring himself at home. Thoreau, perhaps more than any American writer, has an uncanny sense of *place,* of actually being situated on a certain tract of land at a certain time. And just as there is in the end something ludicrous about raging after an ever-receding frontier, so Thoreau also finds something particularly relentless about the place one is at: "Think of the consummate folly of attempting to go away from *here!* When the constant endeavor should be to get nearer and nearer *here*....A man dwells in his native valley like a corolla in its calyx, like an acorn in its cup. *Here,* of course, is all that you love, all that you expect, all that you are. Here is your bride elect, as close to you as she can be got" (17:275). At times Thoreau could almost convince one that his persistent lamentations are all a ruse, that Nature is no mystery at all and that "travellers generally exaggerate the difficulties of the way." "If a person lost would conclude that after all he is not lost," the *Week* continues, "but standing in his own shoes on the very spot where he is, and that for the time being he will live there; but the places that have known him, *they* are lost,—how much anxiety and danger would vanish" (1:193). But since his anxiety will not vanish sheerly on command, the best way for Thoreau to keep his project going is to keep it dangerous.

Neither can that anxiety be disconnected from the eroticism implicit in Thoreau's figuring of *here* as his "bride elect." As in the case of so many American writers, the question of sexuality in Thoreau is continually refracted into the lust of exploration and the hunt, even when those enterprises go under the banner of a chaste disavowal of intimacy or matrimony. Thoreau's *here* echoes Natty Bumppo's final declaration, a haunting utterance of "Here!" spoken into the fading sunset of the West.[22] Natty's cry is the dying warrior's password, a last affirmation of natural right and heroic asceticism. Like Natty, who with the exception of a momentary lapse in *The Pathfinder* always chose Nature over woman, or like Ike McCaslin in *The Bear,* who repudiates his marriage and finally can take only the woods for "his mistress and his wife,"[23] Thoreau simply declares, "all nature is my bride" (15:337). Given such a remark, the nature of Thoreau's *sanctum sanctorum*, his wilderness chasm, begins to shape up differently. It is even clearer, if a little vulgar, in this spirited remark from the *Week*: "If we look into the heavens they are concave, and if we look into a gulf as bottomless, it would be concave also. The sky is curved downward to the earth in the horizon...I draw down its skirts" (1:353). Thoreau draws down its skirts— with himself inside. Getting inside—inside of Nature, of Silence, of *here*— is at once an advance toward the Eden of the West and a return to a primitive paradise, the womb of America. Thoreau's insurgent vocabulary of invagination—whether flower, folds, buried depths, portals, recesses, and even bottoms, which take on a lurid tone at times[24]—reinforces his figure of Nature as a virginal mistress or bride. But the status of Nature as a virgin land corresponds as well to the elusive mistress of Silence: her enticement depends upon remaining inviolate, which in turn excludes cultivation.

Richard Poirier has remarked that the greatest American writings "are alive with the effort to stabilize certain feelings and attitudes that have, as it were, no place in the world, no place at all except where a writer's style can give them one."[25] This is evident enough in Thoreau's case, and all the more an accurate way of putting it since, as Thoreau says in his essay on Carlyle, "literally and really, the style is no more than the *stylus*, the pen [one] writes with" (4:330). Thoreau wields his own *stylus* as a tool of cultivation, a literary plow which is at once a brutal weapon of incision and an instrument of insemination. His interest in the alignment of writing and cultivation situates Thoreau in the line of American narratives that link eroticism and regeneration with acts of totemic violence. If the question of violence in Thoreau is often channeled off into moments of sheer spectacle—his Trojan war with weeds in his bean field, say, or his lurid delight in the mock civil war fought by red and black ants enclosed in the theater of a glass tumbler (2:178, 255–56)—we must nevertheless be attuned to the way in which the same violence, however sublimated or diffused, underlies the transactions which engender the drama of his own settlement. To do so, we must follow out a peculiar detour on his map of the primitive.

Thoreau's insertion of himself into the feminized landscape of America is marked by the imperialistic eroticism which Annette Kolodny has observed throughout American literature and so accurately summed up in the commonplace phrase, "the lay of the land."[26] But as in the case of *Pierre*, where a mother and a sister are converted into the receptacles of Melville's tortured version of manifest destiny, or *Home as Found*, where Cooper builds an enclosed garden around his American Eve and fosters an incestuous marriage in hopes of retrieving the shattered Edenic dream, so

Thoreau's intimacy with his mistress Nature has its own ties to family romance. Thoreau's early life in a household that included a mother, two sisters, and two aunts, and his Leatherstocking-like avoidance of intimacy with women may have no small bearing on the sensuality with which he charged the accounts of his various pioneering enterprises.[27] Yet if Thoreau enforced his own chastity with rituals of purification and so saved his higher energies for the sacred role of hunter and explorer, it is even clearer in his case than in Natty Bumppo's that the penetration of the wilderness is at least in part a sublimated return to the Mother. "Woman is a nature older than I," Thoreau writes in 1849, "and commanding from me a vast amount of veneration, like Nature. She is my mother at the same time that she is my sister. I cannot imagine a woman no older than I." Thoreau's positioning of "Nature" in the context of a discussion of his enigmatic relationship with women is by no means an accident, for his writings continually make a fetish of troubling the distinction between the two. He goes on to say that his "most intimate acquaintance with woman has been a sisterly relation, or at most a catholic-mother relation," one in which "she has exerted the influence of a goddess over me; cultivating my gentler humane nature; cultivating and preserving purity, innocence, and truth." We will need to reconsider the striking reversal of roles that has occurred—the woman now becoming the cultivator of Thoreau's nature—but should add here that in the ellipsis of the quotation Thoreau remarks of his sister-virgin-mother relationship, "—not that it has always been free from the suspicion of a lower sympathy."[28] What amounts to a "lower sympathy" in Thoreau's eyes is not entirely clear, but we are forced to share his suspicion of it.

Although Thoreau's gardening does not impinge so nearly upon the sordid and the demonic as Cooper's in *Home as Found,* Hawthorne's in *The House of the Seven Gables,* or Melville's in *Pierre,* it is no less overtly mythological and personal. Emerson might have been projecting a career for Thoreau when he wrote in *Nature* that "in the woods. . .a man casts off his years, as the snake his slough, and at what period soever in his life, is always a child."[29] Becoming a child in the garden of Nature is a transfiguration hardly peculiar to Thoreau, and both he and Emerson have a healthy tradition, running at least from Vergil to Wordsworth, to draw on for such sentiments. But one of Thoreau's particular gardens, his bean field at Walden, stands out with enchanting power:

> When I was four years old, as I well remember, I was brought from Boston to this my native town, through these very woods and this field, to the pond. It is one of the oldest scenes stamped on my memory. And now to-night my flute has waked the echoes over that very water. The pines still stand here older than I; or, if some have fallen, I have cooked my supper with their stumps, and a new

growth is rising all around, preparing another aspect for new infant eyes. Almost the same johnswort springs from the same perennial root in this pasture, and even I have at length helped to clothe that fabulous landscape of my infant dreams, and one of the results of my presence and influence is seen in these bean leaves, corn blades, and potato vines. (2:172)

While Thoreau's prose is as carefully cultivated as his garden and laden with the conventions of pastoral, his description of the landscape of his "infant dreams" as "fabulous" locates his garden in a topography halfway between fable and fantasy, between historical tradition and personal memory. His gardening is at once an invocation of eclogic archetypes and a return to the childhood of his own dreams. When he adds in the next paragraph that the arrowheads turned up by his hoe prove "that an extinct nation had anciently dwelt here and planted corn and beans ere white men came to clear the land" (2:172), Thoreau ironizes the violence of his own wars in the bean field at the same time he turns his cultivation, whether by hoe or by pen, into an elegy for a lost moment in American history, a moment which has become analogous for him to a lost scene in his own life.

Perhaps the violence of Thoreau's gardening is not merely a threatrical exhibition, though, but a crucial part of his remembrance of things past. In what may be the most striking episode in the *Week*, Thoreau's rendition of Cotton Mather's capitivity narrative of Hannah Dustan, an act of violent revenge provides him a convenient entrance into American mythology and subtly annotates his own attempted recovery of the fantasized state of Nature. For Mather, the Dustan captives' slaughter and scalping of the Indians who had seized them provides a lesson in just retribution and the occasion for a sermon on Christian perseverance in the satanic wilderness. Thoreau's account, though free from ecclesiastical baggage, follows the details of Mather's narrative fairly closely, except for two remarkable variations. Mather's version of the murder of Dustan's infant child by the Indians is relatively simple: "they dash'd out the Brains of the Infant, against a tree";[30] but in Thoreau's rendering Hannah sees "her infant's brains dashed out against an apple tree" (1:342). The significance of Thoreau's addition is clarified at the end of his account when, repeating himself for good measure, he notes that the Dustan family is "assembled alive once more, except for the infant whose brains were dashed out against the apple tree" and fixes the lesson of *his* narrative by adding "there have been many who in later times have lived to say that they have eaten of the fruit of that apple tree. This seems a long while ago, and yet it happened since Milton wrote his Paradise Lost" (1:345). That Thoreau intends both himself and his readers to be numbered among those who have eaten of the fruit is supported by his subtle conversion to the present tense midway in his story, as though to

recreate the scene of violence as one in which we are directly participating—
as indeed we are. Richard Slotkin has described Thoreau's fruit as "a kind of
Indian-cannibal Eucharist" that "serves to link the present dwellers in the
land to the reality of that bloody revelation of wilderness by means of a sacrament in which the symbolic fruit is perceived as a scant covering, an insig-
nificant palliation or sublimation, of the reality of infant blood and torment."[31] Even if Thoreau's narrative does not have quite the eschatological
thrust Slotkin finds, it nevertheless points up the fact that the seizure of the
American paradise is a complicated second performance of the fall of man,
an act of grim violence that goes hand in hand with settlement. Yet as
Thoreau recognizes, one way to account or atone for the incursion of white
civilization and the violence it provoked, is to render it the source of a for-
tunate fall, one that produces a fruit of communion with the past, a communion in which atonement is never complete and in which the participant,
like the mythographer, is always "in arrears," yet one in which a repeated
memorial incident will allow us "to say" we have eaten of the fruit and thus
settled and naturalized the act.

     That "saying" is of critical importance to Thoreau, and it is not to be
disconnected from his anxiety about his complicity as a writer in the
ravishing of the American Eden. The second important variation he works
on Mather's account is concerned precisely with the act of violence that is
presumably being commemorated as sacrament. While Mather describes the
murder of the Indians as a typological imitation of "the Action of Jael upon
Sisera" (*Judges,* iv), he turns the scalping into a simple act of practicality,
by which the avengers "Received Fifty Pounds from the General Assembly
of the Province, as a Recompence of their Action," and also "a very
generous Token of his Favour" from "Colonel Nicholson, the Governour of
Maryland,"[32] Although Thoreau takes note of the bounty paid for the Indian "trophies," he not only drops the Biblical sanction for the murder,
thus making *it* a simple act of practicality, but also severely complicates the
motive for the scalping when he reports that the captives took the scalps and
put them "into a bag as proofs of what they had done" because Hannah
feared "that her story would not be believed if she should escape to tell it"
(1:343). Immediately after these remarks Thoreau switches to present tense
in his narration, bringing the deed home to the reader and mounting the
suspense of the captives' escape.

     But we must wonder still why Thoreau feels compelled to raise the ques-
tion of the integrity of Hannah's story, unless perhaps it is a reflection of his
fear that his own accounts will not be believed without similar acts of regenerative violence. What proof of his own struggle with the primitive might
amount to in Thoreau's case is open to question; certainly when he notes a

few pages later that "the talent of composition is very dangerous,—the striking out the heart of life at a blow, as the Indian takes off a scalp" (1:351), we suspect Thoreau once more of indulgence in the spectacle of his own invention. Yet we might say as well that Thoreau has replicated the captivity narrative he borrows from Mather, that his variations at once constitute an act of violence against Mather's account yet reap the rewards attendant upon an improved story, one that places the episode in a more valuable context of American mythology and buttresses its sacramental power. The talent of composition *is* dangerous for Thoreau; wielding his pen as a plow or an axe, he burdens the pristine territory under investigation with a "load of thought" analogous to those "superfluous commodities" with which the white man has swindled the savage under the guise of trading for his "fresh fruits." The apple tree in Thoreau's account of Hannah Dustan is all the more an interesting addition to the story in that it stands at once as a sign of the Edenic state Thoreau hopes to discover on his travels and conversely as a sign of the shattering of that Eden. The apple tree is the trophy which Thoreau's violent foray into Mather produces; it is proof of his imaginative venture and the regenerative reward of his communion with a scene which has threatened to become lost from American memory.

Thoreau employs the "trophy"—indeed, the "trope"—of the apple in a number of writings, and we will want to return to its role again; but it is necessary first to consider another aspect of Thoreau's Edenic mythologizing of the captivity tale. That the slaughtered infant of Hannah Dustan may be echoing in Thoreau's mind an incident or threat from his own childhood, we can only speculate; yet that Thoreau's cultivation of the landscape of America's infancy and that of his own "infant dreams" are strangely interfused, seems further evident when he goes on from his invocation of Milton to chart the historical distance from Adam and Eve to the settlement of America and remarks that "the lives of but sixty old women, such as live under the hill, say of a century each, strung together, are sufficient to reach over the whole ground. Taking hold of hands they would span the interval from Eve to my own mother" (1:346). We might take this to be merely a rhetorical flourish were it not for the strong identification Thoreau continually makes between the primitive and the infantile, and between Nature and the Mother (or, as we have seen, the older sister). Thoreau alternates spasmodically in his assessment of Nature, and for every instance in which he finds her to be his mysteriously enfolding bride or mother, a home warm and safe wherever he is when he is *here,* he finds a counterfigure of significant aspect: "Man cannot afford to be a naturalist, to look at Nature directly, but only with the side of his eye. He must look through and beyond her. To look at her is [as] fatal as to look at the head of Medusa" (11:45).

Corresponding to the ambivalence surrounding the trope of the apple, then, is an ambivalence in Thoreau's attitude toward the Mother of Nature. Just as the apple is both the sign of Eden and the sign of its dispersal, so Nature is both comfort and threat; or rather, the fantasized return to Nature is both dream and nightmare. We will have to look to *Pierre* for a full-scale exploitation of this tension in the American topography; but Thoreau forecasts the vague region between incestuous eroticism and the threat of castration Melville will explore when he remarks of his voyage in the *Week* that the traveler who is "born again on the road" will "experience at last that old threat of his mother fulfilled, that he shall be skinned alive. His sores shall gradually deepen themselves that they may heal inwardly . . ." (1:326). Thoreau's being skinned alive parallels his devouring of the raw woodchuck as an act of totemic internalization, but the suggestion seems to be that his own ritual rebirth entails being inversely devoured by Nature, that in his erotic return to the landscape of his infant dreams he must run the risk of mutilation at the hands of that Mother he so cherishes as a virgin goddess. It is as though the "violence of love" which Thoreau speaks of in the famous pages on friendship (1:290) were composed equally of the violence of his own cultivating penetration and of a countering violence of revenge dealt by the Nature he would possess.

It would be a mistake to read these episodes in the *Week* too psychoanalytically, in the vain hope of determining Thoreau's mental condition. Even if that were possible, it would be beside the point, which is to lay out Thoreau's use of figures that are ambiguously psychological and mythic in his narrative. The question of the imaginative rebirth Thoreau undergoes in the course of his voyage, and the way it is accomplished, is completely relevant in this respect, and there is a passage late in the *Week* that suggests the nature of this rebirth and hauntingly echoes the threat of the Mother, which that experience entails. It is "as if our birth had at first sundered things," Thoreau says of the literal birth that his voyage has figuratively reenacted, "and we had been thrust up through into nature like a wedge, and not till the wound heals and the scar disappears do we begin to discover where we are, and that nature is one and continuous everywhere" (1:372). By the point in the *Week* at which this passage occurs, Thoreau has become considerably involved in an overt attempt to cover up the incursion of his voyage and heal the wound *it* has made by turning it into part of a natural process. What is of interest here, however, is that when juxtaposed to the earlier passage in which Thoreau is "born again" on the road by reliving the Mother's threat, his remarks not only encompass the rude violence carried out in the act of birth but also trouble our identification of the wounded. Is it, in fact, the child (Thoreau) or the Mother (Nature) who is wounded at birth and whose scar must heal? And who, then, is wounded by the reenactment of birth Thoreau attempts to perform by his voyage into Nature? The question is complex, and all the more so in that the figures it summons up are so startlingly reminiscent of the opening of Whitman's "Song of the Broad-Axe":

> Weapon shapely, naked, wan,
> Head from the mother's bowels drawn,
> Wooded flesh and metal bone, limb only one and lip only one,
> Gray-blue leaf by red-heat grown, helve produced from a
> little seed sown...[33]

Whitman's lines, among the best in American poetry, brilliantly explicate the tension in Thoreau's narrative. Like Thoreau's "wedge," Whitman's axe is at once child and phallus, the product of birth and the weapon turned back against the Mother Nature that bore it. Both narratives describe a release from captivity and an act of revenge that, whatever its intention, turns back in violence upon its source. Though Whitman's poem breaks into a celebration of the deeds performed by the American axe, his overt eroticism brings the actions of the weapon closer to a drama of incest than is comfortable.

If Thoreau's narrative is not as economically constructed as Whitman's packed lines, his sense of the ironies of that drama seems clearer; for perhaps more poignantly than Whitman, he recognized that his own pen was a weapon that, however much it celebrated the settlement of America, aligned itself unnervingly with the destruction of the new Eden. Thoreau's birth "up through into" Nature like a wedge is inversely repeated in the repenetration of Nature undertaken in his traveling, plowing, and writing. He might well have recalled, though repressing it in his own account, that Mather described the revenging wounds inflicted by the Dustan captives as "Home Blows, [struck] upon the Heads of their Sleeping Oppressors,"[34] for his return to the home of Nature, the primitive landscape of the Mother, is a liberation that also exercises a certain violence against a figure who rules over the home of his infant dreams. The interval between Thoreau's first and second sunderings of Nature, his two births, corresponds to that "memorable interval" between the spoken and the written he elaborates in the chapter on "Reading" in *Walden*. The spoken "is commonly transitory, a sound, a tongue, a dialect merely, almost brutish, and we learn it unconsciously, like the brutes, of our mothers," while the written "is the maturity and experience of that; if [the spoken] is our mother tongue, this is our father tongue, a reserved and select expression, too significant to be heard by the ear, which we must be born again in order to speak" (2:112). Against the feminine primacy of the spoken Thoreau shares with Emerson and Rousseau, among others, he places the power of the written, the father tongue whose *stylus* registers an advance in cultivation and necessarily joins forces with the masculine domination civilization inflicts upon the primitive, the first home of Nature and Mother violently "rent" by the inscriptions of plow and pen.

III

In his attempt to naturalize his traveling and his writing, then, Thoreau's employment of the trope of cultivation is more than a literary convention; rather, it is an exact index of the psychological and mythological motives of his frontier enterprise. But if Thoreau plays out the intimate connection between *grafting* and *graphein,* he does so in full awareness of the risk that his *grafting* may introduce a corrupt economy that issues either in mutation and disease or in illicit profit gained by violence and double-dealing. Thoreau's cultivation of Nature yokes literal seeding with insemination by the letter in a precise way, for his whole project involves implanting himself in the midst of Nature while at the same time concealing the injury generated by that act. When Thoreau notes in the discussion of friendship in the *Week* that "speech. . .follows after silence" at a long remove, just as "the buds in the graft do not put forth into leaves till long after the graft has taken" (1:285), he calls attention to the way in which language grows round the enfolded recess of silence by grafting itself on to Nature's void. Writing for Thoreau, even more pointedly than speech, is an act of implanting, incubation, and labor; and as a "home-staying, laborious native of the soil," he claims in *Walden* that he would work his bean field "if only for the sake of tropes and expressions, to serve a parable-maker one day" (2:173, 179). One constantly feels, in fact, that Thoreau would not undertake half his projects if he did not have before him the prospect of writing about them, or, like Hannah Dustan, bringing home proof of his enterprise, the "trope" and "trophy" of his writing and scalping.

Yet the graft of writing is also a kind of rehabilitation for Thoreau, a cure of the ground which is also the disease itself. To accentuate this aspect of his own mythology, Thoreau continually reverts to the figure of the apple, at once a token of the primitive, innocent paradise, but likewise its most culturally burdened symbol. In the midst of the wilderness of the *Week,* Thoreau strikingly amends the "free aspect of the wild apple-trees" he has just praised, by reporting that in fact they are "not poison, but New English," their "ancestors" imported by his own; these "gentler trees," Thoreau adds, "imparted a half-civilized and twilight aspect to the otherwise barbarian land" (1:246). In "Wild Apples," Thoreau links the apple's role to his own craft even more pointedly when he remarks that "*our* wild apple is wild only like myself, perchance, who belong not to the aboriginal race here, but have strayed into the woods from the cultivated stock" (5:301). More naked yet is his observation in *The Maine Woods* that a particular "orchard of healthy and well-grown apple-trees" unfortunately bears "all natural fruit" and is thus "comparatively worthless for want of a grafter." He goes on to propose, in an open display of his own motives, that "it would be a good speculation, as well as a favor conferred on the settlers, for a Massachusetts boy to go down there with a trunk full of scions, and his grafting apparatus, in the spring" (3:9). Placed against his earlier lamentation that ever since Adam man has been trapped in a "web of speculations" spun from inference and reference, this American apple orchard stops somewhat short of Eden's bliss and brings the "Massachusetts boy" even closer to Thoreau's own *grafting*. The paradise of the natural he keeps projecting as a desirable state shrivels and goes rotten on closer inspection, as though Thoreau had to guarantee his own fall and complicity in the act of settlement which makes its way by graft and trade. In order to obtain the savage's "fresh fruits" Thoreau must enter into trade himself; but since "no *trade* is simple, but artificial and complex" (11:445), and since that which "commerce seizes is always the very coarsest part of the fruit,—the mere husk and rind" (20:277), his search necessarily profanes its object in the very act of obtaining it. Or, in what is at once a more practical but also more disturbing alternative, it may prove to be the case that the wild, untouched fruit is *too* natural to be of use, that only a grafter can make it fit for consumption. In either case Thoreau is in danger: he either engages in an activity which he must continually admit is illicit, or he renounces the tangible proof of an American paradise.

Also subject to the paradox of settlement is the *too* natural Silence that waits like the untouched land or the blank page to be penetrated and engrafted, for it is the act of insemination, the graft of writing or speech, which both domesticates and obliterates Silence, removing it farther West or further within. Like the arrowhead or the blank wall of Ktaadn, unencumbered by interpretation, Silence is that which is always in refuge, most in recess. Of the words which parade and pander about Thoreau's mistress, those which come nearest must be written "exactly at the right crisis," for "poetry. . . is not recoverable thought, but a hue caught from a vaster *receding* thought" (1:350, my emphasis). If "the most excellent speech finally falls into Silence," however, one approach to the "right crisis" is to place it at the very edge of this *falling*. The writing act catches Nature, or the primitive past it represents, on the brink of Silence; yet in holding that Silence in reverence, Thoreau's writing marks itself as an inadequate deterioration and falling away from that which it sets up as unavailable to appropriation. Ob-

viously, *fall* is a word with a razor edge, and we will see eventually how crucial its ambiguity is to the lesson of "Friday" in the *Week*. What is important to note here is that *fall* may connote a natural cycle, like that of the river
itself, "falling all the way" to the sea according to "the law of its birth" and
"an ancient, ineradicable inclination" (1:86–87); or it may indicate a
plunge into the virtual abyss of Silence, a wholesale eradication of intelligibility. On the one hand, language stops short of the abyss and rescues intelligibility; on the other, language is in fact already *fallen*, the perversion of
pure and sacred Silence, and thus the very condition of man's trangression
and violation of an American Eden. These are the choices Thoreau juggles,
but in either case writing becomes subject to the speculative web of reference; its *graft* creates meaning by instituting an economy of reference yet
continually retreats defeated into its own silence to await the next "crisis"
when the arrowhead, the foundation, the bottom, or whatever relic at the
moment represents Nature, threatens to fall into too deep a *recession*.

"Recede" may be the most loaded word in Thoreau's magazine of
puns, having a duplicity as paradoxical as that attached to his notion of the
frontier as the place where facts are "fronted." The true wilderness, the
home of the Indian, is the "Unappropriated Land" (1:334) which Thoreau
seeks to appropriate, but the very act unfortunately dissolves the wilderness
and forces it constantly to recede, its "free" space usurped for profit and
speculation by the agricultural wave whose limit forms the frontier between
the savage and the civilized. That which Thoreau seeks *recedes* into the future, and its economic *recession* is paradoxically its most valuable attribute:
it remains unprofaned by the commerce necessarily introduced by the tilling
of the soil, or by the telling of the story. Since language and possession are
inextricably entwined, it is entirely appropriate that the West is a place of recession, a pocket of virginal Silence; the West across the frontier must be
Adamic and free from the structures of value introduced by the mediating
agencies of language and commerce. But again, because Thoreau is investi-
gating a presumably *natural* American state that has been disrupted by the
white man's entrance, that which recedes—the "vaster receding thought,"
for example—is also what fades into a silent past. What Thoreau pursues is
both past and future, paradise lost and, since "there is an orientalism in the
most restless pioneer, and the farthest west is but the farthest east" (1:157),
paradise still outstanding; yet both may prove to be beyond the frontier of
the intelligible.

Thoreau's Indian, his version of Rousseauvian man, is thus both past
and future, a wraithlike embodiment of Thoreau's projected ideal simultaneously lost in history and still waiting over the horizon; yet his language is
unintelligible and his relationship with Nature troubling. "The Indian's in-

tercourse with Nature,'' says Thoreau, ''is at least such as admits of the greatest independence of each. If he is somewhat of a stranger in her midst, the gardener is too much of a familiar. There is something vulgar and foul in the latter's closeness to his mistress, something noble and cleanly in the former's distance'' (1:56). The white gardener's settlement and cultivation of the land penetrates and befouls it, and provokes a virtual enslavement by appropriation and ownership. Thus when Thoreau remarks further on that ''man tames Nature only that he may make her more free than he found her, though he may never yet have succeeded'' (1:337), his ''free'' is at once wildly ironic and accurate: the taming of agriculture initiates a form of prostitution which erases freedom, but it may at the same time make Nature sexually freer, more fertile. Just so, Silence, verbally chaste, when inseminated by the white man's ''load of thought'' becomes productive, but in doing so loses its seductive charm. Clearly enough, Thoreau's penetration of Nature has two sides. On the one hand, it is a rude despoiling, but on the other, it represents a fathering and impregnation, the necessary cultivation entailed by settlement.

Thoreau has a number of strategies to account for his entrance into Nature, but one he returns to again and again in the journals is the metaphor of the gall. At a local level, Thoreau finds it ''remarkable that a mere gall, which at first we are inclined to regard as something abnormal, should be made so beautiful, as if it were the *flower* of the tree; that a disease, an excrescence, should prove, perchance, the greatest beauty,—as the tear of the pearl. Beautiful scarlet sins they may be. . . . This gall is the tree's 'Ode to Dejection''' (11:210). While Thoreau claims in *Walden,* of course, that he does ''not propose to write an ode to dejection'' (2:94), his career is exactly that, at least in the sense ascribed to the tree's gall. An 1854 journal entry is more exact on this subject: ''Is not Art itself a gall? Nature is stung by God and the seed of man planted in her. The artist changes the direction of Nature and makes her grow according to his idea. If the gall was anticipated when the oak was made, so was the canoe when the birch was made. Genius stings Nature, and she grows according to its idea'' (13:10). Yet another journal passage, of just a year earlier, records that ''Nature [itself] is a kind of gall. . . the Creator stung her and man is the grub she is destined to house and feed'' (11:210). Thoreau's indecision as to whether it is Art or Nature which forms the gall is important, since his whole enterprise is directed at troubling the distinction between the two. Perhaps more revealing, though, is his attempt to make the wounding and impregnating act part of a natural process, thus domesticating its violence and fitting it into a chain fathered finally by God. In the end, Thoreau's metaphor is all-encompassing; since man becomes a center of civilization wherever he is, housed like a grub

in the flesh of Nature, his every attempt to make a home must heal the
wound made and nurse the scar of settlement.

A more classical instance of this confrontation between Art and Nature,
and one which retains the figure of a wounding inscription so important to
Thoreau, is Marvell's "The Garden." Thoreau quotes two lines from the
poem—"Two paradises 'twere in one/To live in paradise alone"—at the
outset of his journals as a beacon to his solitude, but the third stanza must
also have struck home for him:

> No white nor red was ever seen
> So am'rous as this lovely green.
> Fond lovers, cruel as their flame,
> Cut in these trees their mistress' name.
> Little, alas, they know, or heed,
> How far these beauties hers exceed!
> Fair trees! wheres'e'er your barks I wound,
> No name shall but your own be found.[35]

All told, Thoreau's work does just as efficient a job as Marvell's poem of
"Annihilating all that's made/To a green thought in a green shade," and
the wound he makes in Nature is as handily covered up by a healing gall; the
action both satisfies the lust for violation and saves Nature by reconstituting
it at a further remove, some realm presently beyond the reach of domestication. Thoreau's journal of 1851 records that "a surveyor must be curious in
studying the wounds of trees, to distinguish a natural disease or scar from
the 'blazing' of an axe" (9:79–80). Sincere as this may be, it is nevertheless
part of Thoreau's purpose to get to the point where the two scars are indistinguishable, where he can enter Nature undetected and without telltale
trace. His writing itself performs this function while it at the same time
betrays it. Like the "well-built sentence" that a journal entry of 1842 compares "to a modern corn-planter, which furrows out, drops the seed, and
covers it up at one movement" (7:313), Thoreau's own writing gouges out a
clearing in the wilderness, implants itself, and attempts to cover up its violation by apology and oration. Yet that recovery has another side too: since
the prize of the wilderness, the Eden of Nature, is automatically buried
beneath the "load" of writing at the very moment its appearance is proclaimed, the writer necessarily covers up what he has exposed whether he
wants to or not. Thoreau can neither keep his name succinctly carved in the
bark of Nature nor ever find out what, if anything, lies beneath that bark.

The gall of writing ultimately becomes a surrogate for the "fresh fruits"
of Nature that Thoreau has gone in search of, the most valuable product of
his act of violation. As the central figure in a melodrama of naturalization,

the gall represents the union of the savage and the civilized, of the feminine Nature and the fathering Art; and since it enacts both a rebirth and an erotic if violent coupling, the gall is the perfect emblem of Thoreau's ambivalence. We should recall at this point the journal passage quoted earlier in which Thoreau projects the figure of the woman as one who cultivates *his* nature, thus reversing the usual roles; this troubling of the distinction corresponds to the erosion of the frontier between Nature and Art, for as Thoreau remarks in his 1858 journal, "genius is inspired by its own works; it is hermaphroditic" (17:204). As for Whitman, Thoreau's frontier between Nature and Art is the site of androgynous self-generation. The violence of the masculine is countered by the commanding comfort of the feminine, and in many respects Thoreau, like Whitman, finds the artist the perfect union of the two. "The practice of giving the feminine gender—to all ideal excellence personified," Thoreau writes in his 1840 journal, "is a mark of refinement, observable, in the mythologies even of the most barbarous nations. . . . Man is masculine, but his manliness is feminine. It is the inclination of brute force to moral power."[36] And in the *Week,* Thoreau says of Chaucer that "his genius was feminine, not masculine. It was such a feminineness, however, as is. . . not to be found at all in woman, but is only the feminine in man. Such pure and genuine and childlike love of Nature is hardly to be found in any poet" (1:398). If Thoreau's own "childlike" relationship with Nature borders on a fantasy of incest, it nonetheless provides an apt figure for the feminization he found necessary to his craft. "There must be the copulating and generating force of love behind every effort destined to be successful," he writes in 1852. "The poet's relation to his theme is the relation of lovers" (9:253). That relation applies equally to Thoreau's cultivation as a pioneer and his cultivation as a writer; and if his galls of writing come at times to resemble the "bunch" that Whitman onanistically "pluck'd at random from myself" in "Spontaneous Me"[37]—a "bunch" that is at once his sexual seed and the flower of his writing—it is because Thoreau shares with Whitman a tendency to channel off erotic excitement into the act of writing. We might well compare his penetration of Nature's frontier and his admonition that the words which come nearest to Silence be written "exactly at the right crisis" to a rather extravagantly sublimated sexual act, for both may be marked by an exhilaration of conquest and a consequent shame for the befoulment, however great the rewards of the completed cultivation. Thoreau's self-imposed chastity seems in fact designed to further the creative powers of his writing, for he notes in what is, ironically enough, a wedding letter of 1852 to Harrison Blake that "there is to be attributed to sensuality the loss to language of how many pregnant symbols" (6:207). Whatever loss Thoreau himself suffered at the hands of sensuality, it was apparently too little to stifle the insemination he chose to practice in his gardening and his writing.

IV

Because Thoreau's pen is wielded as an axe or a plow, his activity as a writer reflects and endorses, while at the same time attempting to assuage, his actions as a pioneer and settler. "Homeliness is almost as great a merit in a book as in a house," Thoreau writes in the *Week* (1:111); this is not only because, as critics of Thoreau have often recognized, his books are laboriously constructed, but also because writing and cultivation, whether of himself or his property, are almost inseparable. That Thoreau is unable or unwilling to free himself from the "load of thought" inherited even by America is evident in his prodigious learning; and for all his rituals of stripping down, he is just as oppressed by quotation as Cooper. Perry Miller accurately characterizes the manic addiction to collecting his own thoughts and those of others that marks the whole of Thoreau's work, when he notes "the niggardly way [Thoreau] scrapes his mind," preserving every scrap and husbanding his energies in anticipation of the day when he can "construct an edifice. His problem was not, as was Emerson's, to check a stream of expression, but to keep the crevices from showing after he laid one brick on top of another. His existence was an anticipation that the miracle would happen—that the inert bones would join together and become flesh, that the resurrection would come."[38] But the other side of Thoreau's vision of his solitary enclosure as a kind of chrysalis preparing him for a higher life is his constant fretting, as in *Walden,* that his dwelling will become "a workhouse, a labyrinth without a clue, a museum, an almshouse, a prison, or a splendid mausoleum instead" (2:31).

While Thoreau is the essential American *bricoleur,* a skilled builder of hypotheses and spiritual playgrounds, the ingeniously practical collector and constructor who makes do with what is at hand and convinces one that nothing else is necessary, he is equally rabid in his consumption and merchandizing of the materials of the country about him, and is exceeded only by Whitman in his desire to get America *written down* and indexed like a list of native commodities. If he would have concurred with Emerson's remark in the chapter of *The Conduct of Life* (1860) entitled "Wealth," that "a garden is like those pernicious machineries we read of...which catch a man's coat-skirt or his hand, and draw in his arm, his leg, and his whole body to irresistible destruction," Thoreau would also have had to agree that "wealth has its source in applications of the mind to nature, from the rudest strokes of spade and axe up to the last secrets of art." He seems to have directly anticipated Emerson's further observation that the "craft of the merchant" lies in "bringing a thing from where it abounds to where it is costly,"[39] when he writes in 1841 about the act of journalizing: "If I make a huge effort to expose my innermost and richest wares to light, my counter seems cluttered with the meanest homemade stuffs; but after months or years I may discover the wealth of India...in that confused heap, and what perhaps seemed a festoon of dried apple or pumpkin will prove a string of Brazilian diamonds, or pearls from Coremandel" (7:182). That the farthest West is but the farthest East surfaces even in the imperialism of Thoreau's ransacking of his own mind.

More characteristic of Thoreau's attempt to domesticate his writing enterprise is his handiness at treating Nature as a book, a font of type, a hieroglyphic text, and even, finally, a virtual library. Along with Hawthorne, Melville, and Whitman, Thoreau inherited the Puritan fascination with the interpretation of Nature's text, and he comments over and over in his journal on various aspects of his reading of the landscape. Animal tracks are of particular interest, not only since they are a kind of natural writing but also because they represent the most persistent form of Thoreau's search for identity. "Every man," he writes in his journal of 1860, "thus *tracks himself* through life, in all his hearing and reading and observation and traveling. His observations make a chain" (19:79). Tracking is a recuperation of what has been lost or denied at the outset; to track oneself is to return toward the origin, by going up river or deep into the woods, say, or by plowing up some arrowheads. Tracking is a form of reading and vice versa, yet both threaten to become lost, to trail off into the underbrush, or become absorbed in a welter of other tracks. Fast on the heels of the *Walden* passage in which Thoreau clamors for a *point d'appui* upon which to found his wall or state, he adds, among a series of epigrammatic statements, "I know not the first letter of the alphabet" (2:109). Thoreau is not Hawthorne, but his anxiety about the *alpha* of language is just as pressingly tied to his reading of Nature's text. This is why the arrowhead, which Thoreau can only explain by drawing a picture, is in one respect an ideal symbol, though in another it is totally useless. It is also why Thoreau spends so much time elaborating the hieroglyphic leaves on the melting sand back in *Walden,* a beautiful mural in Nature produced by the "Deep Cut" of the railroad, an heroically magnified version of the regenerative gall (2:336–41). As John Irwin has pointed out, Thoreau's exercise at the sand bank "connects the attempt to find a basic unifying form beneath the multiplicity of natural forms with the attempt to penetrate the language of convention and discover within the original language of nature, that basic verbal form with its emblematic relationship between words and things."[40] If the languages of convention and nature are fused by virtue of their hypothetical mirror relationship, though, Thoreau still has to hedge the rhetorical power of their capacity to be differentiated. For however persistent his attempts, Thoreau's desire to root out the emblematic relationship continually shows itself as a snare for the unwary tracker, one in which the pure *figure* of Nature—the illustration of the arrowhead, for example—remains a figure, a trope that ideally represents an unintelligible Eden free from the economy of language and its speculative web of reference, but as figure, is also a coin deposited in the sand *bank* he exploits in his commerce with Nature.

How seriously Thoreau pursued this paradox is revealed in an almost hallucinatory journal passage of 1851, one worthy of Borges, which binds together the rhetorics of archeology and hunting, the archive and the lair:

> I have sometimes imagined a library, *i.e.* a collection of the works of true poets, philosophers, naturalists, etc., deposited not in a brick or marble edifice in a crowded and dusty city, guarded by cold-blooded and methodical officials and preyed on by bookworms, in which you own no share, and are not likely to, but rather far away in the depths of a primitive forest, like the ruins of Central America, where you can trace a series of crumbling alcoves, the older books protecting the most modern from the elements, partially buried by the luxuriance of nature, which the heroic student could reach only after adventures in the wilderness amid wild beasts and wild men. (9:271)

Only *Moby-Dick*'s "Bower in the Arsacides" more insistently ties together the natural and the cultural in an inextricable knot; the churning, smoking textile mill seated inside the vine-covered whale skeleton is the industrial correlative of Thoreau's more respectably learned, but equally exotic, trope for imperialism.

Whether it ventures into landscape or library, however, Thoreau's journey is far from safe. Like writing, "travelling is no pastime," but is "as serious as the grave" and "requires a long probation to be broken into it" (1:326). The restlessness of traveling "is a prevalent disease," Thoreau notes, one "which attacks Americans especially," and though it is "the opposite of nostalgia," still it "does not differ much from nostalgia" (15:252). The *Week*'s rivers are the "guides" and the "constant lure" that urge him to "explore at their invitation the interior of continents" (1:11), and the Merrimack is "the only key which could unlock [New Hampshire's] maze" (1:85). Yet that maze may well issue in a cul-de-sac, a trap whose bait continues to recede on two fronts, whether as buried origin or manifest destiny. At the limit of the voyage Thoreau and his brother pitch their tent near Hooksett Pinnacle, "on the very spot which a few summers before had been occupied by a party of Penobscots" (1:318). This is as close as they come to recapturing the lost primitive state in any physical sense; but in fact they are

hardly away from home at all, for directly below the Pinnacle lies
"Concord"—Concord, New Hampshire, that is—and almost the very port
they left now seems magically to have appeared at the end of the line
(1:322). Thoreau resorts to a similar sleight of hand when he returns home,
but the irony of the doubled name is more than a simple joke here. For what
Thoreau finds at the far limit of the journey is "that the frontiers were not
this way any longer. This generation has come into the world fatally late for
some enterprises. Go where we will on the *surface* of things, men have been
there before us. We cannot now have the pleasure of erecting the *last*
house" (1:323)—the pleasure, that is, of taking the first step of conquest
and cultivation.

Rudely baffled in his attempt to repossess the primitive, Thoreau blurts
out his famous exclamation that internalizes the frontier and by that token
even further and more maddeningly obliterates its mark: "The frontiers are
not east or west, north or south, but wherever a man *fronts* a fact, though
that fact be his neighbor, there is an unsettled wilderness between him and
Canada, between him and the setting sun, or, farther still, between him and
it. Let him build himself a log-house with the bark on where he is, *fronting*
IT, and wage there an Old French war for seven or seventy years, with the Indians and Rangers, or whatever else may come between him and the reality,
and save his scalp if he can" (1:323-24). Almost absurdly, the frontier, or
whatever it hides, is both there and not there; precisely because Thoreau
finds he is there too late and the frontier is gone, he can declare IT still available to possession by an act of imagination or narration. Here the "fact"
fronted is "it," a neutral, even neutered, object—if it is an object at all—at
once concrete and abstract, like the arrowhead, an exact token of the unintelligible. Writing posits "it" as unassailable but violently takes "its" place
and forces "it" into further recession. If, as Walter Michaels has claimed,
Walden's search for a *point d'appui* is "a kind of ontological scavenger-
hunt" in which "the prize is reality,"[41] it would be equally appropriate to
find in this passage from the *Week* a bottom as treacherous as any in
Walden. In view of the labyrinthine quality of the declaration, Thoreau's
remark in *Walden,* that he went to the woods in order "to front only the
essential facts of life" (2:100), almost brings one to despair over its complex-
ity. Fussell notes of this passage that Thoreau's "starting point is the frontier
metaphor compressed in a single word," that "'front,' normally a transitive
verb, under the impact of American conditions quietly turns into a copula-
tive."[42] This is exactly to the point, for since the frontier, like the *point
d'appui,* is unfathomable, it may well be located always at one's fingertips:
"it" is "here," where one "is," and this is why Thoreau is everywhere at
home but nowhere settled. And just as everywhere is a frontier, so each mo-

ment constitutes an origin. Because "all biography is the life of Adam," as Thoreau writes in the Carlyle essay (4:351), his remark in *Walden* that "it is, after all, always the first person that is speaking" (2:3–4) is optimistically accurate. The first person speaks as Adam did when creating himself at the beginning, the *point d'appui*. But *Walden* is not the *Week*, and Thoreau had tricked out his metaphysics more punningly by the second book; for the first, his *fronting* of IT stopped him cold, like the blank wall of Ktaadn. He knew the fact of the wilderness was there, but he could not grab hold of it, not to save his scalp. The *Week*'s frontiers, like the many "realities" in *Walden*, threaten to "all go to pieces in [the] account of them" (2:107).

The paradise of IT, a place or moment free from reference where one's compass points everywhere at once and one could, like Adam, "simply wonder," is a *pokelogan*. It is what writing and traveling strive for but in so doing vanquish. Like Lévi-Strauss, Thoreau finds that his "load of thought" so engulfs the undefiled objects of his inspection that he can reach bottom only by metaphoric ruse. Edward Said's characterization of Lévi-Strauss's predicament is in this regard directly applicable to Thoreau: "Because the observing ethnologist is a product of literate society, and because anthropology itself is subject to the enslaving laws of literacy, the zero state [of Nature] is a forbidden paradise which literacy penetrates only at the critical moment that the paradise is being obliterated."[43] Since the zero state's paradise is lost at the very moment it is *found*, it cannot be successfully written, not even at "exactly the right crisis." It remains a fantasized projection in the topography of a dream, a state which, like the arrowhead, has symbolic value zero and thus a meaning both null and limitless. In his attempted recovery of that state, Thoreau might well have come to the same conclusion as Lévi-Strauss—that "travelling was a snare and a delusion," that "every effort to understand [the specimens of Nature] destroys the object studied in favor of another object of a different nature; this second requires from us a new effort which destroys it in favour of a third, and so on and so forth until we reach the one lasting presence, the point at which the distinction between meaning and the absence of meaning disappears: the same point from which we began."[44] This is the irony endorsed by Thoreau's finding himself, at the limit of his voyage in the *Week*, once again at "Concord." The very point at which he began has become his point of termination, its name almost a mocking repetition of his inability to escape one home and search out another, and moreover a sharp signal that the language of civilization has coincided with, if not preceded, his assault on Nature.

At the same time "we are clearing the forest in our westward progress," Thoreau writes in his journal of 1851, "we are accumulating a forest of books in our rear, as wild and unexplored as any of nature's primitive wildernesses" (9:353). This forest of books matches by obverse reflection the hallucinatory library in the middle of a wild jungle Thoreau imagines, while at the same time it provides a further *naturalization* of his craft. Going forward for Thoreau means going away from history; but it also means digging back through the accumulated strata of what Whitman called in "Slang in America," "the infinite go-before of the present"[45] to reach a primitive past, though the account of such a project only adds to the accumulating facts to which the theorizer is in "arrears." Even "our brave new poets," Thoreau complains in his journal of 1841, "are [as] secondary as [Saxon translators], and refer the eye that reads them and their poetry, too, back and backward without end" (7:290). Since it is precisely the *recovery* of the relics of the past that renders their authenticity suspect, Thoreau's historical task in the *Week* and elsewhere paradoxically affirms the observation made by Rousseau in his attempt to account for the ruptured transaction between the savage and the civilized: "What is even crueler is that, as all the progress of the human species continually moves it farther away from its primitive state, the more new knowledge we accumulate, the more we deprive ourselves of the means of acquiring the most important knowledge of all; so that it is, in a sense, by dint of studying man that we have made ourselves incapable of knowing him."[46] Because Thoreau's journey leads back and forth at the same time, back toward the unfallen garden, forth to the new Eden of the West, it is no wonder that he declares in the 1842 journal, "our eye splits on every object, and we can as well take one path as the other. If I consider its history, it is old; if its destiny, it is new" (7:338).

Since history accumulates like rubbish about the portals of Nature and surrounds the figure of Silence like the gall about a wound in Nature's flesh, Thoreau must further naturalize his pursuit by prophesying that "when out of history the truth shall be extracted, it will have shed its dates like withered leaves" (1:231). Yet as in Wallace Stevens's "The Rock," where "The fiction of the leaves is the icon / Of the poem, the figuration of blessedness... a cure of the ground and of ourselves, / In the predicate that there is nothing else,"[47] the suspicion arises in Thoreau's case too that the ground of truth is perpetually a fiction. To protect that truth, though, Thoreau turns it into mythology, which he can affirm to be more true than history—and more *natural*. Although he admits that "mythology is only the most ancient history and biography," he yet maintains that "in the history of the human mind, these glowing and ruddy fables precede the noonday thoughts of men, as Aurora the sun's rays. The matutine intellect of the poet, keeping in advance of the glare of philosophy, always dwells in the auroral atmosphere" (1:61). This well-known passage from the *Week* fully dramatizes Thoreau's almost comically paradoxical position. While he aligns himself

with an auroral atmosphere, he must move west to keep in advance of the
philosophical "glare" of noon—presumably the facts of history which succeed the ruddy fables of noon—must follow a westward course to the frontier, but one which cannot sustain its own retreat before the facts that his
own narrative generates, that increasing "load of thought" that will itself
one day become mythology. Such a "retreat" is the only kind Thoreau, wittily playing with Emerson's "Circles," found of merit—"an orderly advance in the face of circumstances" (5:107).

A retreat that advances to the frontier at the same time it moves back
through history is in either case the victim of its own project. "Men seem
anxious to accomplish an orderly retreat through the centuries," Thoreau
writes in the *Week,* "earnestly rebuilding the works behind, as they are bat-
tered down by the encroachments of time; but while they loiter, they and
their works both fall prey to the arch enemy" (1:162–63). Whether retreat-
ing to the rear or forward, the pioneer who brings his load to bear upon the
savage accordingly finds himself in the position of Natty Bumppo—"*par-
ticeps criminis,*" as Thoreau says of the satiric poet (1:328). Indeed, Thoreau's account is itself a kind of satire on American settlement, at least on his
own role in it; for while he pursues the unravished and the wild, and
plunges ever more deeply because driven behind by a profane commerce, he
cannot but be himself a harbinger of that white glare. The "fruit" he would
seize characterizes his frustrating enterprise: it is the fresh reward and unblemished sign of paradise, yet the record of its possession, as a figure of
literary mythology, is a dialogue between enslavement and nostalgia, a narrative in which the writer's performance erodes the paradise he would
achieve. Capitalistic and imperialistic, Thoreau's *grafting* disfigures the figure of the landscape and enters it in an account which his speculation generates and tries to close out at the same time.

V

But perhaps I spoke too soon in designating Thoreau's termination at
Concord, New Hampshire, the ironically thwarted goal in his search for the
frontier. In fact, Thoreau's journey up into the White Mountains pushes the
frontier farther, to a point where the travelers breathe "the free air of Unappropriated Land." As though unsatisfied with this ambiguous label,
Thoreau goes on to explain how they "had traced up the river to which our
native stream is a tributary, until from Merrimack it became the Pemigewas-
set that leaped by our side, and when we had passed its fountainhead, the
Wild Amonoosuck, whose puny channel was crossed at a stride, guiding us
toward its distant source in the mountains, and at length, without its gui-

dance, we were enabled to reach the summit of AGIOCOCHOOK'' (1:334–35). Here Thoreau's account stops. The next remark tells us that they returned from the mountain trip one week later. The truncation of the narrative is entirely appropriate, though somewhat surprising. One would expect at least a brief eulogy like the one in *The Maine Woods,* where Thoreau declares that farther upstream than one can penetrate, the Indian ''is lost to my sight, as a more distant and misty cloud is seen flitting by behind a nearer, and is lost in space. So he goes about his destiny, the red face of man'' (3:88). But in the *Week* Thoreau halts at a strange Indian name displayed in full caps, a name which seems to absorb his accomplishment into it as the landscape has done, draining away its power of articulation, almost as though he has undergone, as his journal of 1851 records, one of those ''revolutions which create an interval impassable to memory'' (8:229). AGIOCOCHOOK balks interpretation as stringently as the arrowhead; it is as if Thoreau staked his claim to the frontier, but by putting up a sign of that claim dissolved the possibility of its being understood or communicated, the possibility of its taking on negotiable value. For this reason, Thoreau's consummative trip is essentially *silent,* a pretended if not actual penetration into the heart of darkness, the zero state of Nature which cannot be written. At a certain point, though no identifiably necessary one, Thoreau can only renounce his narrative and stammer out a name or, as in *The Maine Woods,* a nearly mad flurry of inadequate words: ''Talk of mysteries!—Think of our life in nature,—daily to be shown matter, to come in contact with it,—rocks, trees, wind on our cheeks! the *solid* earth! the *actual* world! the *common sense! Contact! Contact! Who* are we? *where* are we?'' (3:79). Writing stops at the frontier which it itself is; the rest is silence.

It is no mistake that Thoreau delimits the penetration of his journey and his literacy by erecting a forbidding Indian name in our path. For when he somewhat jokingly finds, in a story of the Pilgrims's purchase of Indian land in *Cape Cod,* that ''Not Any seems to have been [the name of] the sole proprietor of all America before the Yankees'' (4:43), he not only hits on the sad truth of an imperialism that rode roughshod over a land proclaimed free for the taking but also accentuates the cul-de-sac where his attempted tracing of the American garden ends. ''Not Any'' encompasses both ''not any'' *owner* and ''not any'' *name:* the questions of commerce and language cannot be separated, for it is the conjunction of the two that most defines the American fall, that nick of time in which ownership replaced simple wonderment, and in which the American ''web of speculations'' can be *said* to have begun. Thoreau is not one to squander his sentiment, though, and even the Indian, because his ''memory is in harmony with the russet hue of the fall of the year'' (7:444), means most to him as a replica of Rousseauvian man, an occasion for mythologizing the American discovery and labor of its garden: he is the finest trope that Thoreau's cultivation yields.

But the elegance of that trope does not mitigate the violence that it conceals. Thoreau's writing enterprise must bear the shame of this violence even while it transforms the American settlement by a mythic model of domestication and regeneration. Like Lévi-Strauss, Thoreau is "the less able to ignore his own civilization and to dissociate himself from its faults in that his very existence is incomprehensible except as an attempt at redemption: he is the symbol of atonement."[48] As an elegy to the American Indian, the *Week* poses in part as a cure for the disease of white commerce and involves a dredging up of past affliction in order to cleanse it in confrontation, in order to assuage any doubt that "our bold ancestors who settled this land" struggled not with "a copper-colored race of men," but with "vapors, fever and ague of the unsettled woods" (1:176). The act of writing entails working through what now seems "shadowy and unreal" in order to reach, if only by a recuperative projection, an assertion of the struggle as original and the settlement as a real appropriation, an event that can be documented. Thoreau needs the guarantee of a violent seizure in order to mark a *fall*, a moment of America's beginning, though as continually proves to be the case, locating such a *point d'appui* is no easy matter. Since the frontier between now and paradise in America is at once past and future, both projection and nostalgia, the wilderness of natural man, while hailed as something toward which a journey is made, is equally at home within memory as the relic of a struggle. Fussell points out that "in his passion for Indian relics [Thoreau] desired to anticipate something altogether more wraith-like, the re-emergence of the past, the imaginative return of the dead."[49] One should add to this that Thoreau recognized his activity was problematic at best, one which could not generate the evidence of Nature's lost state without participating in its vanquishing. Always on the lookout for symptoms of America's origin and its initial possessors, Thoreau was more than aware that "inside the civilized man stand[s] the savage still in the place of honor" (1:368), indeed, that "these aboriginal men cannot be repressed, but under some guise or other. . .survive and reappear continually" (18:424–25). In this last remark from the journals, though, Thoreau delineates the way in which the repressed figure of the Indian, like the state of Nature, goes under various guises but is continually displaced into darker, more remote abodes. Because each recovery of the arrowhead only plows under a layer still more primitive and pure, Thoreau's account of that transaction by which the white gardener's intimacy with his mistress the land violently displaces the "innocence" of the Indian's silent intercourse with Nature results in no definitive possession but one which must be continually reenacted, as both as conquest over, and a commemoration of, the lost native fathers.

The act of writing the myth of America, whatever its value as a commemorative act, remains one more commercial incursion in which the white man's "load of thought" further buries that which it would recover. The success of the myth will depend upon its own repression of the telling symptoms of a disease that results from "the grazing of cattle and the rooting of swine" in the American garden, which has been "converted into a stye and hot-bed, where men for profit increase the ordinary decay of nature" (1:379). The health of the commercial labor, even the labor of writing, that inflicts itself on the primitive, hides within itself an illness that the poet uproots and domesticates while he at the same time confirms it as incurable by constantly relocating the site of its origin. Yet even in this case Thoreau is able to convert trauma into restoration by making disease the condition of an empowering ritual. Disease "is one of the permanent conditions of life," Channing records from Thoreau, for "life is a warfare, a struggle, and the diseases of the body answer to the trouble and defects of the spirit. Man begins by quarreling with the animal in him, and the result is immediate disease. In proportion as the spirit is more ambitious and persevering, the more obstacles it will meet with. It is as a seer that man asserts his disease to be exceptional."[50] It is one thing if the animal Thoreau quarrels with is a woodchuck that he can devour raw; but if the animal is the repressed spirit of the aboriginal Indian, Thoreau's cure must wage a more pitched battle with internalization.

Although Thoreau's cultivation of his anxieties yields fruit, the gall of writing, it also breeds a profane trade without making proper restitution to that which has been uprooted and displaced, however shadowy and unreal. The reward of cultivation's "cure," the innocent fruit, remains outstanding, either plowed under by the advancing front of civilization, or recessed beyond the frontier of the intelligible or negotiable, too free to be fertile. Thoreau's plow reemploys the shadows it would disperse and uncovers the Red Man's "mark" only to *re*cover it. Thus he can say that "every sentence is the result of a long probation," that indeed, "the word which is best said came nearest to not being spoken at all, for it is cousin to a deed which the speaker could better have done. Nay, almost it must have taken the place of the deed by some urgent necessity, even by some misfortune, so that the truest writer will be some captive knight after all" (1:107-8)—the Hannah Dustan of his own narrative. It is the "truest writer" who recognizes the necessary "misfortune" of being a fallen "captive" of his own myth, who knows that what he "says" is but a displacement of an act he can never rectify but only dramatically repeat in the interests of his own seizure of power and as a communal sacrifice. Like the Indian's, then, Thoreau's memory is in harmony with the fall of the year. In his ongoing melodrama of America's fall from a paradise it probably never knew nor will know, writing is perpetual elegy. It is "because we naturally look most into the west, as forward into the day," Thoreau notes in the *Week,* that we "in the forenoon see the sunny side of things, but in the afternoon [see] the shadow of every tree" (1:341). Because the fabled future of the West is paradoxically a land of nostalgia, Thoreau's auroras, like those of Wallace Stevens, are of autumn. The *Week,* balked in its recovery of paradise, though not unexpectedly, is a book that elaborates the poetics of afternoon and autumn, a moment in which writing takes account of its own fall. It is this continual conjunction of fate and violence in the *Week,* as Walter Hesford points out, that makes us feel throughout "that we are enjoying a golden moment on the edge of fall."[51] This is the exact message of the book—that Thoreau's America, hardly unsettled but not yet settled, *founded* but not very securely, exists at least temporarily, and perhaps perpetually, in such a moment.

On "Friday" Thoreau "awoke in autumn," the season having changed "in some unimaginable point of time, like the turning of a leaf" (1:356), and commenced the swift downstream journey, the return home from the incursion into the wilderness, falling away from the *point* of penetration at which his probe ended. This mapping of the journey while Nature is "composing her poem Autumn" (1:403), is only the most obvious and suitable closure for a book which deals with *falling* as a poetic. If Thoreau sets up continual categories of innocence, "pure discoveries, glimpses of *terra firma,*" he knows with a keen reflection that these are available only to "shipwrecked mariners" (1:100), only to one who knows himself to be a violator always in arrears to his own project. Only by the end of the *Week* does one see exactly what Thoreau meant when he said even before the voyage began that "the lapse of the current" is "an emblem of all progress" (1:11). That "lapse"—of the river's "current" and whatever else is "current"—has all the resonance which Thoreau assigns it in *Walden* when he derives "lobe" (leaf), "labium" (lip), "labor," and "lapse" from the same etymological roots (2:338–39), thus implicating autumn, his own pioneering labor, the fall of his birth, the language that falls from his lips (or his pen), and the declivity of the river in a panoramic melodrama embracing the loss of Eden, the settlement of America, and the seasonal cycle of nature. Thoreau had written, in a series of translations from the laws of Menu published in *The Dial* in 1843, that "*if* [the Brahmin] *has any incurable disease,* let him advance in a straight path, towards the invincible *north-eastern* point, feeding on water and air, till his mortal frame totally decay, and his soul become united with the Supreme."[52] If Thoreau's voyage in the *Week* was such a spiritual pilgrimage (though once he reached the Merrimack, of course, his journey veered to the northwest), one in which his spirit, as he says of the *Week*'s style, "rise[s] from the page like an exhilaration, and wash[es] away our critical brains like burr millstones, flowing to higher levels above and behind ourselves'' (1:105), the journey of recuperation had still to account for the *lapse* that instigated Thoreau's disease and hung like an afternoon shadow over his every attempt to reach the sanctuary of purity. Though the style of the *Week* is that of "great prose," which "commands our respect more than great verse, since it implies a more permanent and level height, a life more pervaded with the grandeur of thought," that grandeur has its own hand in the disease (the dis-ease or labor) of America; for "the prose writer [who] has conquered, like a Roman, and settled colonies" (1:365) is one who has wielded his own *stylus* with the violence that settlement requires. Thoreau could not be more aware of his own implication in the white gardener's violent and profane closeness to his mistress than when he calls the downstream voyage a "plowing homeward" (1:385). The pen that aligns itself with the plow in a laborious enterprise must abide by its own violation, must, even if it sets up as an innocent sign the untouched fruit, locate its own poetry in that fruit's fall.

What Thoreau awoke from on Friday was the dream in which the return to a silent American wilderness was accomplished, if only with an ironic measure of success. But since "the heroic spirit will not fail to dream of remoter retirements and more rugged paths" (1:55), and since the marks of the past in their purest form are unintelligible, the completion of the return is incident upon a trick turned by the tools of memory. The Thoreau who had at birth, as we noted earlier, been thrust like a wedge into Nature has replicated the experience, turning the violence of delivery back on itself in order to be "born again on the road," in order that his wounds heal and the scar disappear. As traveler or writer, he cures himself by finding that Nature is "one and continuous everywhere" and by declaring his own craft part of Nature, even its improvement. The wedge, like the point of pen or plow, cultivates its own healing gall about that silent chasm of Nature, but because it is only a *graft,* Thoreau concludes at the end of the *Week,* his account cannot write Silence itself:

> It were vain for me to endeavor to interpret the Silence. She cannot be done into English. For six thousand years men have translated her with what fidelity belonged to each, and still she is little better than a sealed book. A man may run on confidently for a time, thinking he has her under his thumb, and shall one day exhaust her, but he too must at last be silent, and men remark only how brave a beginning he has made; for when he at length dives into her, so vast is the disproportion of the told to the untold, that the former will seem but the bubble on the surface where he disappeared. (1:420)

That Silence has in the end become the river itself should not be surprising; for the traveler who had at the outset "resolved to launch myself on [the river's] bosom and float whither it would bear me" (1:11) has dived into the Mother of Nature and been born again on the journey, if only by domesticating the violence of the act and having failed to translate the Silence accurately.

Thoreau's figuring of Silence as both a woman and a book only further underlines the paradox in his interpretive enterprise. "She" remains pure *figure*, what cannot be interpreted, but yet, as figure, can only be interpreted, that is, subjected to the violence of translation. But "is not Nature, rightly read," Thoreau asks, "that of which she is commonly taken to be the symbol merely?" (1:408). Because Nature is a self-emptying term endowed with sacred and feminine mystery, Thoreau can domesticate it endlessly and still leave it untouched. He knows with a vengeance the frontiers beyond which his *telling* and *tilling* of the story cannot go. The *Week* is a text whose power lies in its admission that, as Thoreau would put it in *Walden*, "the volatile truth of our words should continually betray the inadequacy of the residual statement" and leave behind the "literal monument alone" (2:357), as though struck to stone by the Medusa of Nature. In such a narrative it is the "unwritten sequel" that can be held out as the "most indispensible part. It should be the author's aim to say once and emphatically, 'He said,' ἔφη ἑ. This is the most the bookmaker can attain to. If he make his volume a mole whereon the waves of Silence may break, it is well" (1:149). It is an autumnal poetic which can *say* it has eaten of the communal fruit and told its story, yet still hold forth the silent and seductive fruit at a further remove in the wilderness dream.

Yet "all our life," Thoreau remarks in his journal of 1859, "is a persistent dreaming awake. The boy does not camp in his father's yard. That would not be adventurous enough, there are too many sights and sounds to disturb the illusion; so he marches off twenty or thirty miles and there pitches his tent, where stranger inhabitants are tamely sleeping in their beds, just like his father at home, and camps in their yard perchance. But then he dreams uninterruptedly that he is anywhere but where he is" (18:296–97). Thoreau could never escape camping in his own or someone else's yard, not that it would have mattered much; for as he suggests in the journal entry with which we began, "it is vain to dream of a wilderness distant from ourselves. There is none such" (15:43). Even in our dreams, Thoreau discovers in the *Week*, "we but act a part which must have been learned and rehearsed in our waking hours, and no doubt could discover some waking consent thereto. . . . In dreams we see ourselves naked and acting out our real characters" and have a "juster apprehension of things, unconstrained by habit, which is then in some measure put off, and divested of memory, which we call history" (1:315–16, 58). But the contradictions and ambiguity here are also of note, for it is not clear whether Thoreau's dreams are rehearsed or unconstrained by habit, nor whether dreams are divested of memory, and hence of history, or must be divested of memory in order to *become* history. This confusion, however, is in perfect keeping with an enterprise that finds its dream of Eden stuck in an endless historical regression and even finds itself rehearsing the violations it seeks to be shed of. Thoreau's enactment of a return to Nature ends without having clearly succeeded, though it is difficult to say exactly what might constitute success for one who finds, as he writes in *Walden,* that "the wildest scenes" continually become "unaccountably familiar" (2:232)[53] and whose every satisfaction of desire at once estranges him from yet another scene lost in the landscape of the West or that of his "infant dreams."

Thoreau's journey is problematic at best, but since "half the walk is but retracing our steps," as he puts it in "Walking" (5:206), going away from home and returning to it are hardly different. Home, after all, is where one's dreams begin. By the end of the *Week,* the "wild apple-tree" of the American garden is in fact found to inhabit the "native port" to which Thoreau returns, its stem still marked by the wound which the boat's "chain had worn in the chafing of the spring freshets" (1:420). By an exquisite sleight of hand, the regenerative tree is brought *home* from the wild, though its scar stays as a telling sign that the journey, like the writing labor, is a healing gall grown about its own wound. But after all, Thoreau asks earlier on, "where is the skilful swordsman who can give clean wounds, and not rip up his work with the other edge?" (1:234). For the skilled writer faced with this challenge, his task is to be "not like a vine, which being cut in the spring bears no fruit, but bleeds to death in the endeavor to heal its wounds," but to be "as vigorous as a sugar maple, with sap enough to maintain his own verdure" (1:101). Thoreau remarks in "Wild Apples" that he knows of "no trees which have more difficulties to contend with, and which more sturdily resist their foes. These are the ones whose story we have to tell" (5:302–3). The wild itself sturdily resists Thoreau in his attempt to graft himself on by way of a story; but in the end, if the apple tree of the *Week* is proof, he succeeds in domesticating the violence of his act and settling his account with Nature, though perhaps only by a ruse like that which placed "Concord" at the opposite limit of the voyage. Like the figure of the beautiful bug born from the "old table of apple-tree wood" at the end of *Walden* (2:366), a sign of Thoreau's resurrection from the dead wood of society, the stage prop of the apple tree at the close of the *Week* is a sign that Thoreau's pen remains as double-edged as his plow. As a sacrificial trope—the trophy he has brought home—the apple tree counters his pioneering imperialism and justifies his inability to purify his craft, standing at once for that which is obliterated by his labor and for the atonement that his transgression entails. Guaranteeing that his plunder is neither complete nor in vain, it allows Thoreau to *say* he has pursued a home that could not be found but settled for one that can.

THREE

"The home of the dead"

Representation and Speculation in Hawthorne and *The House of the Seven Gables*

Representation, therefore, lies at the root of the entire American system.

Conflicting opinions exist on the subject of the relations between the representative and his constituent, impracticable notions and contradictory errors being equally maintained.... The subject is grave, and all important to a country like this.

—Cooper, *The American Democrat*

If a man has a seesaw in his voice, it will run into his sentences, into his poem, into the structure of his fable, into his speculation, into his charity. And, as every man is hunted by his own daemon, vexed by his own disease, this checks all his activity.

—Emerson, *The Conduct of Life*

Thoreau outdid Hawthorne, if not Poe, on one occasion when he burst out in his 1858 journal, "how much the writer lives and endures in coming before the public so often!... He learns how to bear contempt and despise himself. He makes, as it were, *post-mortem* examinations of himself before he is dead. Such is art."[1] Cooper was normally more restrained about his craft unless pursuing one or another libel suit, though as we have seen in the case of *Home as Found,* explosive frenzies certainly lay in wait beneath the often dead calm of his style. But both Thoreau's staged renegadery and Cooper's anxious polish seem frail assertions of authority's trauma compared to Hawthorne's life-long struggle with the irrepressible faces of his peculiar

American history. If Cooper's style is sometimes deadly calm to no point, Hawthorne's style cultivates both dead calm and spasmodically piercing introspection as weapons in an arsenal stocked alternately against the intrusion and the collapse of the past. Going public meant two things for Hawthorne: it meant, to borrow two of his phrases from *Legends of the Province House,* "keeping jubilee" at the "funeral of departed power" (*TT* 298, 252)[2]; and it meant accounting continually for his own role in that pageant—a role that, since it created and judged what it half acted in, was often in arrears as bothersome as Thoreau's. Were we to say that Hawthorne mastered the *execution* of his craft, we would perhaps come close to locating that particular power in his work which fuses a trenchant and precise command of the problem of representation with an obliquely paralleled interest in revenge. But since Hawthorne himself is so often at the center of sacrifice, like Hester Prynne in "the market-place," his *execution* doubles back on itself as an uncannily familiar visage in the dim mirror of romance. Hawthorne's art is *post-mortem*, in Thoreau's phrase, because his favorite subjects are either dead to start with or arrayed on the scaffold when he takes them up—or rather, when they take him up.

Hawthorne's execution elicits the hazards which accompany both legal and artistic "representation" and transfigures them in a jubilee of his own authorial powers. He comes to the materials of his craft in a moment of crisis, "as if to gather up the white ashes of those who had perished at the stake, and to tell the world—the wrong being now atoned for—how much had perished there, which it had never yet known how to praise" (*BR,* 161). The gathering and praising of ashes, and the atonement for wrong, collide and merge in Hawthorne's representation of his past and of himself; and as the prefix of "representation" would indicate, repetition or re-doing is a central exercise for Hawthorne.[3] This activity can be no more accurately characterized than by noting its alignment with the burdensome skill reputed to belong to Matthew Maule's descendants in *The House of the Seven Gables*— the ability, "by what appears to have been a sort of mesmeric process," to make the House's looking glass come "alive with the departed Pyncheons" and to show them "as doing over again some deed of sin, or in the crisis of life's bitterest sorrow" (*HG,* 20–21). The "doing over again" of some sin reaches such a compulsive pitch for Hawthorne as to become an incantation, a jubilee of remembrance in which the departed personages of America's short history are re-collected so that the moment of crisis they once acted out may be kept alive. Even more so than Cooper, whose representation of the past entwined him in a mire of incest and imitation in *Home as Found,* Hawthorne made his art enact the foundation of American tradition by re-presenting, again and again, the moments in which it most became a tradition, the moments when there was suddenly something to repudiate and revolt against, or perhaps even more significantly, the moment when one could, as in "The Custom-House," act as an editor of old documents in need of reconstruction and interpretation. Hawthorne's lament in *The Marble Faun,* that "there is reason to suspect that a people are waning to decay and ruin, the moment that their life becomes fascinating either in the poet's imagination or the painter's eye" (*MF,* 296), pinpoints the nearly necrological thrill in which he found his power and opens a question about the particular position of the country he had left behind when he went abroad. Not only is that process of decay of vital importance to Hawthorne's work, but his overestimation of European decay is proved unnecessary by his own prior achievement with the materials of American ruin. Certainly Hawthorne has moments in which he conforms to James's version of him as one tormented by America's lack of historical commodities, moments almost Thoreauvian in which he can complain, as in "Sketches from Memory," that "in other lands, Decay sits among fallen palaces" while in America "her home is in the forests" (*MM,* 437); yet the bulk of his work uneasily authenticates the fact that America had reached a point at which one could, like Colonel Pyncheon, "build his house over an unquiet grave" and be sure "his home would include the home of the dead...." (*HG,* 9).

I

Cooper was torn in his allegiance, on the one hand pining for the restoration of Natty Bumppo's and Judge Cooper's era of initial settlement, for a time when the only decay was in fact in the unscarred forests, and on the other vainly anticipating, with Eve Effingham, a period when the Susquehanna Valley might be littered with feudal ruins. He forced the moment by planting a squadron of imposing busts in the middle of his house and by founding *Home As Found* on the legacies of both his own family and that of *The Pioneers* in a fashion whose best and most serious intentions bordered on the grotesque. One might expect that Cooper's obsession with stabilizing tradition by fixing a lineage of families and documents could be countered by Thoreau's mad flight in the face of history; but Thoreau's pursuit of the clean frontier only led him back into history, so that his every complaint about executing the wills of the dead and carting around on his shoulders the relics of his ancestors is matched by the discovery of a library at the heart of his most cherished wilderness—and more bothersome still, one he found he was building himself. Hawthorne's engagement with the past occurs on a ground at first glance quite different from that of Cooper or Thoreau. While one cannot quite say of him, as D. H. Lawrence did of Poe, that he "has no truck with Indians or Nature'' and ''makes no bones about Red Brothers and Wigwams,''[4] Hawthorne, aside from some of the tales and a few important ingredients in *The Scarlet Letter*, would not be wholly misrepresented by such a stricture. Though he remarks in ''The Custom-House,'' for example that the loss of the pre-Revolutionary ''documents and archives of the Custom-House'' is a source of regret, since those papers, ''would have affected me with the same pleasure as when I used to pick up Indian arrowheads in the field near the Old Manse'' (*SL*, 29), his response in ''The Old Manse'' itself is more telling. After a genuinely stirring imaginative recreation of Indian life prompted by his Thoreauvian cultivation of arrowheads, Hawthorne cuts his dreamy recollection short with a quick return to his true source of interest: ''But this is nonsense. The Old Manse is better than a thousand wigwams'' (*MM*, 11). Only the Effingham ''Wigwam'' is whiter than Hawthorne's. We recall too that when Hawthorne purchased Thoreau's boat, he changed the name from ''Musketaquid'' to ''Pond Lily'' (*AN*, 357).

That America's home included the home of dead Indians was not sufficiently menacing for Hawthorne; his dead had to have a stranglehold more convincing, more familial, in order to count as representatives of the past. While Thoreau reported in the *Week* that ''the *past* cannot be *presented*,''[5] it would seem that Hawthorne's career is a storming denial of this proposition, though one that has a grimly self-reflexive twist. Hawthorne adamantly maintains—indeed, cannot escape the fact—that the writer, as Whitman's 1855 Preface has it, is one who ''forms the consistance of what is to be from what has been and is. He drags the dead out of their coffins and stands them again on their feet. . .he says to the past, Rise and walk before me that I may realize you.''[6] Where the comparison falters, of course, is in the fact that Hawthorne locates himself at a point where ''what has been'' is too insistently a part of ''what is to be''; since the haunting memory of Hawthorne's Puritan past is on the brink of dissolution, yet refuses to relinquish its hold, his craft must run a double course which both saves the dark dream by repetition and commemoration, and participates in its vengeful exorcism. His task is to *re*present that past by resuscitating its most critical and cruelest moments, and to stage himself as *representative* of that past. Hawthorne's desire to recuperate the vestiges of terror lurking beneath the foundation of his manse parallels Thoreau's need to prevent the past from *receding* beyond the frontier of memory, though Hawthorne must hold up the added pressure of a conscience more definably cultural that strives to bury and repress those insistent phantasms of culture who in turn claim to *represent* Hawthorne, to draw off his self-presence into them. In this regard, Hawthorne's recurrent term ''threshold'' has much the same function as

Thoreau's "frontier"—it marks the nebulous limit beyond which one cannot go, or can go only at risk, in search of the past.

At Hawthorne's threshold there appears, as in *The Ancestral Footstep,*
the bloody print of a foot, a figure representing an insoluble crime or an untraceable mystery, some event whose reverberations have not ceased to be
felt but which can neither be completely erased nor satisfactorily recon-
structed.[7] The threshold, as we will see, is hardly limited to this function for
Hawthorne, but his many deployments of the device begin here, at a boundary at once psychological and historical. The threshold across which
Hawthorne's remembrance must play belongs equally to his personal life
and to the historical tradition which he finds himself to represent, and at the
risk of placing it in a context that may initially seem foreign, we ought to
compare Hawthorne's representation with Freud's drama of the totem
sacrifice, for both perform a ritual act remembered and fantasized in which
atonement and revenge are fused in the emergency of celebration. The
crime whose outlines Hawthorne must work through to recover takes several
forms, most notably that of an original sin—whether sexual transgression or
a Puritan act of cruelty—that has dispersed the American Eden. Freud's
crime is specifically parricide, though as he notes, it is often the case in the
history of religion that the murder of the father is replaced by the shadowy
and ambiguous concept of original sin.[8] We will find this to be the case in
Hawthorne, but what should be noted at this point is that for both Freud
and Hawthorne, the *representation* of the ancestral crime eventually turns
an occasion of revenge into an act of atonement and commemoration. For
Freud, the murder of the father, which takes place in the name of equalizing
the power among members of a community, induces a guilt whose atonement requires a repetitive and commemorative enactment of the deed. The
totem meal forms a covenant with the slain father by which the society
achieves identification with the ancestor and allays its guilt through a deferred obedience; thus the celebrations which accompany or devolve from
the meal at once comprise "expressions of remorse and attempts at atonement" and serve "as a remembrance of the triumph over the father."[9] The
ritual celebration is thus a *representation* in both senses pertinent to
Hawthorne: it is not only a dramatic rendering but also an event in which
the actors take on the burden of the initial crime and stand in the father's
stead as his representatives. That the crime re-presented, whether by
Hawthorne or Freud, remains shrouded in mystery and inaccessible to exact
reconstruction only augments the urgency of its performance and further
empowers the guilty sway it holds over the community, and particularly over
the artist who takes it upon himself to direct the ritual melodrama.

Yet because the crime is ambiguous, half remembrance and half fantasy, the figures summoned up by the writer to play in that "atmosphere of strange enchantment," as Hawthorne called his "Faery Land" of romance, must run their own risk. If the writer establishes "a theatre" where "the creatures of his brain may play their phantasmagorical antics," he as author and we as readers must beware, in putting any figure "under our microscope," not to "magnify his peculiarities, inevitably tear him into parts, and. . . patch him very clumsily together again," lest we "be frightened by the aspect of a monster, which. . . may be said to have been created by ourselves" (*BR*, 1–2, 69). Such a fear about his own complicity also haunted Freud, who spoke eloquently if inadvertently on the suppressed intent of his own analyses when he wrote that "the distortion of a text resembles a murder: the difficulty is not in perpetrating the deed, but getting rid of its traces." One must give the word "distortion" (*Entstellung*) its double meaning, says Freud, both "to change the appearance of" and "to displace" (or "to mutilate"), since in many interpretations we may "count upon finding what has been suppressed and disavowed hidden away somewhere else, though changed and torn from its context."[10] The reconstruction of an historical event, the proper interpretation of the text, like the treatment of a mental disturbance, must run the risk of further distorting or mangling what it works on, of accomplishing a deed no less suspicious than the crime whose solution it purports to be. When the analyst casts himself as a vengeful Chillingworth, for example, the rigor of his scrutiny may only be overshadowed by the unscrupulousness of his motives. If Hawthorne anticipated Freud in his assessment of the dangers of analytic reconstruction, it is because his own probings of recollection also have as their goal a reparation of past disturbances and crises whose psychic and historical implications are hardly separable. In Hawthorne's narratives, as in Freud's, "remembrance" is often literally that: one re-members what has been dis-membered, reconstructs what has been shattered, and atones for what has been ruined or murdered. And as Freud also found, the monster that appears may loom just across the uncomfortably close threshold of the mirror: "If the person under examination be one's self, the result is pretty certain to be diseased action of the heart, almost before we can snatch a second glance" (*BR*, 69).

To combat the diseased action of his own heart Hawthorne must imaginatively reconstruct the mausoleum of ancestral memory in which his characters and their stories are buried. But while recollection is a means of repairing the ruins of the past, it is a reparation that rebuilds the prison in order to liberate its captives, which nonetheless "fixes up the effigy" of history in order to punish its abuses.[11] "Our age is retrospective," writes Emerson in *Nature*. "It builds the sepulchres of the fathers."[12] That construction, however, has a doubled force: it buries and commemorates in the same act, at once disposing of the fathers and erecting a monument to their vanquished power. Writing, for Hawthorne, is a way of building those sepulchers, and in this respect one is tempted to agree with James M. Cox, who notes that the "morals" of Hawthorne's work "operate in the present in the same way that the actuality of history does: to reject the very past out of which they came. Every experience for Hawthorne is either a deviation from a moral convention or an eventuation into a moral conclusion which condemns the experience from which it arises."[13] But "rejection" is too strong a term, however appropriate, for precisely because the rejection never completely succeeds, the moral of Hawthorne's work, its atonement for the sins of the fathers, is never completely fulfilled. And as in the case of Freud, the very activity that seeks to lay bare the past is what may most threaten it. The analyst of history, like the analyst of memory, will have to flirt with the danger Hawthorne notes in *The Blithedale Romance:* "by long brooding over our recollections, we subtilize them into something akin to imaginary stuff, and hardly capable of being distinguished from it" (*BR*, 104–5). Turning recollection into imagination threatens its veracity, but it may too be the only way to bring about a productive reparation, one that stands the dead on their feet and gives them a convincingly eloquent voice.

Not only does brooding upon recollection unavoidably tamper with the evidence, but as we noted, it is also an exercise that Hawthorne suspects to partake of the very criminality it unearths: the distortion of memory is not unlike a murder. Hawthorne put his hesitations on this count nowhere more bluntly than in a passage from "Fancy's Show Box" that unfolds his acute awareness of complicity:

> A scheme of guilt, till it be put in execution, greatly resembles a train of incidents in a projected tale. The latter, in order to produce a sense of reality in the reader's mind, must be conceived with such proportionate strength by the author as to seem, in the glow of fancy, more like truth, past, present, or to come, than purely fiction. The prospective sinner, on the other hand, weaves his plot of crime, but seldom or never feels a perfect certainty that it will be executed. There is a dreaminess diffused about his thoughts; in a dream, as it were, he strikes the death-blow into his victim's heart, and starts to find an indelible blood-stain on his hand. Thus a novel-writer, or a dramatist, in creating a villain of romance, and fitting him with evil deeds, and the villain of actual life, in projecting crimes that will be perpetrated, may almost meet each other, half-way between reality and fancy. It is not until the crime is accomplished, that guilt clinches its gripe upon the guilty heart and claims it for its own. Then, and not before, sin is acually felt and acknowledged, and, if unaccompanied by repentance, grows a thousand fold more virulent by its self-consciousness. . . . In truth, there is no such thing in man's nature, as a settled and full resolve, either for good or evil, except at the very moment of execution. (*TT*, 225–26)

"Execution," as I suggested earlier, is a loaded pun for Hawthorne, one which not only comprises the like crimes of murder and narration, but also intimates that the punishment that accompanies the act turns the exhilaration of a plot successfully fulfilled as though in dream into the uncanny harbinger of a guilt that will eke out its own revenge. Behind Hawthorne's use of the word is a strangely duplicitous attitude toward his art: his storytelling reenacts and attempts to reverse the executions carried out by the Puritan forefathers; but since it not only mutilates the figures under its microscope but also cloaks itself in the witchcraft of fiction, storytelling executes a deed as suspect as that which was first punished. Thus, for example, *The House of the Seven Gables* revenges the death of Matthew Maule by gleefully presiding over the demise of Judge Pyncheon, only to turn around and implicate its narrator, through his association with Holgrave, in the necromantic act with which the cycle of guilt originated. There are, of course, subtleties and shadows which trouble such a blatant reading; we should only note now the coincidence of actions that makes Hawthorne's attitude toward the execution of his craft a problem. Putting his story on the page often seems to affect Hawthorne in the same way that putting the frayed and tattered rag of scarlet cloth next to his breast in the Custom House does: the letter comes clear by an act of sympathy that incriminates Hawthorne at the same time it instigates his pursuit of the crime.

The warring impulses that combine to produce Hawthorne's strange hedgings and confessions have been well delineated by Frederick Crews, who notes that Hawthorne "is at once the artist-victim of censorship, the Puritan censor himself, and a shrewd analyst of the censor's dubious moral status."[14] The degree to which this is the case appears in Hawthorne's remarkable penchant for representing portions of his own personality in the most diverse and seemingly opposed characters. As though dismembering his own self under the probing eye of a guilty fancy, Hawthorne is at once Hester, Dimmesdale, and Chillingworth, for example, or Holgrave and the Pyncheons. His wild fascination with doubles of himself and with representation by mirrors and portraits is a constant sign of Hawthorne's fractured identity, whether personal or authorial. Like Clifford Pyncheon, who watches a "constantly shifting phantasmagoria of figures" in the haunted waters of Maule's Well (*HG*, 153), or like Old Esther Dudley, who can bring the Province House mirror aswarm with "all the figures that ever swept across the broad plate of glass in former times" (*TT*, 295), Hawthorne is Narcissus with a vengeful difference. Instead of simply withering away in search of a single replica of himself, Hawthorne finds that the mirror of romance contains a host of personages all claiming to be his representatives. When he remarks, then, at the opening of "The Custom-House" that the

office of "the printed book, thrown at large on the wide world," is "to find
out the divided segment of the writer's own nature, and complete his circle
of existence by bringing him into communion with it" (*SL,* 3–4),
Hawthorne has in mind not only that divided segment of his own nature
formed by his ancestral past but also the cruel compulsions and martyred
sympathies which still divide his own nature. Those ancestors who induce in
Hawthorne "a sort of home-feeling with the past" so strong that he feels
compelled to take shame upon himself "as their representative" (*SL,* 9–10)
lurk still in his introjection of his own demonic impulses into the characters
that on the face of it are most the focus of his desire for retribution. Like
Thoreau, Hawthorne makes an *account* of the past that is doubly that, a
combination of narrative and atonement; yet since his own devices reenact
the crime they would obliterate, *representation* is a completely ambiguous
action for Hawthorne: it casts off the burden of shame and at the same time
offhandedly revives it. In this respect, Hawthorne is perhaps most like the
ghost of the first shopkeeper of Seven Gables, still to be seen "poring over
the dingy pages of his day-book. . . in a vain effort to make his accounts balance" (*HG,* 29). As one who originated commerce with the public, the
shopkeeper stands in a disquietingly analogous position to the Hawthorne of
the preface to *Twice-Told Tales,* who attempts with somewhat feigned
timidity "to open an intercourse with the world" (*TT,* 17); both make a
slight break in the prison wall of solitude's enclosure, but at the risk of the
befoulment incident upon the business of making an account. If Hawthorne
too "had the blood of a petty huckster in his veins" (*HG,* 29), his commerce
with the public at least has the saving grace of commemorating and refound-
ing a home even while covertly undermining and exploiting it.

It is difficult now to think of Hawthorne as the tormented artist in isolation, however much he at times cultivated such a picture of himself. Even
though he claims only to be "laying out a street that infringes upon
nobody's private rights, and appropriating a lot of land which had no visible
owner, and building a house, of materials long in use for constructing castles
in the air" (*HG,* 3), Hawthorne's commerce, whether with the past or with
his public, concerns itself as much with the intricacies of exchange and bar-
ter as does Thoreau's assault on his "Unappropriated Land" in the *Week.*
The bizarre edifice in which Hawthorne's narrator finds himself in "The
Hall of Fantasy," one that "occupies, in the world of fancy, the same position which the Bourse, the Rialto, and the Exchange do in the commercial
world" (*MM,* 173), represents with the condensed economy of a dream the
negotiations that Hawthorne's stories play out. It is no fluke either that the
Hall contains busts of Homer, Aesop, Dante, Ariosto, Rabelais, Cervantes,
Shakespeare, Spenser, Milton, Bunyon, Fielding, Richardson, Scott,

Goethe, Swedenborg, and, in an obscure niche, Charles Brockden Brown (significantly identified only as "the author of Arthur Mervyn"); like the travesty of authority at the center of Cooper's Wigwam, these grand heads are at once oppressors and authenticators of Hawthorne's authorial power, and indices of his own desire for public recognition. One cannot help but be reminded, though, of the curious piece on the "Preservation of the Dead" that Hawthorne contributed during his 1836 editorship of *The American Magazine of Useful and Entertaining Knowledge,* in which he recounts Jerome Segato's discovery of a means of instantly embalming and immortalizing parts of the human body by turning them to stone. Seeing what a boon this might be, Hawthorne suggests that rather than "seeking the sculptor's aid to perpetuate the form and features of distinguished men, the public may henceforth possess their very shapes and substance, when the aspiring souls have left them." Indeed, "every mortal, when the heart has ceased to beat, may be straightway transformed into a tombstone, and our cemeteries be thronged with the people of past generations, fixing their frozen stare upon the living world."[15] One need hardly appeal to a Marble Faun for confirmation of the fact that Hawthorne's hallucination of fame is riven by a morbid interest in the ponderous authority of the dead. Hawthorne's repeated obsession with being turned to stone has, as will be clear, more complex motivations, but here we should only note that it demonstrates in an absurdly personal fashion Thoreau's proposition in *Walden*—that "most of the stone a nation hammers goes toward its tomb only. It buries itself alive."[16] Hawthorne hammered, as it were, from inside the sepulcher of the fathers, breaking out and walling in with alternate blows.

Coming out of his tomb leads Hawthorne, as it does Hester Prynne, into "the market-place," though for Hawthorne the market, besides being a scaffold of public scrutiny, is also a board of ancestral exchange, a place to balance his account. Hepzibah Pyncheon's use of "the House of Seven Gables as the scene of...commercial speculations" (*HG,* 36) is, among other things, a flimsily disguised model for Hawthorne's own authorial action. Even more pointedly than the Thoreau who longed for an Adamic era free from a "network of speculations" in which one could "simply wonder, without reference or inference,"[17] Hawthorne was tangled in the web of speculation cast over post-Adamic America; and though he stopped short of Cooper's nihilistic social vision, he nonetheless made the problem far-reaching in his own personal way. One need only count the excessive number of times the word "speculation" is associated with Hester Prynne, for example, to measure its close dependence on transgression. Speculation is both a curse and a mark of liberation in Hawthorne's world, for though it defines a kind of sin in which the powers of capitalism and the imagination are abruptly

fused, the Adamic world in which one could "simply wonder" is relegated
to a prenarrational era, a time either inaccessible or without *interest* (in the
Jamesian sense) to the moralist.

To enter into the realm of speculation is to cross the threshold, to *transgress* it, either as the actor in a drama or as the author of the drama. This is
the point of Hawthorne's odd locution in *The Scarlet Letter* when he finds
the sacramental rose-bush "on the threshold of our narrative, which," he
says, "is now about to issue from that inauspicious portal" of the prison
door (*SL*, 48). Both Hester and "our narrative"—in some sense the same,
yet hardly synonymous—issue from what Hawthorne later calls Hester's
"term of confinement" (*SL*, 78); and in every respect Hawthorne identifies
his own action with Hester's. His "term of confinement," his years of isolation, has been both an imprisonment and a lying-in, a preparation to give
birth to his own narrative. (Hawthorne confirms this linkage when, for example, in "The Devil in Manuscript" he laments the "deformed infant" or
"unborn children" that perished in his immolation of his early productions
[*SI*, 173, 177], or when he writes of the birth of his second daughter that
"Mrs. Hawthorne published a little work two months ago, which still lies in
sheets."[18]) But the similarity has its more problematic side, too, for just as
Hester's childbearing issues from an act of transgression with Dimmesdale,
Hawthorne frets that his writing labor is one that would be deemed "worthless, if not positively disgraceful," by his stern ancestors (*SL*, 10). Hawthorne's art, like Pearl itself, finds its very "principle of being" in "the freedom of a broken law" (*SL*, 134),[19] and by so doing establishes its intimate
kinship with the act of transgression it hopes to root out and account for.
Hawthorne's freedom to speculate matches Hester's, though it has a double
edge: his speculation involves brooding upon dark recollections until they
finally become indistinguishable from imagination, endowing them with
morbid and commemorative interest; and it also involves his own entrance
into the marketplace of commercial fiction, an activity he also broods upon
so intensely as to render it almost imaginary. This is why the Custom-House
preface is such a masterful stroke on Hawthorne's part, yoking together as it
does his confinement and his labor with *customs* that are simultaneously
ancestral and commercial, as complex in their range of association and suggestion as Thoreau's various *economies*. When Hawthorne steps forth from
his confinement to display his wares, he transgresses ancestral law; the illegitimate birth he enacts breaks the rigid dynastic authority of his ancestral
forefathers and ushers him into a fallen world where he becomes the subject
of public observance and interpretation: like Hester, he turns himself into
"the text of the discourse" (*SL*, 85), and it will be his hazard that the text
not resemble a murder.

Speculation ensnares Hawthorne in a web of transgression in yet another, more devious respect. Since to speculate is to reflect, as in a *speculum*, a mirror, the very emblem of his craft of romance necessitates Hawthorne's implication in a fantasy of reference, a web of exchange that proceeds by the powerful but unnerving freedom of a broken law.[20] As Frank Kermode has pointed out, the mirror in Hawthorne's work is one usually "mysterious or distorting, denying the possibility of a simple relation between image and reality, between sign and referent,"[21] the very symbol, then, of a fall from the Adamic world, but a fall upon which Hawthorne's exploitation of transgression and remembrance depends. The mirror of art Hawthorne holds up to his world threatens to turn history into fantasy and simple reality into a monstrous grotesquerie, as when Governor Bellingham's armor reflects Hester's letter in such "exaggerated and gigantic proportions" that she seems "absolutely hidden behind it" (*SL*, 106). This lopsided relationship, at once the product of Hawthorne's historical culture and its obsession with the reading of types out of Nature, and his own fascination with the instabilities of representation, is the motivation behind his insane concentration on the mysterious scarlet *A*. There is an implicit correlation between the fact that the enigmatic letter affords a variety of interpretations and the fact of its association, as the initial letter of the alphabet, with the very notions of origin itself, with the outset of language and its referential web of speculation. But like the act of transgression which is deleted from Hawthorne's story, the *A* itself regresses into a wilderness of enunciation, as deftly shedding attempts at interpretation as the mysterious crime in Freud's text that instigates the sacrificial celebrations of the totemic meal. Since the letter "originates" a world of speculation, a proper reading risks either distortion or redundancy.

In her walk in the forest with Pearl, Hester, responding to the child's persistent questioning about the letter, backs definition of the letter against a blank wall by declaring, at her wit's end, that the scarlet *A* is the Black Man's "mark" (*SL*, 185). Like Thoreau's tautological offering of a picture of the arrowhead as a definition for the Red Man's "mark," Hester's attempt to render an account of the sign halts with Ktaadn-like frustration. What makes the scene more pointed is the fact that the reader must assume that the forest is the site of Hester's and Dimmesdale's original transgression; and Hawthorne seems to confirm this when he moves quickly to a haunting vignette of the forest brook, the "traces" of whose course are soon lost "amid the bewilderment of tree-trunks and underbrush" and granite boulders, which seem "intent on making a mystery of the course of this small brook; fearing, perhaps, that with its never-ceasing loquacity, it should whisper tales out of the heart of the old forest whence it flowed, or

mirror its revelations on the smooth surface of a pool" (*SL,* 186). The
brook's "babble," moreover, since it is associated with the "babble" of in-
famy that continually accosts Hester (*SL,* 85, 118), functions as a metaphor
of the Babel of language that accompanies and defines a state of transgression. Covered with the shadows of the old forest, the surface of the brook
can no more mirror out the secret in a narcissistic pool than any of Hawthorne's mirrors can reliably reflect their secrets. One looks, as Hawthorne
puts it in "The Custom-House," deep within [the] haunted verge" of
romance's mirror in order to "dream strange things, and make them look
like truth" (*SL,* 36); but such *speculation,* which turns recollection into
imagination and which is met not with a sure reflection of oneself but with a
ghostly ancestral pageant that multiplies and disfigures its referent, cannot
hope to free itself from the very bind it investigates. It can hope, however, in
the economy of its desires to augment the wealth of its investment.

Hawthorne makes no mistake when he ties together the origin of *A* with
the Black Man's mark of transgression; since the storyteller and the villain
meet each other halfway, the representation produced by memory's mirror
must either remain a tautological sign of transgression or else lose itself in a
wilderness of fantastic and haunting forms. At the threshold of consciousness is the bloody trace of a footstep; beyond it is the cavern of the unconscious Hawthorne recurs to so fondly. Because his fictive world is decidedly
one in which a state outside of transgression is unimaginable or else the
dreamiest of projections, representation refuses to produce a comfortable relation between sign and thing. Two puzzling notebook entries are of interest
for this issue:

> Letters in the shape of figures of men, &c At a distance, the words composed by
> the letters are alone distinguishable. Close at hand, the figures alone are seen,
> and not distinguished as letters. Thus things may have a positive, a relative, and
> a composite meaning, according to the point of view. (*AN,* 183)

> To make literal pictures of figurative expressions;—for instance, he burst into
> tears—a man suddenly turned into a shower of briny drops. An explosion of
> laughter—a man blowing up, and his fragments flying about on all sides. He
> cast his eyes upon the ground—a man standing eyeless, with his eyes on the
> ground, staring up at him in wonderment &c &c &c. (*AN,* 254)

The passages suggest the degree to which Hawthorne continued to be aroused
by the question of metaphor and the problems of literal versus figurative
language that so claimed the attention of his Puritan forefathers. As with
the "certain affair of fine red cloth" Hawthorne finds in the Custom House,
which "on careful examination, assume[s] the shape of a letter," but which
also "gives evidence of a now forgotten art, not to be recovered even by the

process of picking out the threads'' (*SL,* 31), the mystery of relationship between sign and object balks Hawthorne's effort to unravel it. Were language
accurately to mirror a given chain of events, an absurd situation would be
required, a romance with a vengeance—for example, ''a man standing eyeless, with his eyes on the ground, staring up at him in wonderment.'' Hawthorne, almost unwittingly, finds such an absurd situation in Holgrave's art
of the daguerreotype, whose exact mirroring is an uncanny perfection of
mimesis in the speculative world of romance. The question will remain,
however, whether mimesis is desirable, whether, in fact, the distortion and
play of fantasy is not an advance over the Eden of simple, staring wonderment. When ''writing a romance,'' Hawthorne remarked while at work on
The House of the Seven Gables, ''a man is always, or always ought to be,
careening on the utmost verge of a precipitous absurdity, and the skill lies in
coming as close as possible, without actually tumbling over.''[22] It is no simple matter, in Hawthorne's case, to assign any narrative to the category of
the realistic or the fantastic: in the *speculum* of romance the mimetic itself
careens on the verge of the absurd.

II

In order to understand the complex way in which Hawthorne's theory of
representation animates the dialogue between his writing and his past, we
need to consider one tale where the problem is most in evidence. ''Monsieur
du Miroir'' is on the face of it a simple enough elaboration of the Narcissus
story. The first-person narrator—who can as well as not be called ''Hawthorne''—finds his double haunting him at every location where reflection
is possible, aping his every move until he can ''almost doubt which of us is
the visionary form, or whether each of us be not the other's mystery, and
both twin brethren of one fate, in mutually reflected spheres.'' One might
almost suppose that Monsieur du Miroir is ''a wanderer from the spiritual
world, with nothing human except his illusive garment of visibility'' (*MM,*
170–71). But the significance of Hawthorne's design becomes more insidious when he compares the attempt to escape his reflection to ''the hopeless
race that men sometimes run with memory, or with their hearts, or their
moral selves'' (*MM,* 169). Though Monsieur du Miroir never speaks ''of his
paternity and his fatherland,'' perhaps because he is but a ''dumb devil''
who ''lacks the faculty of speech to expound it'' (*MM,* 160–61), he nevertheless belongs strictly to that domain lodged between ancestry and personality whose pressure prompts Hawthorne to raise the question in genealogical terms. Monsieur is in fact the very sign of Hawthorne's inability to dodge
the issue of ancestry and the peculiar history of his ''fatherland.'' Among

his cast of characters, only Dr. Grimshaw is perhaps truly "an American son of nobody,"[23] a New England Natty Bumppo (or Ulysses). Hawthorne himself, often to his dismay, approaches no such Adamic condition, but is haunted by a throng of ancestral fathers, all waving their paternity before his susceptible imagination like faces in a mirror. Hawthorne's stories lie always in the "dusky region" of "psychological romance," as he puts it in the preface to the *Snow-Image* stories (*SI*, 4)—in a region inside romance's mirror where the storyteller is one's speculative double. Indeed, "a blind man might as reasonably deny that Monsieur du Miroir exists, as we" (*MM*, 170).

A glance at Freud's discussion of the double in his essay on "The Uncanny" illuminates a good deal of Hawthorne's narrative anxiety and helps particularly to divulge the motive for "Monsieur du Miroir." "When all is said and done," Freud remarks, "the quality of uncanniness can only come from the fact of the 'double' being a creation dating back to a very early mental stage, long since surmounted—a stage, incidentally, at which it wore a more friendly aspect. The 'double' has become a thing of terror, just as, after the collapse of their religion, the gods turned into demons."[24] Freud's statement corresponds closely to Hawthorne's belief that since he finds his double "mingling with my earliest recollections. . .we [therefore] came into existence together, as my shadow follows me into the sunshine," and to the mounting frustration which ultimately leads him to declare, "I will be self-contemplative, as nature bids me, and make him the picture or visible type of what I muse upon, that my mind may not wander so vaguely as heretofore, chasing its own shadow through a chaos, and catching only the monsters that abide there" (*MM*, 166, 169–70). Freud, moreover, splits the agency of the double between the critical powers of conscience on the one hand, which keep check over the repressed materials springing from the primary phase of narcissism, and on the other, "all the unfulfilled but possible futures to which we still like to cling in phantasy, all the strivings of the ego which adverse external circumstances have crushed, and all our suppressed acts of volition which nourish in us the illusion of Free Will."[25] This duplicitous characterization also has its match in Hawthorne's man of the mirror:

> I involuntarily peruse him as a record of my heavy youth, which has been wasted in sluggishness, for lack of hope and impulse, or equally thrown away in toil, that had no wise motive, and has accomplished no good end. I perceive that the tranquil gloom of a disappointed soul has darkened through his countenance, where the blackness of the future seems to mingle with the shadows of the past, giving him the aspect of a fated man. Is it too wild a thought, that my fate may have assumed this image of myself, and therefore haunts me with such inevitable pertinacity, originating every act which it appears to imitate, while it deludes me by pretending to share the events, of which it is merely the emblem and the prophecy? (*MM*, 168)

Before the full implications of these correlations can be played out, we need to consider several other aspects of Freud's essay. Since what is uncanny, says Freud, is something frightening that strikes one as repeating or harking back to an experience or fantasy that has been forgotten or repressed, *das Heim-liche* (the "canny": "homely" or "homelike") is easily extended into its opposite, *das Unheimliche*. While one source of the uncanny lies in its association with primitive beliefs in animism, with the command of "secret injurious powers and with the return of the dead," another is constituted by those experiences that start "from repressed infantile complexes, from the castration complex [or] womb-phantasies," although since "primitive beliefs are most intimately connected with infantile complexes, and are, in fact, based on them," the distinction between the two "is often a hazy one."[26] The pertinence of beliefs in animism and the return of the dead to any consideration of Hawthorne is self-evident and is closely tied to the question of mimesis in romance—perhaps in family romance; the way in which Hawthorne's *Unheimliche* springs from infantile phantasies is not quite so evident but is equally important, not least because that infancy impinges upon an American Eden free from the web of speculation.

Freud's explicit connection of the uncanny with the female genitals, as "the entrance to the former *Heim*...of all human beings...the place where each one of us lived once upon a time and in the beginning,"[27] is shadowed forth under a number of guises in Hawthorne's work. The cavern of the unconscious often assumes the characteristics of a physiological landscape, for example in "The Man of Adamant," in which Richard Digby enters a cave that has "so dense a veil of tangled foliage about it, that none but a sworn lover of gloomy recesses would have discovered the low arch of its entrance, or have dared to step within its vaulted chamber where the burning eyes of a panther might encounter him" (*SI*, 162–63); or in the well-known notebook passage where Hawthorne projects a sketch of "the human heart to be allegorized as a cavern" whose entrance is surrounded by sunshine and flowers, but whose deeper recesses contain "a terrible gloom, and monsters of divers kinds." Deeper still, though, one finds the "beauty of the entrance" reproduced, the very seat of "eternal beauty" (*AN*, 237). Hawthorne's allegory, whatever else it might eventually have suggested, indicates a passage through the terrifying realm of the unconscious to a place of peace beyond, a reinscription of the sensual pleasure of entrance at an Eden of beginning. The plunge into the unconscious, the return to an Edenic state, and a nostalgia for home are constantly linked together in one way or another for Hawthorne; and as Edgar Dryden has shown, Hawthorne's "central and repeated experience is one of exile and dispersion from a number of temporary homes" accompanied by a longing for return to a universalized lost home.[28] What may be the most telling passage on this

score is found in *The Ancestral Footstep,* where Middleton is led back to his
ancestral English home in the attempt to puzzle out the crime which has left
a bloody footprint on the threshold of his memory: "he sought out his ancient home as if he had found his way into Paradise and were there endeav-
oring to trace out the sight [site] of Eve's bridal bower, the birthplace of the
human race and its glorious possibilities of happiness and high performance."[29]

How extensively Hawthorne links the mythology of America's Eden to
his own childhood memories is perhaps precociously evidenced by a remarkable passage from his youthful essay "On Wealth":

> When I was a boy, I one day made an inroad into a closet, to the secret recesses
> of which I had often wished to penetrate. I there discovered a quantity of very
> fine apples. At first I determined to take only one, which I put in my pocket.
> But those that remained were so inviting that it was against my conscience to
> leave them, and I filled my pockets and departed wishing that they would hold
> more. But alas! an apple which was unable to find space enough among its com-
> panions bounced down upon the floor before all the Family. I was immediately
> searched, and forced, very unwillingly, to deliver up all my booty.[30]

It would not be sensible to read too much into this passage, but its fusion of
the forbidden fruit of the American garden with that of a childhood remembrance is uncannily prophetic of several of the older Hawthorne's major
themes. Because it was a readily available prop in the landscape, Hawthorne
reverted easily to the figure of the apple or its tree as a sign of America's
simultaneously found and lost paradise; and as for Thoreau, Hawthorne's
apple is usually located halfway between the nostalgic wilderness and man's
profane cultivation of the American garden. "An orchard has a relation to
mankind," Hawthorne writes in "The Old Manse," "and readily connects
itself with matters of the heart....And what is more melancholy than the
old apple-trees, that linger about the spot where once stood a homestead,
but where there is now only a ruined chimney, rising out of a grassy and
weed-grown cellar?" Hawthorne's trees, like Thoreau's, "have lost the wild
nature of their forest-kindred, and have grown humanized by receiving the
care of man, as well as by contributing to his wants." But whereas Nature's
"infinite generosity and exhaustless bounty...can be enjoyed in perfection
only by the natives of the summer islands," that bliss may, Hawthorne
maintains, be shared "almost as well, by a man long habituated to city-life,
who plunges into such a solitude as that of the Old Manse, where he plucks
the fruit of trees that he did not plant, and which therefore, to my hetero-
dox taste, bear the closest resemblance to those that grew in Eden" (*MM,*
12–13). If going *home* is not so wild an adventure for Hawthorne as for
Thoreau, the Old Manse nonetheless occupies a place in Hawthorne's imagi-

nation as colored with the enchantment of America's beginnings as Thoreau's hut on the frontier of the mind. Thoreau transplanted his apple tree from the wilderness to his "native port" in the *Week* as a sign of his own complicity in its uprooting and domestication; and though Hawthorne is less sanguine about the imperialistic vector on the map of white settlement (as in his flippant dismissal of arrowheads), he plays second-hand Adam with equal abandon and desire.

The notebook passage on which he drew for "The Old Manse" also records that Hawthorne found these old apple trees to "form a peculiar link between the dead and the living." Like the rag of scarlet cloth discovered in the Custom House, the trees are animistic tokens for Hawthorne's fancy, doubly powerful because of their mythological associations. That they originate in the same uncanny soil as the severed tree on Three-Mile Point which Cooper insistently linked to the mutilation of his father's authority, is made clear when Hawthorne goes on to say that since his trees "have stood around a house for many years, and held converse with successive dynasties of occupants. . . it would seem almost sacrilege to cut them down" (*AN, 327*). Because they are signs of the powers of the past, Hawthorne's apples stand in the curious position of being objects of both probing scrutiny and reverent guardianship, the hidden treasure whose possession represents both paradise and transgression. The explicitly psychological dimension of Hawthorne's mythology is thus also suggestive of the way in which the apple, as a figure representing not only a lost paradise but its correlative home of the dead, partakes of the fear of castration, the trauma which Freud finds to lie behind the uncanny and its frightening doubles. It would be a mistake, though, to reduce Hawthorne's fiction to a sheet of neuroses; one need not turn original sin into a primal scene—though as I have suggested, the two often become entwined—in order to recognize that the two equally hypothetical moments have a similar force. Both purportedly generate a fallen world of transgression in which fantasy and guilt evacuate the recovery of a simple relationship between image and reality, and in which remembrance must piece together a shattered self never properly *present*. In this respect, Hawthorne's "neuroses," whatever they might be, are of interest only to the extent that they inform his own fictional record of a larger American experience. The figure of the apple is particularly serviceable to his drama because as a forbidden fruit it stands at once for paradise and the transgression by which it was obliterated, just as the *home* of the female genitals stands in Freud's mythology both for the comfort of the womb or the relationship with the mother, and in its *unheimlich* repetition for the eventuality of its disruption by the violence held out as a threat against the child's acquisition of sexual power, whether fantasized or actual.

What is to be made, we might wonder, of the weird coincidence between Hawthorne's characterization of Chillingworth, in his rapid assault on Dimmesdale, as "a thief entering a chamber where a man lies only half asleep. . .with purpose to steal the very treasure which this man guards as the apple of his eye" (*SL*, 130), and Freud's reading of the commonplace expression "[to] treasure a thing as the apple of our eye" as an example of the way in which "anxiety about one's eyes, the fear of going blind, is often enough a substitute for the fear of being castrated?"[31] (Perhaps no more than is to be made of the fact that the subject of Freud's analysis of Hoffmann's "The Sand-Man" in "The Uncanny" is a child named Nathanael.) Though Chillingworth is a striking figure of the analyst at the height of complicity, Freud hardly elaborates his expression on a mythological scale like that which Hawthorne's, given his concern with an act of original transgression, suggests; but there are other factors that make the parallel seem less fortuitous. We noted earlier Hawthorne's belief that his work is designed in part "to find out the divided segment of the writer's own nature" and began to suggest why Hawthorne's doubling of himself proceeds either by explicit mirror reflections or by his splitting of his own personality into seemingly opposed characters. This most often takes the form, as Dryden has pointed out, of Hawthorne's fear of being subjected to the "gaze of the Other" and his obsession, in turn, with voyeurism and detective-like surveillance.[32] Thus one has the Hawthorne who casts himself as a self-absorbed paranoid like the narrator of "Monsieur du Miroir" or like Dimmesdale, whose "viewing [of] his own face in a looking-glass" typifies "the constant introspection wherewith he tortured, but could not purify, himself" (*SL*, 145), and the Hawthorne who gleefully probes the secret life of another through such surrogate representatives as Chillingworth, Holgrave, and Coverdale.

It is the latter two who reveal most clearly the sexual dimension of Hawthorne's scrutiny, particularly Coverdale, who admits of his fascination with Priscilla that though "it was a kind of sacrilege in me to attempt to come within her maidenly mystery. . .I could not resist the impulse to take just one peep beneath her folded petals" (*BR*, 125). The shadowy compulsion that underlies Coverdale's desire for penetration is given a darker turn in the legend of the Veiled Lady (Priscilla's professional guise), whose shimmering mask some believe "covered the most beautiful countenance in the world," while others consider "that the face was the most hideous and horrible, and that this was her sole motive for hiding it. It was the face of a corpse; it was the head of a skeleton; it was a monstrous visage, with snaky locks, like Medusa's" (*BR*, 109–110). The cutting down of the ancestral apple trees and the voyeuristic penetration of Priscilla are both called "sacrileges" by

Hawthorne; and Priscilla, "whose impalpable grace lay so singularly between beauty and disease" (*BR*, 101), certainly is the apple of Coverdale's (or Hawthorne's) eye. His desire to probe beneath her veil, like Richard Digby's entrance into his cavern through "a veil of tangled foliage," is a forcibly covert sexual entry which has as its reward either the tasting of forbidden fruit or, just as likely, the horror of that emasculation that may be boded, according to Freud, by the representation of the female genitals in the figure of Medusa. Richard Digby, we recall, is turned to stone, an event to which we will want to return.

But seeing the female genitals in the guise of Medusa, or vice versa, suggests too that there is a question about perception that may have no simple answer. What is *seen* is perhaps not the same as what is *perceived;* but if perception is riddled by guilt and fantasy, and its objects transfigured by the atmospheric medium enclosing a world of romance, it must be asked whether "seeing" is possible for an observer who regards the subjects of his drama as though through a speculative and distorting mirror. Precise vision may, like mimesis, be relegated to a prelapsarian moment lost in memory. D. H. Lawrence cannily noted the conjunction of voyeurism and transgression—a conjunction crucial to an attempt to read original sin and castration trauma as complimentary moments in sexual mythology—upon which Hawthorne's psychologizing of the legends of an American Eden depends, when he remarked in his essay on *The Scarlet Letter* that, in their sexual relations after the fall, Adam and Eve "kept an eye on what they were doing, they watched what was happening to them. . . . Before the apple, they had shut their eyes and their minds had gone dark. Now, they peeped and pried and imagined. They watched themselves."[33] The self-conscious peeping and imagining that Lawrence so acutely brings to the fore as constitutive for Hawthorne's notion of original sin animate the Oedipal drama in its relation to the *Unheimliche* as well and, moreover, are central to the problems of perception and mimesis in Hawthorne's "romance." If Coverdale's perception of Priscilla fixes not on the complete figure but on a face in whose features are sublimated his own sexual anxiety, it is not only because the face's veil is the only one that Hawthorne could in all propriety lift, but also because it is the face that mirrors back, in fantastic distortion, the gazer's own troubled perception.

The fear that reality will not correspond to fantasy introduces the possibility that the *real* can never be seen and that a projected desire will not find correspondence *except* in fantasy, leaving the subject himself to hover between perceptions of beauty and disease. The fear of castration, according to Freud, springs from the (male) child's disappointed expectation: he expects to "see" a maternal penis but does not, and hence refers the possibility of a similar loss to himself. What he "perceives" is not simply *not there,* but rather is posited (or fantasized) as initially *there* but then suddenly removed or concealed; his act both imagines and hides its object in the act of finding it absent. It would seem that Hawthorne indicates a correlative frustration of desire when, in the legend of the Veiled Lady—whose performance, we should notice, is advertised "in red letters of gigantic size" *(BR,* 108)—he records Theodore's attempt to uncover the face which he jokingly suspects may be composed of "the lips of a dead girl, or the jaws of a skeleton, or the grinning cavity of a monster's mouth":

> Grasping at the veil, he flung it upward, and caught a glimpse of a pale, lovely face, beneath; just one momentary glimpse, and then the apparition vanished, and the silvery veil fluttered slowly down, and lay upon the floor. Theodore was alone. Our legend leaves him there. His retribution was, to pine, forever and ever, for another sight of that dim, mournful face—which might have been his life-long household fireside joy—to desire, and waste life in a feverish quest, and never meet it more! *(BR,* 114)

Hawthorne's Veiled Lady disappears only to rise up simultaneously "amid a knot of visionary people" *(BR,* 114), there, eventually, to subject the book's narrator-Narcissus, Coverdale, to a fate similar to Theodore's; and one would not wish to overplay the psychological aspects of the legend at the expense of its function in the whole of Hawthorne's narrative. Neither would it be reasonable to read the legend as an exact correlative of the child's primal scene of perception, though it is precisely the challenge to the veracity of perception posed by the child's traumatic experience that introduces the threat to his bodily integrity and disrupts *his* powers of exact correlation. When the child's identity is no longer mirrored in that of the mother, his own figure in the mirror figuratively embodies the portion of himself that has been threatened with dismemberment: the pleasure of narcissism is replaced by the possibility of his own loss, and the double confronted in the mirror uncannily represents both the transferral to himself of the wound he perceives in the mother and his consequent inability to trust the desires of his own eyes. The threat to the organs in question is displaced to, and exacerbated by, the organs of perception that must confront and interpret that threat.

What this might mean for Hawthorne's psychomythology will be clearer if we hark back to Thoreau's journal entry which runs, "man cannot afford to be a naturalist, to look at Nature directly, but only with the side of his eye.... To look at her is [as] fatal as to look at the head of Medusa,"[34] and then compare it to the following passage from Hawthorne's notebooks:

> I have before now experienced, that the best way to get a vivid impression and feeling of a landscape, is to sit down before it and read, or become otherwise ab-

sorbed in thought; for then, when your eyes happen to be attracted to the landscape, you seem to catch Nature unawares, and see her before she has time to
change her aspect. The effect lasts but a single instant, and passes away almost as
soon as you are conscious of it; but it is real, for that moment. It is as if...you
caught a glimpse of a face unveiled, which veils itself from every wilful glance.
The mystery is revealed, and after a breath or two, becomes just as much a
mystery as before. (*AN,* 485–86)

Like Thoreau, Hawthorne treats Nature as the object of a clandestine gaze
whose sexual overtones are unmistakable, though the threatening aspect of
his exhibitionistic landscape is not so immediately evident. The status of
Nature is quite the same in both cases: just as Thoreau's Nature is that
which ultimately can hardly be seen, much less described, without either
risking despoilment or else figuratively dismembering its observer, so Hawthorne's Nature is glimpsed only to be hastily covered up again, or, like the
Veiled Lady, to disappear altogether, leaving her observer with the dubious
comfort of his own loss and despair. Hawthorne peers beneath the folds of
Nature's petals to find something which is immediately removed to a further reach of fantasy. His somewhat nasty interest in voyeurism parallels
Chillingworth's searching out of that secret which is the "apple" of Dimmesdale's eye; but like Nature or the Veiled Lady, the secret of transgression, the book's primal scene, lies behind the story of *The Scarlet Letter,*
severed from the tale which it ostensibly produces and which almost futilely
attempts to reveal its significance: it cannot be *seen* but only *perceived* in
the manifestations of its disappearance. It is no mistake that we are tempted
to link together an American "original sin" and a compulsion to unveil the
secret of Nature, whether that belonging to a mysterious virgin or to an unappropriated landscape; the two are inextricably bound for Hawthorne, as
unheimlich as possible. Like Thoreau in his desperate chase after pristine
Nature, or like Chillingworth and Coverdale in their compulsive pursuits,
Hawthorne is unable to tell whether he will find anything other than a fig-
ment of his own imagination, whether what he has perceived is really there
at all.

This ambivalence belongs to the stress of the child's primal perception
as I have been outlining it, and moreover to the very structure of the uncanny, which is comprised of the repetition of the stress. In an incisive reading of Freud's essay on the uncanny which I have been drawing on, Samuel
Weber has demonstrated the importance of vision and voyeurism for a
proper understanding of the uncanny. According to Weber, the threat of
castration, particularly as it instills in the subject a fear of being blinded, is
provoked by a frustrated perception, one which perceives not what it had expected or imagined, but rather a lack, the absence of a maternal phallus.

Since the child is henceforth led to doubt the veracity of his perceptions, the threat of castration is not necessarily something that can be fixedly *represented* (by a visible surrogate for the castrating father, for example); rather, says Weber, "what is designated by the term 'castration' is precisely the impossibility of seeing directly, right on or straight ahead. Castration can never be looked at, en face, for it is always off to the side, off-side, like the uncanny itself." What is "discovered" by the child is "a kind of negative perception," one that separates "desire" from its "object" and thus "structures the future identity and experience of the subject, by confronting it [him] with its unconscious desire as a violent and yet constitutive difference, preventing the subject from ever being fully present to itself or fully self-conscious." Castration then cannot be treated "as one phenomenon among others," Weber maintains, but only "as the *crisis of phenomenality,* as such, since it marks a new differential and symbolic contextuality which can no longer be simply *perceived,* but rather [only] *read* and *interpreted.*" Because the uncanny is "bound up with a *crisis* of perception" and with a threat that poses "a mortal danger to the subject, to the 'integrity' of its body and thus to its very identity," it also implies a necessary defense against this crisis, one which "expresses itself in the compulsive curiosity, the Wissgier, the craving to penetrate the flimsy appearances to the essence beneath...the desire to uncover the facade and to discover what lurks behind."[35]

Weber's reading gracefully illuminates the questions of perception and fantasy in Hawthorne, and I would only contradict Weber's own use of the word *perceived;* as I have been using it, "perception" belongs exactly to the moment when the subject can no longer "see," or see exactly: in a subject partially blinded, perception is itself an interpretation. *Seeing* belongs to the Eden of simple wonderment in which the child's identity was whole and safe and in which referentiality posed no problem: the narcissistic relationship between child and mother, and between word and thing (image and reality) occurs in a hypothetical realm of perfect mimesis buried in memory. The crisis of perception Weber defines is thus a figure of original sin in that it comprises simultaneously an act of transgression and the threat of punishment meted out for that act. Like the Medusa, which for Freud stands at once for the phallus and its absence (an ambiguity we will return to), that which the child *perceives* fails to correspond to his expectation of identity but at the same time suggests that some *thing* which was once there *to be seen* has vanished; the disappearance is represented by a wound, a mark of transgression. In this sense Weber underestimates the capacity of castration to be "represented" visibly, for exactly because the maternal vagina only "represents" a loss—that is, it is not clear to the child that one has actually taken place—the child's referral of a similar loss to himself is equally capable of "representation" in the visible form. Since the child cannot believe his eyes, there is no basis for privileging a negative perception over one with a visible content: both are *perceptions* in which a loss *can only* be "represented," not mimetically "presented" (see also note 35).

"My eyes fastened themselves upon the old scarlet letter, and would not be turned aside. Certainly, there was some deep meaning in it, most worthy of interpretation, and which, as it were, streamed forth from the mystic symbol, subtly communicating itself to my sensibilities, but evading the analysis of my mind" (*SL*, 31). What does Hawthorne see, or rather, almost see but not quite: would it be legitimate to read this famous passage as the allegory of a castration trauma? When Hawthorne places the letter on his own breast, he does, after all, experience "a sensation not altogether physical, yet almost so, as of burning heat; and as if the letter were not of red cloth, but red-hot iron" (*SL*, 32), an experience not unlike Richard Digby's encounter of "the burning eyes of a panther." Hawthorne takes the wound the letter represents upon himself, prefiguring its ambiguous appearance on Dimmesdale's breast later in the book. But to repeat, though: if we read Hawthorne's act as a figurative shadowing forth of the castration trauma, such a reading neither claims to be primary nor dismisses the significance of his act as a recreation of Hester's and Dimmesdale's punishment for adultery. Yet having said as much clarifies the way in which these acts partake of the same motives, for it is precisely the point for Freud that castration be understood as the threat held out against the child's fantasy of committing adultery with his mother, a desire apparently coincident with the child's perception of a "wound" at once enticing and repulsive. (Neither is it idle to recall that Hawthorne wrote *The Scarlet Letter* and its preface in a time of emotional crisis brought on not only by the loss of his job as a surveyor of customs but also by the recent death of his mother.) The trauma represents a crisis of perception and belief introducing something which can no longer be simply *seen* but rather, as Weber has it, only *"read* and *interpreted."* Hawthorne's "discovery" of the scarlet letter does exactly that: the cloth turns into a red *A* only upon his imaginative reconstruction, and even then it has a meaning which is never established but which it is the whole point of the novel to try and work out. Because the brand of the *A* is stuck halfway between imagination and reality, as in its questionable transference to Dimmesdale's breast, one can say no more clearly than Freud can of castration that it poses a "real" threat; its significance lies in undecidability. What the child sees is not the object expected, but its absence, and hence the very act of perception raises the question of his own identity; its significance also lies in undecidability. Hawthorne abides in a world of transgression where only speculation is possible.

Hawthorne's most overt and often-remarked representation of the

threat of castration appears in "The Maypole of Merry Mount," where Endi-
cott's disruption of the sylvan masque and his sword's severance of the
phallic festival pole enact the threat as an allegory of Puritan mastery and
gloom. What castration "stands for" in this instance is the domination and
cruel authority of Hawthorne's Puritan ancestors in their dispersal of the
American Eden. Yet that Eden, as we have suggested, remains problematic;
it appears for Hawthorne only as a fanciful projection, as something that
cannot quite be glimpsed before hiding itself again. It is a face under a veil,
or Nature itself, which one sees at a *side-glance* and only for a moment: to
borrow from Weber, Eden cannot be looked at, en face, for it is always off to
the side. Like the Sylvan Dance in *The Marble Faun*, which Hawthorne cannot help but liken to "the sculptured scene" on a "sarcophagus," where "a
festive procession mocks the ashes and white bones that are treasured up
within," but which on closer inspection reveals the flaws of failure and grief,
Hawthorne's Eden constantly collapses under the pressure of perception:
"Always, some tragic incident is shadowed forth, or thrust *sidelong* into the
spectacle; and when once it has caught your eye, you can look no more at the
festal portions of the scene, except with reference to this one slightly suggested doom and sorrow" (*MF*, 89; my emphasis). In this scene, Miriam's
glance reveals Donatello, and the spell of Arcadia is replaced by the ponderous *malaria* of Rome and its history of sin and crime. What Hawthorne and
his characters continually perceive is the displacement of paradise by a fallen
world, as what is expected or hoped for gives way to threat and transgression,
and that Edenic moment that might be said to have been disrupted disappears behind a veil of fantasy or recedes into an almost unimaginable time.
Hawthorne's scene is always analogous to that which the artist Kenyon, speculating on Donatello's crime, finds at Monte Beni: it may be "the site of an
ancient Eden," but one whose "loveliness" can only be beheld "through
the transparency of that gloom which has been brooding over those haunts
of innocence, ever since the fall. Adam saw it in a brighter sunshine, but
never knew the shade of pensive beauty which Eden won from his
expulsion" (*MF*, 276). In Adam's sunshine, one could, to recall Thoreau's
phrase, "simply wonder," free from the "web of speculations." This is precisely the stupified condition that Hawthorne imagines for his New Adam
and Eve, in the tale of that name, who are baffled by the "witchery of
dress," the "elaborate perversities" of art, the "unintelligible hieroglyphs"
of commercial signs, and the "columns of mystic characters" in the books of
the library (*MM*, 247–66). In the world of transgression one cannot perceive
without *speculating*, reading, repeating, and interpreting. Like Hester,
Hawthorne *speculates* because that action is the very condition and embodiment of transgression; he cannot unravel the mystery of the *letter* because

the transgression—call it original sin, adultery, castration trauma—is a crisis of perception: in a fallen state, one can neither simply wonder and stare nor wholly believe one's eyes. The scarlet *A* succeeds so marvelously for Hawthorne's narrative exactly because it is the very token of speculation itself, of the web of referentiality induced by the crisis. What Hawthorne might have *seen* is no longer there; it has been displaced by the red brand of an enigmatic sign which both represents and fails to represent it, which represents at once transgression and its triumph of repentance, just as in ''Fancy's Show Box,'' the guilt accompanies the act—whether murder or narration—at the precise moment of its fulfillment.

Yet as I have insisted, it is the coincidence of guilt and speculation through which the writer augments and commemorates the power of his transgression, his power, that is, to transgress the stifled Adamic moment in which his art would be pointless. The ''shade of pensive beauty'' won by Adam's expulsion from Eden defines a fallen condition which is precisely the material of the writer's drama of repentance, a drama in which he re-enacts his own complicity, even compulsively repeats it in his craving to peer beneath the petals of Nature and discover the ''crime'' that lurks behind the speculation in which he is engaged. It is the tragic incident cast sidelong into the felicitous spectacle that at once issues a challenge to perception and creates a crisis in which ''representation'' is possible and necessary. Whether we read that crisis as an original sin that introduces the web of speculation and referentiality or as the primal scene in a castration trauma that introduces a rupture in vision and a consequent need for interpretation, transgression marks the beginning of the play of fantasy that must at once posit an Eden of mimesis it can never recuperate and at the same time engage in the ritual deployment of its own devices to transfigure and commemorate in repetition the loss it has purportedly sustained. *Trauma* and *drama* enact an ambivalence in performance that corresponds to the ambivalence that marks the crisis itself: what is introduced by reference and representation is the possibility, even the necessity, that one cannot believe one's eyes, that the identity of the subject is no more integral than the relationship between image and reality or word and thing. Yet it is the very dispersion of the hypothetically monadic state of affairs that makes that state *desirable,* inscribes *it* as a figure in the representation of dream and drama, and holds it forth as the fruit to be tasted. The lost realism of mimesis becomes, uncannily enough, the most fantastic of desires in a world of transgression and romance. In the atmospheric medium of Hawthorne's imagination, the disjunction between sign and referent, between the desire of the subject and the object of his desire, becomes the occasion for his exploitation of the ''witchery'' of dress, the ''perversities'' of art, and the ''hieroglyphs'' of commerce, all in the name of transfiguring a transgression *against* the sacred into a transgression *of* the sacred in a celebration of desire. Hawthorne adulterates "Adultery" in order to turn it into "Able" and "Angel," and as many readers have noted, he might well have added "art," not to mention apple, Adam, authority, autobiography, America, arche, or alphabet. The *A* is at once a wound and a symbol; like the wound of castration, it refers itself indefinitely, represents an ambiguous loss, has no particular and identifiable content, and marks the beginning of guilt, speculation, and fantasy. Like Thoreau's arrowhead, it is a pure *figure* which cannot but must be interpreted: it can only *represent*, whether in trauma or drama.

Henry James appears to have apprehended this quality in Hawthorne's work when he wrote in an essay of 1897 that Hawthorne lived unavoidably in a symbolic world, condemned to "a presentation of objects casting, in every sense, far behind them a shadow more curious and more amusing than the apparent figure."[36] Though James more properly should have said "representation," his statement is ambiguously acute, for the burden of Hawthorne's world (it is not clear that it is always an "amusing" one) is that the "figure" can only be "apparent," or rather, is always a *figure* to be interpreted, never merely the letter with a fixed meaning. Thus it is that Hawthorne can wildly speculate, in the notebook entries we looked at earlier, upon the possibility of literal renderings of figurative statements. But as we saw, the hallucination leaves him with things that seem sometimes figures of men, sometimes letters, sometimes both; depending on his "point of view." Or more notably, it leads him to project as one of his examples "a man standing eyeless, with his eyes on the ground, staring up at him in wonderment." It is hard to imagine a more pointed and anxious representation for the crisis of perception that leads to the hallucination itself: the fear of blindness (the fear of dismemberment Freud finds transferred to perception itself) is reflected in the very act which seeks to recover the lost moment of mimetic identity, its fulfillment reintroduced into the desire to eliminate that fear's possibility. Freud notes at one point in "The Uncanny" that "an uncanny effect is often and easily produced when the distinction between imagination and reality is effaced, as when something that we have hitherto regarded as imaginary appears before us in reality, or when a symbol takes over the full functions of the thing it symbolizes."[37] Is this not the case in Hawthorne's dream of turning figurative statements into literal events, where his example itself is completely uncanny? In the romance, the distinction between imagination and reality is always a question; but at the extremity of the fantastic it is pure mimesis, the symbol encroaching upon and mastering its referent, that is most uncanny, most absurd. This too is why Hawthorne's scarlet *A* is uncanny—not only because it produces a sympathetic burning on his breast, but because in the opposite extreme it refuses to assume the function of the thing it symbolizes, that is, so refuses to stand reliably for any one thing and thus draws all significance into itself that all referents disappear into the function of symbolizing. Here the villain and the storyteller can barely meet halfway because the crime itself is effaced and displaced by the welter of its results, and hence it may be the case after all that the symbol has taken over the function of the act it stands for: it becomes the Black Man's "mark," a sign whose function shadows forth a transgression, but a transgression that gets buried behind it or transfigured into the limitless tropes of fantasy. The *A* is a wound, a frontier, a threshold: on one side is the world of speculation and desire, on the other, if there is an other, the virtual blank of an inaccessible Eden that can only be looked at off-side, utterly fantastic and uncanny.

III

We have come by a necessarily circuitous route back to the problem of Hawthorne's double, which has at least two roles it is important to take account of. It is first of all, says Freud, "an insurance against the destruction of the ego. . .a preservation against extinction [that] has its counterpart in the language of dreams, which is fond of representing castration by a doubling or multiplication of the genital symbol. That same desire led the ancient Egyptians to develop the art of making images of the dead in lasting materials." Yet when this initial stage has been surmounted and the double has become a figure for the mind's censorship of itself, for its "conscience," the role of the double as "an assurance of immortality" gives way to its role as "the uncanny harbinger of death."[38] The double, then, originally represents a protection of the self, the preservation of its continuity and identity (though such a characterization, since it is retroactive, must itself be admittedly speculative). But when one apprehends that the double may likewise scrutinize and command, may wield authority over the self, its role as a representative not of identity but of fragmentation, of the possibility of the self's loss of its own authority, comes into play. The double is uncanny because it *is* and *is not* the self at the same time: it is a portion of the self that has been cut off, dismembered, but its exact status as real or fantasized is no more determinable than that of "castration." Freud does not make the translation between the two stages clear, but this is attributable to the fact that the double continues to partake of both, which is precisely why it is most uncanny. The appearance of the double is the very sign of a crisis in the ego's development that renders perception problematic. Freud does, however, provide a clue that for our purpose is completely to the point—

namely, his remark about "the art of making images of the dead in lasting materials." We have noticed several times the way in which the fascination of being turned to stone, the Medusa's threat, signifies castration, but we have hardly yet begun to see what role this plays in Hawthorne's struggle with *representation* and how, consequently, his renditions of "the home of the dead" are completely *unheimlich*.

The eyes that stare back from the ground, from a canvas, or from a mirror are indeed the apple of Hawthorne's eyes, a sign of the crisis of perception and the world of *speculation* introduced by that crisis; they are the focus of a desire which has been dislocated and thrust into a double who mockingly enacts that dislocation by mimicking the loss of identity. The threat of castration, as Weber puts it, confronts the subject with the possibility of its never "being fully present to itself, or fully self-conscious." What is at stake is the subject's ability to account for its own bodily wholeness, its *presence*; the eyes of the double refute that ability by embodying presence elsewhere, at a distance from the subject. The double is almost the same yet almost other, the very function of the self's fantasized dismemberment. Reflection is not identity; at best it is an exact re-presentation, and in the distorted mirror of romance it shifts, slides, will not stand still. Thus Hawthorne finds a madman in "The Hall of Fantasy" with "a scheme for fixing the reflections of objects in a pool of water, and thus taking the most life-like portraits imaginable" (*MM,* 178). But like Thoreau, who presents an illustration of the arrowhead as its only possible definition, Hawthorne's schemer may suffer from a deluded dream of identity. If a mirror image (or a photograph, to drop a hint about Holgrave's role) *is* identical, a perfect double, then why does Hawthorne need a madman to enact the process? For the same reason he must speculate about turning figures into letters—because mimesis itself is fantasy, the property of a lost Eden, and its attempted recovery leads to an absurd Swiftian utopia where things, rather than words, are exchanged, or to the paradox Plato describes in the *Cratylus:* "how ridiculous would be the effect of names on things, if they were exactly the same with them! For they would be doubles of them, and no one would be able to determine which were the names and which were the realities."[39] The play of representation incident upon transgression, even if the crime is a hypothetical one, locks language and portraiture into a world of romance where imprecisions of representation are matched by the ancestral pageant that troops out of Hawthorne's mirror in place of a simple reflection of himself. Hawthorne's *speculation* leaves him a Narcissus of history, no more able to see only himself in the mirror of romance than he is able to turn the figurative into the literal or read a single meaning out of the scarlet *A*. And when there is "only" himself in the mirror, as in "Monsieur du Miroir," he is in fact in a position just as bad, if not worse: instead of fragmentation and dislocation in the form of the return of the dead, he has sheer tautology in the form of a double as maddeningly ungraspable as the meaning of the red letter. The letter and the double are signs marking a crisis of perception and identity, signs that, because they can only be read and interpreted, represent a self whose bodily integrity has been called into question by being thrust into a speculative network of representation.

The Hawthorne of "Monsieur du Miroir" is, in effect, the madman of "The Hall of Fantasy," not only because his scheme seems unwittingly to have succeeded, but because the fated double, "originating every act which it appears to imitate," is finally little different from the host of ancestral personages that have been channeled into it. The returning dead and the double are both masters of the self, though the latter is at once more comforting and more horrifying precisely because it *is* and *is not* the self, appearing to be the same as one's self but actually embodying the host of others—the fathers of ancestry—who initially affirm continuity and identity but ultimately become harbingers of death and deny the subject's ability to be fully *present* to itself. If it is Hawthorne's continual task to elaborate "the truth," as he puts it in the preface to *The House of the Seven Gables,* "that the wrong-doing of one generation lives into successive ones, and divesting itself of every temporary advantage, becomes a pure and uncontrollable mischief" (*HG,* 2), what most haunts him in the forefathers who stream forth from his mirrors is that *they* are in control of him: the past controls the present, the men of the mirror control his *presence* by appearing to originate rather than imitate. This is a conventional enough claim on the fact of it. Certainly, the origin of the present lies in the past, and present generations imitate those of the past, if only approximately or unintentionally, insofar as they repeat and reconstitute inherited forms of behavior and expression. But Hawthorne's claim is, of course, more diabolical and uncanny, for his ancestors continually appear to *originate* in startling ways—by the fulfillment of curses, the control of dreams, the retribution of past sins, and so forth. Though they are no simple repetitions or copies of the self, the ancestors in the mirror are, in a fantastic and uncanny way, literal renderings of figurative statements, symbols which have come to life, as it were, and taken over the very function they symbolize.

Hawthorne's ancestors, then, are animistic to an astonishing degree; they threaten the self with encroachment and intimate the form of repetition into which the self finds itself drawn but over which it has no control. If the self reflected in a mirror is the double who represents a perceptual crisis by calling into question the subject's command over self-presence, by first duplicating then dislocating genital authority, the multiple faces in the mir-

ror do the same with a vengeance: doubling the self back through an interminable ancestral chain, they dislocate authority to a degree undecipherable
and seize the power of the subject by turning the initial comfort that the
double provides into a mocking repetition of *presence* which no longer
belongs to the self. The problem of originality for Hawthorne, then, is one
with a decided torque, for it is no simple matter of tracing back the beginnings of customs and curses but rather of finding that the very identity of the
self has no origin, no moment of presence that can be confidently articulated. That moment of presence lies behind the *speculation* that issues
from it, behind a world of dislocation and transgression haunted by doubles
of the self who deny its authority by drawing it into their selves. The
speculative web of language and reference that flows out of the mysterious
A, the letter of origin and transgression, is matched by the *speculative* web
of doubles—whether mirror reflections, portraits, or ghosts—that flows
from the crisis of perception, the moment at which self-presence has been
posited and effaced.

Mirrors, Hawthorne wrote in "The Prophetic Pictures," "present us
with portraits, or rather ghosts of ourselves" (*TT,* 173). His indecision in
phrasing is important, for he could not say clearly which it should be— portraits or ghosts; his verb "present" seems innocent enough, too, but as we
have seen, it may be ironic at best, whether or not Hawthorne was aware of
it. He was aware of something like it, though, in his obsession with marking
off the "now" from the past and future, as in the well-known passage about
the half catatonic, half childish Clifford Pyncheon: "With a mysterious and
terrible Past, which had annihilated his memory, and a blank Future before
him, he had only this visionary and impalpable Now, which, if you look
closely at it, is nothing" (*HG,* 149). Clifford here is a version of the New
Adam (with whom he is several times identified), dumbly cut off in a stupor
of simple wonderment. Hawthorne's collapsing of the present, the "now,"
into what is so much *present* that it is "nothing" in itself, also lies darkly
behind his remark that *The House of the Seven Gables* "comes under the
Romantic definition" in its "attempt to connect a by-gone time with the
very Present that is flitting away from us" (*HG,* 2). Characteristically for
Hawthorne, the present is engulfed by the past, swallowed up by what is *not
present,* and hence can only be *represented.* The inherent paradox in
Hawthorne's craft thus begins to come clear: on the one hand, he wishes to
take responsibility for the past and act, as he says in "The Custom House,"
as its *representative*; but on the other, his past demands that it *represent*
him, insofar as it shatters the *presence* of his self, kinging over it in the form
of doubles and haunting portraits which deny the integrity of his identity.

We must, then, distinguish two problems of representation but note as well that they are functions of one another. It belongs to the world of romance that, since the Eden of self-presence has been dispersed, only *repre*-sentation of the self, like any other hypothetical reality, is possible. At the same time, however, a representation that takes the form of exact duplication or repetition is held out as the ideal to be recovered, though it in turn becomes itself a fantasy. *Speculation,* as the play of referentiality *and* as the desire for duplication, is the paradoxical hinge of a transgression whose commemoration, like Freud's totem meal, takes the form of a ritual repetition of the crime that at once enacts and affirms the present community's or self's difference from the past and yet establishes a penitential covenant that seeks identity with, and derives its power from, that past. The ambivalence in the relationship of the living to the dead, as Freud notes, gives rise to beliefs in animism and generates two "opposed psychical structures: on the one hand fear of demons and ghosts and on the other hand veneration of ancestors."[40] In the commemorative sacrifice fear and veneration get merged, and the community's attempt to disavow the ancestor's animistic power of representation is countered by the avowal of its own power to represent the ancestor in deferred obedience. A representation that both challenges authority and identifies with it, a writing that both transgresses and redeems authority, must find its appropriation of power uncanny, at once its affirmation and its haunting denial.

The speculation of the romance, as of the sacred ritual, works by a power that is alternately excised and augmented, and its economy is not unlike that "work" Freud finds performed in dreaming whereby repressed wishes strive for contact with "reality" by converting themselves into figures, concrete forms that are *"capable of being represented."*[41] The repressed wish or fantasy thus takes a form that is representative and hence must be interpreted, and at the same time its appearance, like the appearance of the ancestral faces in Hawthorne's mirror, affirms the subject's lack of conscious self-presence: he is under the control of the unconscious, which represents his self. In an attempt to provide a "psychogenetic theory of figurative thinking,"[42] Geoffrey Hartman has expanded Freud's insight in a way that brings its power more into line with Hawthorne's by pointing out that though the initial character of the dream-wish (the repressed material) is sexual for Freud, "its passage from latency into the content of the dream can only be explained in terms of a *communication-compulsion.*" In Hartman's model, "the autoplastic character of symptom formation" (pictorial representation of dream material) substitutes "action upon self for action upon others," thus limiting "the *demand* placed on others" for a desired response; hence, "the idealism of art" can be understood "as a therapeutic modification of this demand. . . for achieving self-presence despite or through the presence of others." The work of art "'represents' a self which is either insufficiently 'present' or feels itself not 'presentable,'" just as "the dream-wish cannot be admitted into our presence" but can only be "'represented.' As in legal or ritual 'representation' a subject needs a 'representative' because it cannot be present in its own right. It requires advocacy or seconding." Moreover, when the demand for response in question is that "placed by the self on itself" (by way of the super-ego, what in Hawthorne's case is an ancestral "conscience" in the form of a double or doubles), then, says Hartman, "the limitation of demand we call introjection (internalization) may raise the specter of a *further* limitation: of something more properly called a *sacrifice*. . . . The sacrifice feared by one who has internalized demand is simply that of the whole principle of *mimesis:* of a magical correspondence of internal action and external effect, of a mimetic aiming at 'The Real Thing.' In semiotic terms, of wishing to convert symbols into signs with real, immediate reference."[43]

Such a wish for mimetic power is a fantasy of presence that, though it cannot be fulfilled, is not easily given up, and in this respect, Hartman's use of "sacrifice" is interestingly ambiguous; for it is exactly the limitation of demand by internalization that "sacrifices" mimesis in the sense that it precludes mimesis, prevents the subject from being present to itself or making itself present and forces it into poses of representation. But it is precisely the case, too, that representation is a "sacrifice" *on behalf of* mimesis; that is, if representation is a ritual reenactment of repressed wishes or unconscious desires by which the self seeks to assert its autonomous power (by slaying the father, say, or by making literal renderings of figurative statements), then the communication-compulsion of the artist, like the totem meal, is one in which the desire for "a magical correspondence of internal action and external effect" (or, for that matter, external action and internal effect) can never be satisfied but only repeated. Without calling attention to it, Hartman has returned us into the animistic structure of the uncanny, and the importance of his findings (whether in general or in the particular case of Hawthorne) only becomes evident when they are viewed in this light—or rather, in this shadow—for if the correspondence Freud finds between animism and trauma, and between ritual and representation, is to have its proper force, the "sacrifice" of communication must find its power in an implementation and augmentation of the repressed wish, even if at the same time it falls short of an actual conversion of that wish into reality. Hawthorne's work "represents" a self in the basic sense of rendering his dreams (the content of his communication-compulsion, a phrase wholly appropriate for Hawthorne's simultaneously obsessive and retiring narrators) in the form of fiction; yet because these fictional representatives often take the form of autobiographical doubles whose very function is to disrupt the *presence* of Hawthorne's self, it is not enough to say they represent a self that feels itself not presentable: rather, they *keep* the self from being presentable at the same time they are enlisted in the interest of the identity of that self. Their representation is legal and ritual, to be sure, but it is precisely because this is the case, because they master Hawthorne, that he can never be fully present in his own self. In Hawthorne's case, the autoplastic formation of symptoms (the capability for representation) does not so much substitute "action upon self for action upon others" (an audience, say), as it plays out action upon self *through* action *by* others who for Hawthorne constitute an ancestral audience he must represent in both senses and whose redemption he has made his task. This makes the therapeutic aspect of the model much clearer, for if the demand for response devolves not only upon a self whose fragmentation is enacted by others who preside over that demand, the act of *representation* is not nearly so simple: there is for Hawthorne, then, simultaneously a loss of presence (to other representatives) and an attempt to cure or make up for that loss (by becoming their representative).

Because Hawthorne's representatives are legal and dynastic, and because his limitation of demand is so internalized (so much so that those representatives can be said to be inverted into the limitation itself), Hartman's characterization of the "sacrifice of mimesis" is exactly to the point and lies behind the very structure of the uncanny as it appears in Hawthorne. For if we say that Hawthorne would like to achieve *presence* through *representation*, we must add that it is representation itself that denies Hawthorne's presence, by dislocating it and burying it in dynastic repetition, most notably in his double, who as the (seemingly) real embodiment of a figurative condition (loss, transgression, castration) in fact enacts "a magical correspondence of internal action and external effect...mimetic aiming at 'The Real Thing.'" Since representation and speculation are so inextricably bound for Hawthorne, mimesis itself nearly becomes a sacrificial threat; his inability to find presence through representation corresponds to a loss of identity that began as a crisis of perception—the very origin, though one that is effaced, of the speculative split between sign and referent that left only a monstrous symbol, the scarlet wound of *A*. The moment at which *A* had "real, immediate reference" (a moment present only as fantasy) marks a hypothetical point of transgression—the bloody footstep on the threshold—behind which lies *presence*, an Adamic state wherein one could simply wonder, free from speculation and the need of representation; yet the mark itself splinters and disperses that state, leaving Hawthorne to hark back to its point of origin as what can now only be veiled and barely represented. Mimesis is a lost Eden, and as such, its occurrence thereafter is magical, an uncanny moment in the execution of the artist's craft. It becomes, strangely enough, the sacrifice romance must make, and at the same time, that in the name of which the sacrifice is made.

If, as Jean Normand remarks, "Hawthorne had within him a Holo-fernes in search of a Judith,"[44] such a wish is not merely attributable to a personal neurosis but forms a vector of desire which animates Hawthorne's whole craft and career. Perhaps, though, it would be more appropriate, if overly heroic, to say that Hawthorne had within him a Perseus in search of a Medusa. That is, after all, the subject of his twice-told tale in *A Wonder Book* entitled "The Gorgon's Head." It is more than slightly disquieting to think that Hawthorne retold the famous story specifically for children, but then everything we have been saying goes to indicate that the trauma played out in the tale belongs to the province of childhood in an uncanny way, par-ticularly for a writer who feels that his craft itself enacts an illegitimate birth. Hawthorne's rendering of the story is relatively straightforward, but it is worth recording one passage in detail since it bears so directly on his struggle with the problem of representation. Perseus has discovered the Gorgons and recalls Quicksilver's advice to avoid the gaze of Medusa by looking "at the reflection of her face and figure in the bright mirror of [his] shield":

> Perseus now understood Quicksilver's motive for so earnestly exhorting him to polish his shield. In its surface, he could safely look at the reflection of the Gorgon's face. And there it was—that terrible countenance—mirrored in the brightness of the shield, with the moonlight falling over it, and displaying all its horror. The snakes, whose venemous natures could not altogether sleep, kept twisting themselves over the forehead. It was the fiercest and most horrible face that was ever seen or imagined, and yet with a strange, fearful, and savage kind of beauty. (*WB*, 29–30)

Hawthorne's terrifying description is more extensive, though we have enough here to gauge its correspondence to the exhibition of the Veiled Lady. Perseus looks into the shield's mirror in order to see and not see at once: he perceives the Medusa by a *side-glance*, in the protection of the mir-ror, and is thus able to sever her head, dealing her the fate that, presumably, she would figuratively have dealt him with a direct gaze. But to recur to Freud's essay on the Medusa, Perseus's act may shadow forth an acute am-bivalence in Hawthorne's interest in the story. The terror of the Medusa is the terror of castration, according to Freud; yet the snakes (a substitute for the female genitals) "serve actually as a mitigation of the horror," since they multiply the penis symbolically and hence reaffirm its presence. And though the sight of the Medusa "makes the spectator stiff with terror, turns him to stone," says Freud, this in fact "offers consolation to the spectator:

he is still in possession of a penis, and the stiffening reassures him of the fact."[45]

We may well wonder about the bluntness of Freud's assertions, yet they do explicate the function of the Medusa in Hawthorne's work. The snakes of the Medusa perform the same office that the double does, at once affirming the presence and integrity of the subject, and shattering or dislocating it; similarly, their power of turning one to stone both affixes presence and destroys it. But such a power is intimately bound up for Hawthorne with the power of representation, with his art's ability to make images of the dead in lasting materials. Busts are heads, portraits are heads, and both are turned to stone, either literally or figuratively; yet they are inherently uncanny in that whereas they spring from a desire for immortality, they also remain haunting harbingers of death: they embody presence at a distance, draw it out of the subject into their *representation*. His recounting of the story of Perseus and Medusa could easily enough be taken as a disguised allegory of Hawthorne's own anxiety about his craft, for the moonlit shield which protects Perseus from the gaze of Medusa is not at all far from the moonlit mirror of "The Custom-House" into whose "haunted verge" Hawthorne looks in order to "dream strange things, and make them look like truth." Perseus sees Medusa by a *side-glance;* Hawthorne sees—what? He sees, presumably, the story that lies behind *The Scarlet Letter,* but he sees it by a *side-glance,* in romance's mirror: what he sees is a transgression, a sexual crime, which cannot be shadowed forth, the motive for *A* which induces speculation and guilt but which nonetheless affords the materials of his triumph and commemoration. Perseus's act is also, significantly, a public act of revenge. He returns with the Gorgon's head, displays it to King Polydectes, and thus, by turning Polydectes to stone, contravenes the king's threat to cut off his head. Just so, Hawthorne's work enacts the risk lodged in ancestral threat by attempting to double it back as revenge, by exposing the Medusa-like threat of the Past in the public forum, in the marketplace. If Hawthorne never finds himself in a position free from anxiety and threat, he still shares Perseus's victory, for his craft performs a sacrifice that, like the totem meal, slays the fathers and erects a monument in their honor at the same time. When he suggested that *The Scarlet Letter* and the tales he originally planned to publish with it "be considered as the POSTHUMOUS PAPERS OF A DECAPITATED SURVEYOR" written "from beyond the grave" (*SL,* 43–44), we cannot doubt that Hawthorne was thinking, however consciously, of a threat more profound than the political loss of his surveyorship in the Custom House: he had in mind *customs* closer to *home*. Those marble heads arrayed in the Hall of Fantasy, the world's great authors, are all decapitated surveyors of customs; and like the busts in Cooper's Wigwam, they grant authority while at the same time mocking it, deriding its instability and threatening the *present* author with his own loss. An author anxious enough about his powers and reputation, as Hawthorne undoubtedly was, would see himself as though in a hall of mirrors, doubled ridiculously and turned to stone.

While Hawthorne's mirror of romance, like Perseus's shield, is a form of protection, it is also an uncanny reminder that his own authority and identity are constantly at risk. Looking deep into the mirror of romance, Hawthorne might, like Roderick Elliston in "Egotism; Or, the Bosom Serpent," "catch a glimpse of [a] snake's head, far down within his throat" (*MM*, 280). Yet it is precisely in his willingness to hazard himself as representative that Hawthorne keeps jubilee at his "funeral of departed power," that he transfigures the threat undergone by his own identity into the materials of a fantasy reenacted in celebration. If Hawthorne's communication-compulsion is provoked by the longing for an impossible Eden of mimesis, it is in the fictional fulfillment of the desire of his craft, where he can "dream strange things, and make them look like truth," that his purported loss becomes currency for his most real and powerful dreams. Were we to overestimate the darker side of transgression, whether as original sin or primal scene, and its consequent inscription of the self in an unfathomable web of speculation and referentiality that shatters self-presence, we would lose sight of the fact that the paradise of self-presence is, as Thoreau had it, a state of dumb wonderment, a moment that we hypothecate as a beginning but could never inhabit. Because the limitation of demand placed on Hawthorne's self is so internalized as to become that which authenticates his wishes and authorizes his commemoration, the need for representation is no mutilation at all; and the sacrifice of mimesis, even if it is a sacrifice in the name of returning to an impossible condition of presence, is one in which the self and the community achieve the only kind of presence possible—that authorized by the past in the ritual victimage of art. The sacrifice, by hedging the desire of identity, is the atonement and triumph by which the artist and his audience profit: he and his work *are* the *sacrifice of mimesis*.

IV

"Shall we never, never get rid of this Past!" cries Holgrave, in what is perhaps the most notorious passage in *The House of the Seven Gables*. "It lies upon the Present like a giant's dead body! In fact, the case is just as if a young giant were compelled to waste all his strength in carrying about the corpse of the old giant, his grandfather, who died a long while ago, and only needs to be decently buried." Holgrave mounts his tirade about our repetition of Dead Men's jokes, diseases, creeds, and so on. "Turn our eyes to what point we may," he continues, "a Dead Man's white, immitagable face encounters them, and freezes our very heart! And we must be dead ourselves, before we can begin to have our proper influence on our own world, which will then be no longer our world'" (*HG,* 182–83). Holgrave's outburst, warranted though it may be, is somewhat in vain, and he almost admits as much when he suggests how the present generation will itself be inscribed into the chain of repetition and dominion, and freeze posterity with its own Medusa-like face, denying the efficacy of the Present. I suggested early on that Hawthorne often unwittingly, sometimes intentionally, finds himself repeating the very sin he would exorcise, but in *The House of the Seven Gables* this takes a decidedly odd turn. Ostensibly, Hawthorne is again atoning, as in *The Scarlet Letter,* for the punishment dealt suspected witches by his ancestors, notably by Judge Hathorne (Nathaniel changed the spelling of the family name), now represented by the Pyncheons; not only atonement, though, but also revenge is Hawthorne's motive, the fulfillment of Maule's curse against the Pyncheons through the agency of the artist-necromancer Holgrave, who "in this long drama of wrong and retribution. . . represent[s] the old wizard, and [is] probably as much of a wizard as he ever was" (*HG,* 317). Holgrave's claim to representation is completely ambiguous, for though he appears on the face of it to say that old Maule never was a wizard (and hence that he is not), Hawthorne so dissembles and cloaks Holgrave's actions in the story that it is impossible not to read his responsibility as witchcraft, in however tentative a way. His necromancy is doubled, moreover, in Hawthorne's narration, which constantly hides behind veils, peeps voyeuristically at the private lives of the Pyncheons, asserts then discounts rumors and legends, claims then denies supernatural powers—in short, repeats at the level of telling the story the very ambiguity attributed to Holgrave's powers. Cotton Mather remarked in *A Brand Pluck'd Out of the Burning* (1693) that "if I should now venture to suppose, That the Witches do sometimes come in person to do their Mischiefs, and yett have the horrible skill of cloathing themselves with Invisibilities, it would seem Romantic."[46] Hawthorne would have known the passage and might well have taken it as the emblem of his own "Romance," which cloaks and exposes its author's fantastic powers at the same time, lets the reader almost but not quite see, or see only at a *side-glance,* the manipulations that mobilize the drama before his eyes.

Earlier I cited (but truncated) Hawthorne's report that Colonel Pyncheon, following his crime against Matthew Maule, would "build his house over an unquiet grave. His home would include the home of the dead and buried wizard, and would thus afford the ghost of the latter a kind of privilege to haunt its new apartments, and the chambers into which future bridegrooms were to lead their brides, and where children of the Pyncheon blood were to be born" (*HG*, 9). If Hawthorne's homes are continually *unheimlich*, shadowing forth an act of transgression but quickly covering it up, his narration does so with a vengeance. He barely represses Holgrave's necromantic power below the surface of the story and continually affords it a kind of privilege which is advanced and sacrificed at the same time: he keeps it uncanny. "Modern psychology, it may be," says Hawthorne of the Maules' reputed power "of exercising an influence over people's dreams," "will endeavor to reduce these alleged necromancies within a system, instead of rejecting them as altogether fabulous" (*HG*, 26). But here, as elsewhere, Hawthorne's remark performs the very function it describes, asserting the supernatural and explaining it away in the same statement. The capacity for "careening on the utmost verge of a precipitous absurdity" that Hawthorne found necessary to romance, the ability to approach the fantastic without giving way to it, is the focus of his narrative power. It is an attitude neither flippant nor "merely" figurative; but he was perhaps even closer to the true nature of his anxieties when he wrote in a later letter about his inability to get started on *The Dolliver Romance* that "there is something preternatural in my reluctance to begin. I linger at the threshold, and have a perception of very disagreeable phantasms to be encountered if I enter. I wish God had given me the faculty of writing a sunshiny book."[47] One reason Hawthorne's perception is troubled, though, is that among those phantasms, he is bound to find Monsieur du Miroir dogging his steps "as my shadow follows me into the sunshine" (*MM*, 166).

As we have seen, Hawthorne's interest in the "threshold" often lies in the pursuit of a bloody footstep that marks the boundary between a hypothetical Eden and the speculative world of transgression. In the *House* what lies beyond the narrative threshold is a world of phantasms Hawthorne must enter in order that he may find that first threshold marking the Pyncheon crime against the Maules, bring it into the sunshine, and recover an Eden lost in the Puritan past. But since the world before the transgression is as problematic as in *The Scarlet Letter*, Hawthorne's operation is no simple matter. He will not disavow Maule's witchcraft, but in fact repeats it in Holgrave's revenge, and the second threshold thus overlies the first to such an extent that they often seem the same. This is why Hawthorne's narration teeters on absurdity, for however strong his conviction that old Maule was wronged by Colonel Pyncheon in his greed for property and his apparently spurious condemnation of him as a witch, Hawthorne's own craft is pierced by his anxiety about its necromantic power. Again, Hawthorne plays two parts; on the one hand he revenges the ancestral crime, but on the other he finds himself offhandedly reviving the act which that crime punished. His story itself contains the "home of the dead and buried wizard" within it as the repressed power of the "Black Man," whether witch or artist. Plunging over the precipice of the absurd into romance's abyss would mean claiming actual necromantic power, for Holgrave or himself, an uncanny mimesis that aims at "The Real Thing"; Hawthorne's duplicity leaves this only as a possibility, a shadow which will not go away—a Black Man's "mark." In the very guise, then, of casting off the corpse of the past, Hawthorne presses the spirits of the past into his service and dresses up in traditional costumes to make a more disturbing pageant in his newly staged scene of history. Hawthorne's attempt to write a sunshiny book cannot free itself from the shadow of the past, or the shadow of his double; and *The House of the Seven Gables*, "if you would see anything in it," as he says of his *Twice-Told Tales*, "requires to be read in the clear, brown, twilight atmosphere in which it was written; if opened in the sunshine, it is apt to look exceedingly like a volume of blank pages" (*TT*, 16)—as indeed a truly mimetic work would.

But having said as much, we are returned to the fact of Holgrave, who makes "pictures out of sunshine," who "misuse[s] Heaven's blessed sunshine by tracing out human features, through its agency" (*HG*, 91, 46). Holgrave's portraits, his daguerreotypes, purportedly reveal their subjects' secret characters, exposing some grotesque mannerism or desire not observable in the normal countenance. In this way the daguerreotype performs instantly what only the process of decay can bring about in a painted portrait, that of Colonel Pyncheon, say, which on the one hand has "almost faded into the canvas, and hidden itself behind the darkness of age," but on the other seems to be "growing more prominent, and strikingly expressive," with the "bold, hard, and, at the same time indirect character of the man... brought out in a kind of spiritual relief... after the superficial coloring has been rubbed off by time" (*HG*, 58-59). The mechanical swiftness of Holgrave's mode of representation matches his desire to throw off the corpse of the past and finish up the business of revenge on the Pyncheons, but his very technique conjures up another kind of specter that runs in the face of his intention. It is important to remember that even as Hawthorne wrote, daguerreotyping was viewed by many with as much suspicion as Holgrave's other talent of mesmerism, and appeared to some—the writer for the London *Spectator* who reported on Daguerre's invention in 1839, for example—to be "more like some marvel of a fairy tale or delusion of necromancy than a practical reality."[48] Clearly enough, Hawthorne intends that we associate Holgrave's daguerreotyping with his necromantic powers, but the full import of that correlation has seldom been made an issue. Poe suggested the appropriate line of inquiry when he noted in 1840 that "the closest scrutiny

of the photographic drawing discloses only a more absolute truth, more perfect identity of aspect with the thing represented."[49] The photograph, then,
enables the artist to produce a perfect *representation,* an exact double: it is
truly, or as truly as possible, *mimetic.*

For all his speculating on the theory of romance and its capacity for al-
lowing the fantastic to be intermingled with solid reality, Hawthorne nonetheless displays a longing for mimesis, for confidence in his power veritably
to reproduce something, anything. The madman in the Hall of Fantasy, we
recall, had a scheme for turning out such perfect representations. But as we
have noted, the category of mimesis, like Thoreau's Nature, is nearly an
empty one; Hawthorne belongs to a speculative world of transgression in
which language is "babble," in which sign and referent are irremediably
divorced or skewed. In such a world, the virtual occurrence of mimesis—
when one sees oneself in a mirror, for example—is uncanny: it is a tautological reminder that sheer *presence* resides outside the power of *representation.* By an odd inversion of our usual notions, it is the frustrated desire for
true mimesis that is the most romantic element in Hawthorne's conception
of art. Mimesis is magic, a form of transgression, even (to put it somewhat
clinically) a kind of hallucination or psychosis that appears as the desire to
make literal renderings of figurative statements or to make *exact* pictures of
people or things. This obviously overstates the case, but I want to suggest
that, unless such considerations are brought into play, it is difficult for us,
accustomed as we are to photography, to gauge its full import for Hawthorne. As with the case of fingerprinting in *Pudd'nhead Wilson* (a book
equally haunted by the problems of doubling and mimesis), the very revolutionary nature of photography in Hawthorne's story can now hardly be felt.
Even more clearly than in *The Scarlet Letter,* where the moral complexities
of properly reading the *A* are further lost on us than they were even on Hawthorne's audience, the *House* is a period piece subject to a certain decay at
the hands of history. Despite their differences in style, tone, and setting,
both books are for Hawthorne head-on confrontations with the problem of
representation, and the anxieties that get channeled into the mysterious red
letter in the first are paralleled by those which lie behind Holgrave's craft in
the second.

Kermode gets at the heart of this matter when he notes that "only in
the photograph does one abolish the need to *accommodate the image to the
syntax of the medium.* Without intervention by the human mind the truth
is *wholly* inscribed; hence a daguerreotypist might well name himself Holgrave."[50] Kermode's play on "engrave" suggests another pun latent in Holgrave's name which we will return to; and while he is only half right about
the accommodation of image to medium that photography requires, his

remark clarifies the problem of mimetic representation in Hawthorne we have been accounting for. If one evades the accommodation of the image to the medium's syntax, the object in question can be removed from the web of referentiality and instability that forms the syntax of language and painting; the object (at least hypothetically) can be exactly reproduced without fear of loss or misrepresentation. That technical or theoretical objections might be raised against this notion does not discredit its capacity for marking the daguerreotype's vast difference as an artistic tool, at least at the time at which Hawthorne wrote. The photograph has the power to realize its object as a mimetic double, free from the vagaries of words and paint; it exists in a kind of Edenic realm in which the artist can indeed simply wonder, since he has next to nothing to do with the craft he practices. Like Swift's philosopher who simply holds up the thing he wishes to represent in his discourse, the ideal photographer points himself toward the thing that he wishes to reproduce; the machine does the job for him, cleanly and without the bothersome intrusion of mind, and hence, the possibility that misinterpretation will lead him astray. The daguerreotype would seem to be completely removed from that "wild babble" of "Tradition" (*HG*, 17) from which Hawthorne must gather his story.

There is another aspect of the daguerreotype which should be suggested, though, and one that also bears on the issue of mimesis and representation. Holgrave lauds his craft's ability to delve into the hidden recesses of his subjects; rather than "depicting the merest surface, it actually brings out the secret character with a truth that no painter would ever venture upon, even could he detect it" (*HG*, 91). Yet as Holgrave's remark suggests, not only does the daguerreotype have magic powers of penetration, but by affording a kind of objectivity that lets the artist work at a remove, it covertly frees him from direct participation in his craft. It is Hawthorne's dream of Paul Pry come true, the possibility for cold and clinical, if delightfully stimulating voyeurism. Or, as Walter Benjamin has observed of photography, "a different nature opens itself to the camera than opens itself to the naked eye—if only because an unconsciously penetrated space is substituted for a space consciously explored by man. . . . The camera introduces us to unconscious optics as does psychoanalysis to unconscious impulses."[51] We will want to return to this statement and consider its implications for the psychoesthetic reading of mimesis, but we need first to weigh Holgrave's craft as a response to the "babble" of "Tradition" he apparently seeks to overturn. What we should note is that the daguerreotyping employed by Holgrave is at once an attack on tradition, a weapon in his revenge, and at the same time a weapon whose magic aligns him with the necromantic powers of his ancestors that he disavows. In other words, the mimetic authority of the daguerreotype, in its capacity to search out the secrets of the unconscious in the Pyncheons, is what exposes the animistic powers Hawthorne both asserts and denies in Holgrave's art and his own.

Holgrave takes one daguerreotype that is of particular interest, one visible picture of what Hawthorne most muses upon in the course of his narrative. We should recall that the early subjects of daguerreotyping were beset by the tortures of maintaining a rigidily fixed position for the many minutes it took the process to be completed; the experience rendered the achieved picture grim almost by necessity, and as often as not it was spoiled by the subject's inability to pose so long without the slightest movement. This should sound familiar: it is the very motivation of Hawthorne's almost insane treatment of the corpse of Judge Pyncheon in the chapter bearing his unfulfilled title, "Governor Pyncheon," like the label on an old portrait. The dead judge is the perfect specimen for a daguerreotype, which Holgrave of course does take (*HG*, 302), and his spectacular interlude is one of Hawthorne's best set-pieces, at once a black mass, a mocking Beckettian trial and judgment of a judge who is not allowed to testify, a ritual killing of the king who has cursed the land, and a revenge on the dominating and castrating ancestral father, who in turn takes his place among the throng of ancestors who descend from Colonel Pyncheon's portrait to examine him. "Alice's Poesies" and "The Flower of Eden," the chapters that follow Hawthorne's meditation on the dead Judge, depict a magical restoration of fertility, and Alice's crimson-spotted flowers, "flaunting in rich beauty and full bloom," seem "a mystic expression that something within the house was consummated" (*HG*, 286). The curse is lifted and order restored, with the corpse of the Judge served up like part of that garbage Uncle Venner comes to collect for his pigs on the morning following his death. We do not know who killed Judge Pyncheon, if indeed he was killed; and though Clifford has been made the villain by some readers, Holgrave remains the most likely candidate. His explanation of the Judge's death as apoplexy, part of his idiosyncratic inheritance, and his disclaimer that "Old Maule's prophecy was probably founded on a knowledge of this physical predisposition in the Pyncheon race" (*HG*, 304), are ambiguous at best, almost but not quite convincing.

The control which Holgrave exercises explicitly over Phoebe in his tale of "Alice Pyncheon" is implicit throughout the book, and his revenge on the Judge is not to be separated from his near, perhaps more than near, seduction of Phoebe. In the *House* Hawthorne's Edenic impulses, as clearly as his impulse toward revenge, are funneled into the daguerreotypist, who labors with Phoebe to revive the desiccated Pyncheon garden, which is "now contracted within small compass" (*HG*, 86). But while Holgrave has checked the growth of the garden's "rank weeds" "by a careful degree of labor'' and cultivated ''a few species of antique and hereditary flowers,'' as though ''either out of love or curiosity, [he] had been anxious to bring them to such perfection as they were capable of attaining'' (*HG*, 86–87), his labor is not without suspicion, for he cultivates the Pyncheons in exactly the same way, and it is hard to say in that case too whether his labor springs from love or curiosity. ''I dig, and hoe, and weed, in this black old earth,'' says Holgrave, ''for the sake of refreshing myself with what little nature and simplicity may be left in it, after men have so long sown and reaped there'' (*HG*, 91). Like Thoreau's hoeing for tropes, Holgrave's gardening is more mercenary than he first lets on, his refreshment more devious. It is Holgrave who sets up Hepzibah in her humiliating role as the hucksteress of a cent shop; it is Holgrave who admits that, had he the opportunity Phoebe has, no scruples would prevent him from ''fathoming Clifford to the full depth of [his] plummet-line'' and searching out his ''holy ground where the shadow falls!'' (*HG*, 178); and when Clifford nearly dives from his balcony into the street below, ''the sport of some fiend, whose playfulness was an ecstasy of mischief'' (*HG*, 167), that fiend is more probably Holgrave than Judge Pyncheon. Holgrave indeed *does* represent the Maules, and he *is* demonic in his treatment of the Pyncheons. He treats the old house and its inhabitants like a theater spectacle, but as Phoebe accuses, ''the play costs the performers too much—and the audience is too cold-hearted!'' (*HG*, 217). His necromancy, like Hawthorne's own, is split in its desire between a revival and regeneration of the collapsing family and its vested interest in bringing about the collapse. Holgrave's proclaimed interest in democratic reform is figured in the cannibalism of Ned Higgins, ''the very emblem of Father Time'' (*HG*, 115), who represents the process Hawthorne himself carries out, destroying the Pyncheon aristocracy and feeding on it at the same time, like Holgrave ''in quest of [the] mental food'' of revenge (*HG*, 178). Like Hepzibah, who has only the miniature of Clifford ''for her heart to feed upon'' (*HG*, 32), Hawthorne has only the picture that his book is, a portrait both of revenge and of his awesome anxiety about its completion.

Holgrave's and Hawthorne's ''feeding,'' though, retains the ambivalence of the totem meal, at once enacting revenge and slaying the ancestral father by settling the family debt, but at the same time forming a covenant of identification with what has been destroyed. Holgrave makes his daguerreotype of the Judge not only as ''a point of evidence that may be useful to Clifford'' in exonerating him from blame, but also, he says, ''as a memorial valuable to myself'' (*HG*, 303). His art both revenges and commemorates, and this is the other side of the pun latent in Holgrave's name and in his cunning lament that it is unfortunate that the first daguerreotype of the Judge reveals a grim countenance, since ''he is a public character of some eminence, and the likeness was intended to be engraved" (*HG*, 92). As in Hawthorne's other stony images, the Judge is both killed and unwittingly memorialized at the same time, avenged and kept around as a reminder both of his continuing influence and of the present generation's own loss of authority: like Monsieur du Miroir, he is the subject of "grave reflection" (*MM*, 159). The "engraver" Holgrave, though he begins the story "home-less. . . continually changing his whereabout. . . putting off one exterior, and snatching up another, to be soon shifted for a third" (*HG*, 177), desires in the end "a house of stone" (*HG*, 315). In this respect, Holgrave's career matches Hawthorne's, and his wish for a stone house stems not just from his desire to destroy the illicitly founded Pyncheon house, but also from a corre-lative need to repossess it by his lost power. But we should postpone the question of Holgrave's relationship to Hawthorne for a moment and return to the significance of the daguerreotype. And as we do so we want to bear in mind Freud's equation between the totem sacrifice and the Oedipal com-plex, one that we have found central to a consideration of mimesis and representation.

In his "Salon de 1859," Baudelaire joined the many artists who re-sponded to the early vogue of photography with disgust, attributing its pop-ularity to the unformed taste of the masses and the less benign aspects of in-dustrialism. To the masses who sought Truth rather than Beauty and wished only to be astonished by art, he attributes the mocking *Credo:* "I believe that art is, and can only be, the exact reproduction of nature. . . . thus if an industrial process could give us a result identical to nature, that would be absolute art." "An avenging God has heard the prayers of this multitude," Baudelaire adds. "Daguette has his messiah." Because of his invention, "our idolatrous [*immonde*] society rushed, like Narcissus, to contemplate its trivial image on the metallic plate. A form of lunacy, an extraordinary fanaticism, took hold of these new sun-worshippers." Moreover, Baudelaire describes daguerreotypes as the "adulterous" and "abominable" produc-tions of "failed painters" possessed not only of "blind and imbecile infatu-ation" but also of "revenge," productions in which "some democratic writer" might find "a cheap means of spreading the dislike of history and painting amongst the masses, thus committing a double sacrilege."[52] Hol-grave's democratic tendencies, his abomination of the oppressive corpse of history (announced in his famous speech and symbolized in the dead Judge), and his elevation of the powers of photography over those of paint-ing, could well have made him the model of Baudelaire's scorn. That Bau-delaire describes the obsession with photography as a narcissistic madness is a point we must return to, but it is the sacrilege against history that is of first interest. Benjamin echoes Baudelaire when, in his essay on "The Work of

Art in the Age of Mechanical Reproduction,'' he remarks that what "withers in the age of mechanical reproduction is the aura of the work of art,'' that "the technique of reproduction detaches the reproduced object from the domain of tradition. By making many reproductions it substitutes a plurality of copies for a unique existence.''[53] What is threatened, then, is the sacred quality of the work; its cheap reproduction and democratic dispersal threaten the mystical authority that resides in the single original work. Photography, whether it is employed as an art in its own right or as a tool to duplicate masterpeieces, is an attack on sacred authority because, as Baudelaire writes, it is "allowed to transgress [*d'empieter*] the sphere of the intangible and the imaginary, to transgress all that has value solely because man adds something to it from his soul.''[54]

The art that Holgrave practices resides somewhere between the two theories of photography's sacrilegious power offered by Baudelaire and Benjamin. It is exactly in the daguerreotype that Holgrave commemorates his revenge against Judge Pyncheon and obliterates the tradition he stands for, substituting his seemingly egalitarian principles for the aristocratic dominion of the Judge and his forefathers. Against the romantic painting that embodies, almost literally, the Pyncheon ancestors and their powerful authority, Holgrave's daguerreotype, which might indeed be intended for "public engraving,'' displays the secret character of the Judge, exposing his greed and meanness in a contorted dead image. But if one aspect of Hawthorne's interest in the daguerreotype lies in its mimetic power of producing a stone image, an image whose truth disrupts the romantic aura that accumulates about the painted portrait, he nonetheless shares Baudelaire's suspicion that photography's encroachment onto history and painting is a sacrilege against the power of art, a transgression of the ineffable and imaginary. Photography is mimetic, even if only loosely so in a technical sense, and as such it is the successful enactment of Hawthorne's desire to make literal renderings of figurative statements; it is what in the world of representation and speculation he inhabits is most uncanny—the narcissistic perfection of his desire for exact presentation, rather than representation. But it is also—and this is what is of note in Baudelaire's description of the rage for photography as a narcissistic fanaticism—the most fantastic thing imaginable: it is a return to the Eden of mimesis which lies behind Hawthorne's speculative world, a return to that hypothetical time in which an emblematic relationship between image and thing was possible, when, to put it another way, a narcissistic relationship of identity prevailed between child and mother. We have found that moment to correspond for Hawthorne to a lost Eden and have identified his voyeuristic obsession with peeping beneath the woman's veil or the petals of Nature as an attempt to restore that moment, an attempt that sees only at a *side-glance* if at all, leaving him to pine like Narcissus for his lost lover and meet only his own haunting double in a mirror. But the camera might penetrate the forbidden space of Nature, enter swiftly enough to catch Nature offguard. Samuel F. B. Morse must have thought so, when he observed that by the use of the daguerreotype a naturalist might import Nature into his studio for study since daguerreotypes *"cannot be called copies of nature, but portions of nature herself."*[55] Morse is outlandish, of course, but his remark characterizes the response to the daguerreotype's seemingly animistic powers, powers whose penetration, as the perfection of voyeurism, is nearly sexual in character.

We can find no better designation for Holgrave's daguerreotyping than that available in Leo Marx's fine phrase, "the machine in the garden,"[56] for all the same resonances and pressures that surround the nineteenth-century confrontation between the mechanical and the natural that Marx describes also inhered in the artifice of photography at the same time. "The love of obscenity, which is as vigorous a growth in the heart of natural man as self-love," writes Baudelaire of the sacrilege of photography, "could not let slip such a glorious opportunity for its own satisfaction. . . . I once heard a smart woman. . . say to her friends, who were discreetly trying to hide such pictures from her, thus taking it upon themselves to have some modesty on her behalf: 'Let me see; nothing shocks me.'"[57] Baudelaire is speaking figuratively, of course, but only partly so: the close relationship among the feminine, the beautiful, and the sacred is implicit throughout his essay, and the daguerreotype's vulgarity is as clearly sexual as it is industrial and material. Moreover, Baudelaire's equation of narcissism and obscenity makes clearer the link between mimesis and sacrilege, a link at the very base of Holgrave's craft in the *House*. Initially, Holgrave is said to be hesitant about revealing the Judge's death to Phoebe, since it "was like dragging a hideous shape of death into the clean and cheerful space before a household fire" (*HG*, 302). Yet it is exactly his intention to bring the corpse into Phoebe's sunshiny space and expose its latent and hidden character, for his revenge and his courtship go hand in hand. It is the daguerreotype's "image of awful Death, which filled the house, [and] held them united in his stiffened grasp," that hastens "the development of emotions that might not otherwise have flowered so soon" and leads to the couple's Edenic declaration of love (*HG*, 305–6). Clearly, more than one affair has been "consummated" by the Judge's demise. We should recall too that only a paragraph before Holgrave's tirade against the past's dead body, which is addressed to Phoebe, Hawthorne's narrator, "peep[ing] at them through the chinks of the garden-fence," declares that "the young man's earnestness and heightened color might have led you to suppose that he was making love to the young girl! (*HG*, 182). Yet the "stiffened grasp" of Death's image that unites Holgrave and Phoebe has a double edge similar to that of all Hawthorne's stony images: it both reaffirms potency and possession and mockingly subverts it, though here in a slightly different way, since Holgrave not only plays out his revenge on the dead Judge and at the same time makes a memorial representation of his "defunct nightmare" (*HG*, 252), but also draws the collapsing potency of the Pyncheon line into the charge of his own highly sexualized necromancy. If Holgrave's revenge is a reversal of Old Matthew Maule's fate of being "hunted to death for his spoil" (*HG*, 8), his "spoil" is not only the Judge and his property, but also Phoebe.

This is nowhere more clearly the case than in his seduction of Phoebe through the story of "Alice Pyncheon," and there is good reason to consider Hawthorne's chapter and its interpolated tale as a correlative to, perhaps a substitute for, the photographic craft Holgrave has earlier proposed practicing on Phoebe ("I should like to try whether the daguerreotype can bring out disagreeable traits on a perfectly amiable face") but which she skirts by objecting that its results "are so hard and stern; besides dodging away from the eye, and trying to escape altogether" (*HG*, 91). Like young Matthew Maule, who is fabled "to have a strange power of getting into people's dreams, and regulating matters there according to his own fancy, pretty much like the stagemanager of a theatre" (*HG*, 189), Holgrave stages his tale for Phoebe in order to mesmerize her, just as Matthew Maule does Alice in his revenge of Gervayse Pyncheon—though with the important difference, of course, that Holgrave foregoes complete "mastery over Phoebe's yet free and virgin spirit," forbids himself "to twine that one link more, which might have rendered his spell over Phoebe indissoluble" (*HG*, 212). Or does he? By the book's close Holgrave has fulfilled his revenge and taken virtual possession of the Pyncheon property and its owners, particularly of "the village-maiden, over whom he had thrown love's web of sorcery" (*HG*, 319), through both the sublimated agency of the "stiffened grasp" of the daguerreotype and the tale he tells. The felicitous finale has been berated often enough, but Crews is correct to point out that the ending is "psychologically urgent, an ingeniously ambiguous gesture of expiation for a dominant idea that has been warping the book's direction."[58] The exact nature of Holgrave's "sorcery" is kept under wraps, but it is hardly dispelled by Hawthorne's finely shaded phrase. Even more so than Chillingworth's, Holgrave's is an "intimate revenge" (*SL*, 139), one in which his daguerreotyping and his mesmerism have played no small part. Hawthorne was startled by the powers of mesmerism, and before their marriage, he wrote revealingly on the matter to Sophia, who had thought to seek a mesmeric cure for her headaches: "supposing that his power arises from the transfusion of one spirit into another, it seems to me that the sacredness of an individual is violated by it; there would be an intrusion into thy holy of holies—and the intruder would not be thy husband!"[59] As much as young Matthew Maule, who converts "the mind of Alice into a kind of telescopic medium" and uses "the clear, crystal medium of [her] pure and virgin intelligence" to search out the missing deeds of the Pyncheon claim (*HG*, 200), Holgrave may be said to have penetrated into Phoebe's virgin territory in the interest of his pending acquisition of the Pyncheon property.

Phoebe is the apple of Holgrave's eye, the chance for his return to and repossession of a *home*, as Hawthorne's many points of connection between Phoebe and "home" suggest (e.g., *HG*, 71, 82, 141, 156); and the distance between Phoebe's virgin mind and that Freudian *Heim* Hawthorne is always looking for in Nature is not all that far. Though Hawthorne leaves the question of Holgrave's mesmeric possession, like nearly every other suggestion of his necromancy, uncanny, something seen at a *side-glance*, it is hardly separable from the courtship in the garden in which the stone image of the Judge consummates his passionate suit. The mesmeric penetration of Phoebe's "holy of holies" and the daguerreotype's reproductive penetration of secret character are equally animistic delvings into the unconscious, and both are attacks on tradition. Holgrave's necromancy is a transgression—against the sacred and feminine domain of the beautiful that Baudelaire describes and against the traditional aura of the unique work of art that Benjamin describes. But "transgression" is a loaded word in our context. If it is defined as that original sin or "crisis of perception" that provokes Hawthorne's world of speculation and representation, dispersing the narcissistic Eden of identity and mimesis, we must be wary of introducing the same term to account for the attempt to overturn that world and return to art its lost mimetic powers. Yet as I have been insisting, a seeming actualization of mimesis is perhaps the most extraordinary fantasy in a speculative world. Indeed, it is a new and more startling "crisis in perception," which is exactly the phrase Benjamin provides in his essay "On Some Motifs in Baudelaire" to describe the threat of mechanical reproduction. "What prevents our delight in the beautiful from ever being satisfied," he writes, "is the image of the past," that sacred aura of tradition that expands the "play of the imagination" and resides, we would say, in the endless extension of the web of speculation and fantasy. "What [the painting] contains that fulfills the original desire [of the viewer] would be the very same stuff on which the desire continuously feeds," and what distinguishes photography from painting, then, is that, "to eyes that will never have their fill of a painting, photography is rather like food for the hungry or drink for the thirsty. The crisis of artistic reproduction which manifests itself in this way can be seen as an integral part of a *crisis in perception* itself'' (my emphasis).[60] Photography thus partakes of that immediate satisfaction of desire Baudelaire finds an obscenity, a narcissistic indulgence; it makes the sacred manifest and defuses the mystical authority of tradition. The metaphors of consumption and cannibalism that accompany Holgrave's demolition of the Pyncheon dynasty and the overtly erotic character of his relationship with Phoebe are in this respect completely appropriate to the hazard posed by his craft to the aura of tradition, the corpse he so wants to throw off but in whose employ he nonetheless dresses up in uncannily traditional costumes.

Holgrave's working of his machine in the Pyncheon garden is no tame affair, then, no more so than the work Hawthorne performed in the garden at his Manse. After several delightful paragraphs describing the "bliss of paternity" afforded by the pleasant labors in his garden, labors than which "Art has never invented anything more graceful," Hawthorne adds that "not merely the squemish love of the Beautiful was gratified by my toil," for indeed, "the hugest pleasure is reserved, until these vegetable children of ours are smoking on the table, and we, like Saturn, make a meal of them" (*MM,* 13–15). As pointedly as Ned Higgins's appetite for the Pyncheon gingerbread, Hawthorne's toil may be read as an emblem for the artist's craft, particularly Holgrave's. As I suggested earlier, Holgrave's revenge has the character of the sacrificial totem meal, a character we can see even more clearly now that we have located within his art two important moments in the "crisis of perception" central to a "sacrifice of mimesis." The camera's ability to introduce us to unconscious optics is a means of returning the full powers of vision presumably lost in the original "crisis of perception"; by means of the photograph we can *see* rather than merely *perceive* (or so its initiates thought). And yet, as Benjamin notices, such power of vision is a threat to the play of unquenched desire upon which the aura of tradition, in its compelling drama of infatuation and worship, so much depends. Photography appears indeed to be a sacrifice in the name of mimesis, a sacrifice in which the aura of tradition that inheres in speculation is totemized and consumed, its "beauty" replaced by a realistic "truth." That such a distinction does not finally hold up, and that photography does not achieve the devastation of mimesis but becomes entwined itself in the speculative aura of tradition, is obvious enough; yet it does not mitigate the power a truly mimetic craft must initially have seemed to possess.

The apparent perfection of a desire that had hitherto remained sheer fantasy is finally a sacrifice of fantasy itself. Like the uncanny mechanical butterfly created by Owen Warland in "The Artist of the Beautiful," the daguerreotype unites "the hidden mysteries of mechanism" and "the beautiful movements of Nature," but finally at the expense of the dream that enacted its perfection. The artist aiming at "The Real Thing," whether Warland or Holgrave, may indeed feel "the impulse to give external reality to his ideas, as irresistably as any of the poets or painters, who have arrayed the world in a dimmer and fainter beauty, imperfectly copied from the richness of their visions," but he will also have to face the risk that he may "chase the flitting mystery beyond the verge of his ethereal domain, and crush its frail being in seizing it with a material grasp!" (*MM,* 450, 458). Yet Hawthorne's characterization of Warland's craft is telling, for though he attributes a mimetic perfection to his mechanical butterfly, that perfection remains a function of the artist's "ideas" and "visions"; the fulfillment of the fantasy transgresses the "ethereal domain" wherein the artist finds his power and, far from bringing that fantasy to lasting external perfection, undercuts and dissolves its reality. Desire is left unfulfilled and by the same token reaffirmed as the ground whereon the artist works out the continuing sacrifice of his craft. While Owen Warland is left with a shattered dream, pining like Narcissus for his lost reward, Holgrave's perfection of artistic mimesis issues in success and regeneration of a sort, a highly suspicious sort. It may be that his intrusion into Phoebe's "ethereal domain" is accomplished with the result that her "frail being" is crushed in the "material grasp" of his revenge. But if Hawthorne whitewashes the book's ending or simply gives in to sentiment, he nevertheless allows the tale of Matthew Maule and Alice Pyncheon to play its haunting shadow over the sunshiny conclusion.

The tale of "Alice Pyncheon" is perhaps itself a kind of daguerreotype, for just as Holgrave's daguerreotype of the Judge exposes his secret character, the inserted tale exposes the desire latent in Holgrave's (and Hawthorne's) performance of his craft. Richard Brodhead has suggested that for Hawthorne and Melville, "interpolated tales serve as a kind of auxiliary heart for their books, gathering in, purifying, and reenergizing their animating concerns and then pumping these back into the narratives that envelop them."[61] This is acutely the case with the *House*'s interpolated story, which functions as a kind of play-within-the-play, a tableau not unlike the proposal scene in *Home as Found* that acts out in a stylized or ritualistic manner the overall action of the work. We may further interiorize the drama of interpolation by noting that Freud takes up a similar, and for our purposes highly relevant, theme in his consideration of "the enigma of the 'dream within a dream,'" a problem closely linked to that of the dream's capability of representation. "To include something in a 'dream within a dream,'" says Freud, is "equivalent to wishing that the thing described as a dream had never happened." Because the "dream-work makes use of dreaming as a form of repudiation,'' the insertion of a particular event into the dream as a further dream "implies the most decided confirmation of the reality of the event—the strongest *affirmation* of it."[62] Freud's use of the term "reality" is extremely questionable; it would be more convincing to say that the dream within a dream offers confirmation of the reality or power of the "fantasy" that the interpolated dream plays out, but that nonetheless remains a figure, that which can only be *represented* and which, like the stern daguerreotype, "dodges away from the eye" that looks for a mimetic reality. Yet his reading of the inserted dream as a form of repudiation—a repudiation in whose denial there is indeed a confession to the true power of the fantasized event—illuminates the function of the tale of "Alice Pyncheon." It is Alice's poesies whose blossoming marks the consummation of Holgrave's sorcery, placing their own reproduction alongside Holgrave's mechanical reproduction. Just as the legend of the Veiled Lady in *The Blithedale Romance* economically acts out Coverdale's final Narcissus-like frustration, the tale of Alice forecasts the mastery Holgrave finally achieves. If Hawthorne uses the story to dissipate the demonic and lustful undercurrent that keeps threatening to warp the book's direction, the interpolated tale, like a daguerreotype, only shows more clearly the repressed drive that animates Hawthorne's whole spectacle.[63]

While we can read the haunted Pyncheon house itself as a monstrous *camera obscura* into which sunlight has slowly but surely been allowed to enter, developing the image latent in the plate of the book's characters and their history, we must note that the completed picture is no sanguine resolution. Amid the welter of theories offered about the appearance of the *A* on Dimmesdale's breast at the conclusion of *The Scarlet Letter,* Hawthorne exhaustedly remarks: "The reader may choose among these theories. We have thrown all the light we could acquire upon the portent, and would gladly, now that it has done its office, erase its deep print out of our brain; where long meditation has fixed it in very undesireable distinctness" (*SL,* 259). The picture brought into the sunshine at the conclusion of the *House* is finally just as much a problem, and Holgrave's role has threatened, like the wound of the *A,* to become fixed—rather, "engraved''—on Hawthorne's brain with an undesirable distinctness. He must cover it up, as he does the scarlet letter itself. But if he hides it under a veil of renunciation and realism, he certainly does not erase it. In this respect, one might say that the tale of Alice is Holgrave's or Hawthorne's daguerreotype, a picture within a picture in a book filled with pictures and the problems of portraiture, and presenting in fact a portrait of the artist as a young necromancer. The tale offers the possibility that Holgrave's "speculative" disposition toward "acquiring empire over the human spirit" (*HG,* 212) might issue in more than figurative possession. Conscious of the grim image of desire beneath a happy public facade, Hawthorne might well have feared, as Holgrave does, that "the faculty of mesmerism" was in his blood (*HG*, 217); he might too, again like Holgrave, have adopted publication as "one method of throwing . . . off" the haunting tales that seemed to possess him (*HG*, 186).

Holgrave's story is the mirror image of Hawthorne's self, an image not identical but speculative, representing a self that finds itself not presentable, fractured not only by the mastery of a Puritan ancestry but by those things they punished. Because the Maules are as much in his blood as are the Pyncheons, his writing at once accomplishes a revenge on the repressive ancestors and revitalizes and fulfills the repressed desire. Hawthorne remarked in his notebooks that getting into print is "a trial which few persons can sustain, without losing their unconsciousness" (*AN*, 336). Maintaining his own public performance on the very threshold of the unconscious is what most charges Hawthorne's stories, and if the tale within the *House* is evidence, the trial of print can be subversively skirted and "unconsciousness" brought home, like those many facts and scenes said to be "brought home" to Clifford's blank mind (*HG*, 22, 105, 142), in the disguise of another story. Hawthorne's narrative is the voyeuristic double of Holgrave's; it is the tale of "a disembodied listener" (*HG*, 30) who peeps, creeps, slinks about, and teases with hints and guesses, but is unwilling to venture a blunt statement about Holgrave's power until the force so builds up that it must be unleashed as an inserted piece of fiction, a dream that uncovers what cannot be restrained. Holgrave is Hawthorne's public double, *speculative* in his thought, his craft, and his role; he makes voyeurism and revenge into an art, one able to drag a hidden corpse into the sunshine and get the girl at the same time. But Hawthorne might well say of Holgrave what he says of Monsieur du Miroir: "I will be self-contemplative, as Nature bids me, and make him the picture or visible type of what I muse upon, that my mind may not wander so vaguely as heretofore, chasing its own shadows through a chaos and catching only the monsters that abide there" (*MM*, 169–70).

V

The narrator of Poe's "The Oblong Box," an obsessive rationalist, delights in his carefully worked out solution that projects the contents of the mysterious box to be a treasure trove of pictures. The box contains, of course, a corpse, the revelation of which drives the narrator over the brink of madness. Hawthorne would seem to have come at the problem from the opposite angle, turning corpses into pictures; but the similarity of the two keeps coming back to him in a fashion at once dispiriting and invigorating.

And while James complained that the characters in the *House* "are all pictures rather than persons,"[64] this hardly seems a feasible objection to a book that has picture-making so at its center. The risk of losing "unconsciousness" by being put into print was a real enough one for Hawthorne, yet his need to fathom the secret in the mirror of the Seven Gables and "transfer its revelations to our page" (*HG*, 20) is equally real. Hawthorne's memories and fantasies both gain and lose on the page, gain in commemoration what they lose in vindication: they too are very much something to be "engraved." Perhaps, as he admits in the passage from *The Blithedale Romance* we noted earlier, long brooding over his recollections subtilized them into imaginary stuff; perhaps too, as Alice Vane observes of Edward Randolph's portrait, "the original picture can hardly be so formidable as those which fancy paints instead of it" (*TT*, 261). Such a fear is equally part of Hawthorne's need to turn his fantasies into pictures, into *representations* that he can control while still bowing to their control of him. It is "as dear an object as any," says Hawthorne of his writing in "The Custom-House," "to win myself a pleasant memory in this abode and burial-place of so many of my forefathers" (*SL*, 44). To be remembered, Hawthorne adds himself to the gallery of portraits—itself a kind of *grave,* though an open one—which his fiction half remembers, half creates, a fantastic world where the two are often indistinguishable. In the *House,* Hawthorne adds himself in two pictures—one of the dead Judge, one of the live Holgrave, both his representatives.

In Hawthorne's communal sacrifice, the one representation is not to be divorced from the other, and both have to occur in the public forum of "the market-place." No more than he is willing to repress Holgrave's witchcraft is Hawthorne able to stifle that desire for public recognition and financial gains that leads him, like Hepzibah, to choose "the House of the Seven Gables as the scene of his commercial speculations" (*HG*, 36). The rhetoric of title and claim in Hawthorne's preface, the allegories of art's commerce presented in Hepzibah's humiliating cent-shop trade and in the organ-grinder's "pantomimic scene" and rudely gesticulating monkey, "symbolizing the grossest form of the love of money" (*HG*, 162–64), Holgrave's desire to publish his tale of Alice Pyncheon's ruin—all these match the book's instigating action, an illicit seizure of property, and uncover Hawthorne's deepest fears not just that his materials might be useless, fit only "for constructing castles in the air" (*HG*, 3), but that his craft might be sinfully exploitive in its own desire for possession. When Hepzibah, recalling Hester, issues "forth over the threshold of our story" (*HG*, 31), it is to enter her own marketplace; and though Hawthorne fears that the "shop-door" of the House "may damage any picturesque and romantic impres-

sion" he has thrown over his "sketch of this respectable edifice," that is the
very door by which the reader enters Hawthorne's House to "be let into the
secret" of its history (*HG*, 28). Like Hepzibah's, Hawthorne's may be but a
"ghostly or phantasmagoric reflection" (*HG*, 35), but he knows as well
that once he opens shop and enters the marketplace, the "sordid stain" of
"copper-coin" cannot be washed from his hand (*HG*, 51). That "malevo-
lent spirit" who does "his utmost to drive Hepzibah mad" by unrolling
before her imagination a hallucinatory panorama of shops, fixtures, and
merchandise, with "noble mirrors at the farther end of each establishment,
doubling all this wealth by a brightly burnished vista of unrealities" (*HG*,
48), is no doubt Holgrave; but the scene is only more convincing evidence
that Hawthorne found his desire for possession and reputation to be the
haunting double of his revenge and atonement.

In a yet harsher way than *The Scarlet Letter*, the *House* enlists Hawthorne in a *speculative* world that issues from a crime whose exact nature is
still shrouded in rumor and legend, and in which his deepest fear in "The
Custom-House" threatens to be realized—that his "imagination" might
become "a tarnished mirror" and his "power" be "bartered...for a pit-
tance of the public gold" (*SL*, 34). I suggested early on that Hawthorne is
like no one of his characters so much as the original Pyncheon shopkeeper,
doomed "to spend eternity in a vain effort to make his accounts balance"
(*HG*, 29). That Pyncheon, like all the rest, is in debt to old Maule, the
"ghostly creditor" who has "his finger in all the affairs of the Pyncheons"
(*HG*, 189). Unfortunately for Hawthorne, Maule's finger is in his affairs
too, and the role in which he casts the artist Holgrave brings him perilously
close to Chillingworth, who works on Dimmesdale "like a miner searching
for gold; or, rather, like a sexton delving into a grave, possibly in quest of a
jewel that had been buried on the dead man's bosom, but likely to find
nothing save mortality and corruption" (*SL*, 129). Hawthorne, of course,
backs off from this extremity, represses it, but not successfully. Holgrave's
revenge stays close to its root meaning: *vindicare*, "to lay claim to." But
then Hawthorne's hope that he not "be considered as unpardonably of-
fending, by laying out a street that infringes upon nobody's private rights,
and appropriating a lot of land which had no visible owner" (*HG*, 3) is itself
no idle remark. His revenge also lays a claim, however much it attempts its
own pardon. "Dispositions more boldly speculative may derive a stern enjoyment from the discovery" of evil, observes Hawthorne of good Phoebe's
perplexity over the Judge (*HG*, 131). The stern enjoyment belongs not just to
Holgrave, but to the equally speculative Hawthorne himself. The New
Adam and Eve can liken the vault of a bank "to a magician's cave, when the
all-powerful wand is broken, and the visionary splendor vanished, and the

floor strewn with fragments of shattered spells, and lifeless shapes once animated by demons'' (*MM,* 261); Hawthorne, however, lives in no such Eden, but rather in a transgressive and speculative world where the potency of his wand has a commanding currency of its own, one neither lifeless nor free from debt.

The "mirror with a memory" is what Oliver Wendell Holmes called the daguerreotype.[65] We are urged to say that Hawthorne was hardly in need of such an invention, since his mirror of romance continually thronged, much to his horror and delight, with ancestral memories. Hawthorne lived in a thoroughly *speculative* world, haunted by doubles and fathers, fathers and doubles, who stare back at him like a pair of eyes on a canvas, on a page, in a mirror—his own eyes. The camera box used in daguerreotyping is in this respect an uncanny emblem of Hawthorne's art; it is a pair of eyes itself, eyes not one's own that can be used to speculate and represent, used as a tool of art even, perhaps, by a blind man. The mirror of the daguerreotype on the one hand offers the capacity for exact duplication, the means to fix the image in a lasting way; but on the other, it is precisely because the image is lasting and so perfectly a double that the daguerreotype is most unnerving for Hawthorne. Like that "seer, before whose sadly gifted eye" the palatial facade of public character collapses, revealing "the decaying corpse within" (*HG,* 230), the daguerreotype perfects Hawthorne's fantasy of himself as the voyeur who sees all without being implicated in the scene. But Hawthorne *is* implicated in the scene, and to a remarkable extent. The mirror *with* a memory makes the mirror *of* memory lasting: it executes a sign of revenge and conquest, and a reminder of submission to the forms of the past. As both an assurance of immortality and an uncanny harbinger of dislocation and death, it offers the hedged triumph that sacrifice must be.

It is hard to imagine that symbolism could be raised to a higher power than Hawthorne's scarlet *A,* a symbol raised so high that, as James says of its appearance in the sky during Dimmesdale's midnight vigil, it approaches "not moral tragedy, but physical comedy." James adds that in the practice of symbolizing, "discretion is everything, and when the image becomes importunate it is in danger of seeming to stand for nothing more serious than itself."[66] But then that is why Hawthorne's red letter works and why *The Scarlet Letter* is a remarkable achievement—because the *A* finally stands only (though an expansive "only") for the web of speculation and interpretation it is said to originate; only for the act of transgression after which there is need of symbols; only, in the last analysis, for itself as the embodiment of a powerful and inscrutable dream. If there is a more highly charged symbol in Hawthorne (which we must doubt), it is the daguerreotype itself, which is—contrary to Kermode, perhaps—both a symbol and a syntax of a kind, but one as mysterious as *A*. It is the mirror raised to the power of exact and lasting duplication: it makes the creation of doubles the essence of its nature, and like the *A,* is a Black Man's "mark." Were *A* actually to stand for something single and identifiable, mimesis would come true, an occurrence impossible in Hawthorne's world; when it appears to come true, in a mirror or daguerreotype, say, it is uncanny. There seems to be little doubt that Hawthorne was a romancer rather than a realist; but any dispute as to what these terms might mean must take into account the fact that a real fear of *mimesis*—the usual watchword of "realism"—is betrayed paradoxically in the narrative veneer of rationalism that Hawthorne uses to cover over the fantastic. Romance for Hawthorne lay in the fact that realism was hardly a possibility, since the way it kept coming back to him—as an uncanny act of mimesis, witchcraft itself—was altogether too fantastic, *too* romantic, in fact. Hawthorne's teasing narration, the voyeuristic double of Holgrave's artistic power, keeps repressing and sidestepping true (fantastic) mimesis, looking at it askance, from a distance, in a mirror. Seeing it head on would be like looking at Medusa, or at one's double, its very product and symbol. It would be like bringing back to life the home of the dead before our eyes.

FOUR

"At home in his words"

Parody
and Parricide
in Melville's
Pierre

> In the midst of this tumult old Maheyo came to my side, and I
> shall never forget the benevolent expression of his countenance.
> He placed his arm upon my shoulder, and emphatically pro-
> nounced the only two English words I had taught
> him—"Home" and "Mother."
>
> —Melville, *Typee*

> There is a time in every man's education when he arrives at the
> conviction...that imitation is suicide...
>
> —Emerson, "Self-Reliance"

> I have lost my stick....The stick, having slipped, would have plucked me from
> the bed if I had not let it go. It would of course have been better for me to relin-
> quish my bed than to lose my stick....Now that I have lost my stick I realize
> what it is that I have lost and all it meant to me. And thence ascend, painfully,
> to an understanding of the Stick, shorn of all its accidents, such as I had never
> dreamt of. What a broadening of the mind. So that I half discern, in the
> veritable catastrophe that has befallen me, a blessing in disguise. How comfort-
> ing that is. Catastrophe too in the ancient sense no doubt.[1]

The narrator of *Malone Dies* (there is small guarantee it is actually Malone),
like most of Beckett's articulate catatonics, has been reduced to an immo-
bility that seems as much commensurate with his own desires as with some
unpredictable environment. Malone abides in bed—eating, excreting, and
writing the book which we read. His world is defined by the objects that he
can reach with a long, crooked stick, the loss of which produces a profound

crisis and rewarding lesson, to put it that way. The trouble with putting it
that way is that while Malone and his stick—and his writing pad and pencil
and whatever other props get briefly introduced—are insistently something
more than they seem, they cannot be allegorized without sounding foolish.
Beckett's simple items creep up on importance then retreat, taking back
whatever they give. The Stick remains, in the end, a stick, and hardly that.

If it seems we are taking the back door into *Pierre* and at the same time
flying in the face of Melville's warning that "analogies" are "sweet in the
orator's mouth, [but] bitter in the thinker's belly" (*P,* 42),[2] we ought to
recall the following description of Melville's author-hero, near the end of his
lamentable and farcical career: "'Is Pierre a shepherd, or a bishop, or a cripple? No, but he has in effect, reduced himself to the miserable condition of
the last. With the crook-ended cane, Pierre—unable to rise without sadly
impairing his manifold intrenchments, and admitting the cold air into their
innermost nooks,—Pierre, if in his solitude, he should chance to need
anything beyond the reach of his arm, then the crook-ended cane drags it to
his immediate vicinity" (*P,* 301). The sticks of Pierre and Malone are the
gimmicks of dark romance, supercharged equipment that suggest more than
they can possibly account for and bring the Gothic to impinge precariously
upon vaudeville. This is not to slight their differences: Malone's stick, in the
context of his denuded story, is by itself a strong enough emblem to warrant
his anguish over its loss. Pierre's stick, however, is part of a larger tableau,
equally nightmarish and ludicrous, representing the cripple that Pierre has
become and that Melville as author fantasized himself to be in 1851, after
the relative public failure of his masterpiece a year earlier. The professional
writer Pierre sits immobilized in the frozen Church of the Apostles, muffled
in diverse garments and warmed by hot bricks folded in the old military
cloak of his grandfather, a fitting stimulus for the book "he seems to have
directly plagiarized from his own experiences, to fill out the mood of his apparent author-hero" (*P,* 302), a book, like Malone's, that seems to be the
one we have been reading all along. Pierre does not lose his stick, except insofar as he has already lost it—has, that is, been "dismasted" even more certainly than Ahab before him. Pierre, as Richard Brodhead wittily puts it,
"sorely lacks a Moby Dick."[3] In context, Brodhead's point is, of course, that
the action of *Pierre* does not warrant the mountainous and often ridiculous
philosophical inquiry that accompanies it, that the book, with no white
whale to bear the brunt, flounders in its own excess. This is true enough, but
it can be made clearer how the joke is a more significant part of Brodhead's
statement than he lets on, how Pierre's (or Melville's) loss is the very subject
of Melville's (or Pierre's) book.

D. H. Lawrence believed *Moby-Dick* to be an assault on "the last phallic being of the white man,''[4] and though this is hardly the last case, Melville might have taken it that way. One could, no doubt, give numerous plausible readings of *Moby-Dick* without ever broaching its central issues in psychoanalytic language; the book would be no less an achievement. It is doubtful the same can be done with *Pierre,* for the later book is the record of Melville's exhaustion and burning out on the themes of authority and genealogy, which are so carefully posed and well integrated into the mass of the whaling book. In *Pierre* the lack of a Moby Dick is precisely at stake, not only because its hero undertakes a hunt in which the object of his quest has been more violently internalized and sentimentalized, but also because Melville, having taken the frontier impulse that defines much of America's best literature almost farther than it could go, seemed to have nothing left but dramatically to recoup what remained of his shattered and orphaned self and exploit its seemingly thin substance for whatever could be found of worth. Insofar as *Pierre* is an American *Hamlet,* as F. O. Matthiessen called it,[5] many readers would be willing to apply T. S. Eliot's observations on Hamlet and his problems to Pierre and his; but to say *Pierre* lacks an objective correlative (a Moby Dick, for instance) and ''is dominated by an emotion which is inexpressible, because it is in *excess* of the facts as they appear,'' pinpoints a source of the book's power exactly by begging the question. Since we are told that ''Pierre had always been an admiring reader of Hamlet'' (*P,* 169), the comparison is not an idle one, though we may nonetheless be tempted to follow Eliot's lead and conclude that in the character Pierre ''it is the buffoonery of an emotion which can find no outlet in action,'' while in Melville ''the dramatist it is the buffoonery of an emotion which he cannot express in art,'' and ''is doubtless a subject of study for pathologists.''[6]

I have suggested in earlier chapters that America in the nineteenth century had, from one angle of vision or another, Hamlet's problem. For Cooper in *Home as Found,* Hamlet's anguish erupts into the Effinghams' carefully cleared domain in Templeton, exposing Cooper's severest doubts about America's foundation and turning his home into a near travesty of its highest democratic principles. His desire to vindicate and perpetuate his father's name takes the form of an incisive inquiry into the problems of incest and imitation placed disturbingly at the very basis of the new country's sense of its own enterprise. Hawthorne and Thoreau would seem to stand opposed to Cooper's glorification of the family dynasty, the one engaged in throwing off the incubus of his Puritan history and burying the sins of the fathers, the other becoming a lifelong Natty Bumppo dedicated to shedding the garments of the past in favor of an Adamic bareness. Yet both, as we have seen, are able to take their revolutionary projects only half seriously;

just as Hawthorne's revenge turns out to contain its own commemorative *engraving,* so Thoreau carries the baggage of civilization with him into the wilderness, *grafting* the past onto a virgin land with every stroke of his pen or plow. It is not so much the case that Cooper, Thoreau, and Hawthorne were left in Hamlet-like postures of inaction as that they were all torn between the desire to repudiate the paternal authority of the past and the need to act on behalf and in the stead of that authority, repeating its strictures while avenging its faults. It remained for Melville and Pierre to embody and articulate a true American Hamletism, a point of crisis figuring authority at an impotent crossroads where the struggle is so internalized that it can generate only a wild, self-reflexive parody. The various governing concerns we have found central to the first three writers—incest, authority, imitation, the double, the frontier, and so forth—are all reworked and grotesquely exaggerated in *Pierre,* as though Melville were reading the themes of an incipient American tradition through those bookmarks made of whale skin which magnify their subject into an even taller tale (*MD,* 259). He was also, of course, reading them through *Moby-Dick* itself and through his own life and career. Like Pierre, he was plagiarizing from his own experiences; and as for Thoreau, Hawthorne, and, perhaps most notably here, Cooper, that plagiarizing comes so much to be Melville's haunting double that book and author consume one another in the very act of dramatically exploiting the question of American *authority.*

I

We should perhaps revert for a moment to the terms taken in earlier chapters to be of critical importance—*home* and *found.* The terms and their kindred reverberate continually throughout the texts of Cooper, Thoreau, and Hawthorne that we have examined, and we can only find their relative absence from *Pierre* odd, given the themes of the book. But everything we would wish to say about Melville's book indicates how much the act of founding a home is at its very heart, though with a consistent ironic inversion. While the frontier is almost gone from *Pierre*—having been depleted as a subject in *Moby-Dick*—what it represents is not; but as Edwin Fussell notes, "the image of the interfusing frontier rarely suggested to [Melville] peace, mediation, and richness of inclusion, as it was supposed to, but rather chaos, hemorrhage, insanity, hostility, horror, or an inscrutable disjunction."[7] *That* frontier is still very much a part of *Pierre,* as Melville's numerous renderings of psychological struggle and fragmentation in geographical or exploratory terms suggest. The virgin Eden of Nature that Cooper, Thoreau, and Hawthorne all seek in their different ways remains an issue for Melville; and, as in the case of Hawthorne in particular, Melville's search leads him full in the face of the uncanny and the mockery of his own authorial double. If we can enlist the terms "home" and "found" only at a remove from Melville's own text, then, it is not because they are impertinent to it; rather, founding a home, one startlingly *unheimlich* in every sense I have outlined, is what *Pierre* is about, both in its action and its chaotic form, which in the end are mirror images of one another. *Pierre* is also in an important way the double—perhaps the obverse reflection—of *Moby-Dick,* and as a number of readers have noticed, the later book is a direct development of the most hallucinatory moments in the earlier book. As though unleashing a world that had to be repressed or mutantly suggested in the masculine whaling voyage, Melville creates a domestic fiction in which man submits or succumbs to the feminine, to the woman who is half Madonna, half Medusa. In both action and narration *Pierre* seems to issue from that "opium-like listlessness of vacant, unconscious reverie" that Ishmael threatens to fall into at his post on the mast-head; but while Ishmael only hovers precipitously over "Descartian vortices," where the narcissistic wedding of subject and object entails a suicidal plunge into the abyss (*MD,* 140), Pierre actively seeks out the frontier of metaphysics and transgresses it at will. Had Melville left only *Moby-Dick,* readers of a psychoanalytic persuasion would still have their hands full; with the addition of the sister volume *Pierre,* which, as Raymond Weaver puts it, "is a book to send a Freudian into ravishment,"[8] we might well wish to throw over the whale and head straight for *home.* But a word on the first is nonetheless in order.

"Where is the foundling's father hidden? Our souls are like those orphans whose unwedded mothers die in bearing them: the secret of our paternity lies in their grave, and we must there to learn it" (*MD,* 406). Orphaned Ishmael joins the pursuit of Moby Dick in part as a hedge against his melancholy, a "substitute for pistol and ball" (*MD,* 12); but as the passage suggests, the melancholy which, side by side with the exhilaration of the hunt and an addiction to frontier bravado, afflicts the crew of the Pequod is often refracted into a specifically American question of genealogy. There is so much of *Moby-Dick* itself and so much commentary on it—to the point that it might nearly be regarded as the sacred text of America—that we need make note here of only one central theme. The sacred quality of the book is very much to the point, however, for *Moby-Dick* is the great text of sacrament and slaughter, at once a tall tale and a reverent legend of the beast as holy Father. If Hawthorne had all the fathers he could handle, it has also belonged to the American experience documented by Cooper, Melville, and Faulkner, to name only the most prominent, that paternity and the authority it represents, whether legal, cultural, or religious, have been defined by instability or absence; and one result of the genealogical schism which the American repudiation of historical or traditional constraints entailed has been the location of figures of paternal power not among European ancestors or the founding fathers of America (though this has also been the case), but among beasts of the wilderness, animals whose sublime violence and availability for totemic murder have endowed them with sacred mythological status as surrogates for either actual ancestors or God the Father himself. Thoreau's woodchuck, Cooper's deer and sogdollager, Faulkner's bear, and Melville's whale are objects of sacrifice, and their murder and consumption, whether literal or figurative, retain the ambivalence of Freud's totem meal in that it is precisely in their sacrifice that the power they hold is at once appropriated and augmented: they are converted into sacred fathers by virtue of their concurrent murder and worship. But they have also, in the concision of their dramatic configuration, made clearer than Freud's reading of the totem meal the Oedipal impulse lying behind the sacrifice. Because the slaughter of the American totem has so often been represented as an Adamic ritual that is simultaneously a murder and a marriage, a wedding in which the father is symbolically slain and the mother possessed (though in the very name of the renunciation of real marriage), we would go astray were we to read the totem animal singularly as a figure of the sacrificial father.

If we find in *Moby-Dick* a concomitant search for the father and attempt at his murder, then, we must nevertheless note that the whale is a strangely androgynous creature for Melville. When Tashtego is employed in hoisting buckets of sperm out of a whale's head, for example, it is as though he dips out "a dairy-maid's pail of new milk"; and when he tumbles into the head and is momentarily "coffined, hearsed, and tombed in the secret inner chamber and sanctum sanctorum of the whale," his "delivery" by Queequeg is pointedly a lesson of "great skill in obstetrics" (*MD*, 288–90). The head, which only a few chapters earlier was a "blood-dripping head hung to the Pequod's waist like the giant Holofernes's from the girdle of Judith" (*MD*, 263), is now an explicit womb. Because the totemic animal must comprise both the traditionally masculine authority of history and religion, and the feminine authority so many American authors have read in the text of Nature, Moby Dick is both mother and father, womb and phallus. In the hunt as sacrificial marriage, the ambivalence that Whitman so powerfully represented in the opening lines of his "Song of the Broad-Axe" ("Weapon shapely, naked, wan,/Head from the mother's bowels drawn") is fully dramatized: simultaneously a birth and a violation, the confrontation of technology and Nature in America has, under the pressures brought to bear by the yoking together of revolution and imperialism, been posed by its most psychologically attuned interpreters as a problem of decidedly Oedipal dimensions, one in which the relationship with the feminine has either skirted or directly avowed the incestuous and in which the father has been made the object of both parricidal desires and sacrificial internalization.

We have seen that for Cooper, Thoreau, and Hawthorne, the feminine and the masculine, though they are at times easily polarized, have at the most critical moments of artistic power been fused in a more subtle melodrama of family romance in which the writer is intimately involved, a romance in which the writer finds his own authority in a hybrid disjunction and interaction of his *own* desires, and in which the foundling's father and unwedded mother become the American dream family. Thus, if we read *Moby-Dick* as a text of American family romance, it is not sheerly at the expense of the countless other critical narratives it can evolve, but because it is a book pointedly about the fragmentation of family, the dismemberment of the father, the sacrifice of the totem animal, and the violation of Nature: it is—a fact that is difficult to repress, though some readers have tried—a book about Moby-*Dick*. Leo Marx has clarified the centrality of Melville's totemic metonym by noting the transition that occurs in the chapters ''A Squeeze of the Hand,'' ''The Cassock,'' and ''The Try-Works.'' Between the homoerotic and democratic bathing in sperm of the first, and the ghastly representation of the capitalist enterprise as a mechanical, orgiastic ritual of the last, Melville inserts, in Marx's words, ''a brief Rabelaisian tribute to sexual energy as figured in the 'grandissimus,' or phallus, of the whale.''[9] But this interlude may be more important than Marx lets on, for the stripping of ''Bible leaves'' by the ''archbishoprick'' mincer (*MD,* 351) functions as a rite in small of the sacramental phallic harvest which, at the limit of Ahab's madness, the whaling enterprise has become. ''The Cassock'' pointedly fuses tall-tale humor with commercial mission and, more importantly, legislates between Ishmael's sunny, domestic celebration of sperm in the preceding chapter and the sperm's fiery trying-out in the following chapter, where the ''scraps or fritters'' of the tried-out whale, nearly in mimicry of Ahab's monomania, feed its own pyre, like that of ''a plethoric burning martyr, or a self-consuming misanthrope'' (*MD,* 353). It is the interlude, in which the totemic status of Moby Dick is diminutively accentuated in the mock worship of a phallus that is ''longer than a Kentuckian is tall'' (*MD,* 351) and whose skin is donned like a Thoreauvian garment of psychological cannibalism, that most aggressively links the conflicting impulses of the American hunt—the sexual *consummation* of the dramatic frontier pastoral and the *consumption* of frontier bounty in industrial exploitation.

The chapter on the whale's phallus concentrates into a brief episode the tension Melville's narrative must maintain between a ludic "affair of oil" and the plundering of a rich "bank of sperm" (*MD*, 357, 297). Between the erotic marriage and the violent commercial sacrifice stands the mock totem around which Ahab's revenge and Ishmael's melancholy revolve. Yet if in *Moby-Dick* Melville goes in wild pursuit of the phallus of authority, in *Pierre* he returns home to find it—perhaps just as he had suspected all along—safely, or treacherously, in the possession of the Mother. The "Descartian vortices" into which Narcissus-Ishmael peers are transformed in *Pierre* into a hallucinatory landscape of the Mother or a haunting feminine face whose "nameless beauty" summons up before Pierre "many an old legendary family scene" (*P*, 49–50), pointing backward to "some irrevocable sin" and forward to "some inevitable ill" (*P*, 43), and threatening to swallow up completely that "image of the ungraspable phantom of life" (*MD*, 14) that Ishmael goes in search of. The simultaneous *consummation* and *consumption* which governs the cannibalism of *Moby-Dick*— whether literal or figurative—are entwined in the totemic festival; and not least because, as modern anthropology has often confirmed, copulation and eating, and particularly incest and cannibalism, are so often fused as either prohibited or requisite functions in a community's ritual observances. The gap between *Moby-Dick* and *Pierre*, then, may be no gap at all, not only because the questions of authority and authorship are explicitly at stake in both, but also because the issues of totemic cannibalism in the first and incest in the latter are of a piece. In this regard, we might also note in passing from one to the other that Lévi-Strauss takes care to point out that among several African tribes the eating of the totem and incest have equivalent linguistic forms, to such an extent that among two tribes in particular "the word 'totem' also means 'sister's vulva.'"[10]

No one can fail to be struck by *Pierre*'s insanely pastoralized opening. Henry A. Murray is quite correct to point out that the artificially heightened beginning represents "an overcompensatory Eden, a poetical feudal paradise in which woman is zealously elevated to the highest place in the order of nature."[11] It is as though Melville were at once confirming and mocking Cooper's contention in *Notions of the Americans* that America is a virtual "Paradise of woman," where she fulfills "the very station for which she was designed by nature."[12] Yet the transition that occurs between *Moby-Dick* and *Pierre* is one version of the American dream come true: the death of the Father, the overthrow of paternal authority and its replacement by the goddess of Nature, the Mother. In the Eden of the Mother, Pierre is a purely Adamic hero, particularly because his relationship with her, however suspicious, is nonetheless chaste. Their union is marked by "that nameless and infinitely delicate aroma of inexpressible tenderness and attentiveness which...is contemporary with the courtship, and precedes the final banns and the rite'' of marriage. Since it is not limited ''in duration by that climax which is so fatal to ordinary love,'' it partakes of the ''Paradise to come, when etherealized from all drosses and stains, the holiest passion of man shall unite all kindreds and climes into one circle of pure and unimpairable delight'' (*P*, 16). A true Adamic hero, Pierre can neither marry nor climax, since to do so would destroy Eden. His relationship must verge on passion but renounce it, in this case, verge on incest but deny it, as Melville's narration does. Melville treats the sexual and the incestuous in *Pierre* much as Hawthorne treats witchcraft in *The House of the Seven Gables*, repressing and suggesting it at the same time. The sexual in *Pierre* is almost but not quite, as it must be for an Adam in Eden, an eros of concurrently offered and stifled temptation.

Legend has it that Melville's mother, Maria Gansevoort Melville, used to make her eight children sit on stools around her bed while she took an afternoon nap, dismissing them when she awoke. This is hardly enough to account for the grotesque figure that makes up half of Melville's portrait of Pierre's mother, but it is a useful balance to the well-known fact that Melville, upon the birth of his second son, Stanwix, unwittingly entered his own mother's name in place of his wife's on the birth certificate.[13] In the face of evidence no more conclusive, it is not worthwhile to turn Maria Gansevoort Melville into Mary Glendinning in any strict sense; but then fantasy plays fast and loose with the problem of representation, and if Pierre's career contains extraordinary versions of Melville's own, his relationship with his mother may be no safe fiction either, but one whose drama is as intensely personal as the attempted slaughter of the white whale. Forceful as it is, though, Pierre's arrangement with his mother is untenable, if not absurdly dangerous, in 1852. Besides, it is the fact that ''a sister had been omitted from the text'' of Pierre's otherwise ''sweetly-writ manuscript'' which at least in part accounts for his designs upon his mother, even though the ''fictitious title'' of ''sister'' that ''he so often lavished upon his mother'' cannot ''at all supply the absent reality.'' Being sisterless, Pierre ''is as a bachelor before his time,'' since ''much that goes to make up the deliciousness of a wife, already lies in the sister'' (*P*, 7).

But perhaps more significant is the fact that Melville attributes Pierre's yearning for a sister to ''that still stranger feeling of loneliness he sometimes experienced, as not only the solitary head of his family, but the only surnamed male Glendinning extant'' (*P*, 7). The position of the Glendinning dynasty is analogous to that of the Effinghams in *Home as Found*, though neither Melville's nor Cooper's own family lines were in danger of running out, either when they wrote *Pierre* and *Home as Found* or at any other time for that matter. In the case of Cooper, it is his attention to the letter of his father's will that leads him into the ritualized charade by which Paul Powis becomes an Effingham, thus insuring the continuance of the family name. The incestuous marriage saves the Effingham dynasty and protects the family from the dissolution of name and blood which Templeton's democratic addiction to constant change has legislated. Cooper's book, however close at times to the self-parodic and however unnerving the impulses at work in his artificial garden, is nonetheless a strict statement of belief and a warning against the decay of the institutional standards of family and law he so cherished. The case of *Pierre* is similar but much more intricate. Since Pierre's marriage to Lucy would presumably continue the Glendinning line, his renunciation of her in favor of his half-sister Isabel, with whom he can hardly found a family, only insures the dissolution of the Glendinning name. Whereas Cooper's Effinghams suggest an inbreeding that may lead at last to deformity and collapse, Melville's fictional family enacts a virtual suicide of generation, which is, of course, what the book literally ends in. We cannot hope to recover exactly the psychological motivations that led Melville to place an incestuous entanglement at the heart of his first and only piece of truly domestic fiction. There are no biographical facts, like Cooper's longing for his dead sister Hannah and the charge of Judge Cooper's will, which would help account for the relationship of Pierre and Isabel. Yet neither can the question of incest be dismissed as an unhappy effect of Melville's known reading of Gothic fiction. It is clear early on that Melville intends the book, at whatever a fantastic and parodic level, to raise a specifically American issue, one that is as much a real question for the still newly founded nation as that addressed by the inquiry into primitivism and imperialism in his earlier books.

It is a question of breeding. The monarchical world errs, Melville suggests, in thinking "that in demagoguical America the sacred Past hath no fixed statues erected to it, but all things irreverently seethe and boil in the vulgar cauldron of an everlasting uncrystalizing Present.... With no chartered aristocracy, and no lawful entail," the European observer must ask (as so many had by the time Melville was writing), "how can any family in America imposingly perpetuate itself?" (*P*, 8). But Melville goes on to conclude that since most current English peerage can trace their genuine pedigrees back only to Charles II and even at that discover there mere "byeblows" of royalty, many American families—the Van Rensellaers, for example, from whom Melville was descended through his mother—have equal right to hereditary title. Because the blood of English peerage has been "artificially conducted" through both bastardy and the manufacture of titles, creating "grafted families" that thrive only on "the empty air of a name,"

America could, if it chose, "make out a good general case with England in this short little matter of large estates, and long pedigrees—pedigrees I mean, wherein is no flaw" (*P*, 10–11). The irony, of course, is that Isabel is herself a "bye-blow" and that as a result the Glendinning peerage is as flawed as the dukedom of Buccleugh. In a strangely complex situation, Melville manages both to mock an artistocracy of breeding that hides or suppresses its own flaws and to expose America's own fascination, despite democratic allegiance to a leveling of privilege, with the authority of heredity.

The power of such political authority has obvious and important consequences for the writer, though, and Melville shares with his contemporaries a pressing interest in the way in which the issue of legitimacy necessarily informs the claims of literary authority. Cooper's anxious concern for poet Paul's legitimacy—that he not be an "accident" or bye-blow—reflects his dramatic attempt to rescue the threatened authority of both his family and his fiction. The question of breeding haunted Hawthorne as well, for he found in Hester's illegitimate childbearing and in Holgrave's revolutionary conquest of the Pyncheons probing analogies for the democratic craft he practiced. As all three writers noticed, the legitimacy of their authorship entailed a sacrificial confrontation with the past that brought "romance" to verge perilously upon "family romance." In *Pierre,* however, the issue of authority is nearly engulfed by the romance Melville summons up at the outset of his hero's career, as though at the most grotesque and self-reflexive limit the suffocation of the American dream Cooper so feared has,come to pass. "Columbus ended earth's romance: No New World to mankind remains!" Melville wrote in *Clarel*;[14] unlike Thoreau, who could delight in the face of such a challenge, Melville seems after *Moby-Dick* to have accepted the ironic situation in which the American enterprise was thus placed. Yet as I will want to suggest, that irony—which turns finally to awesome parody—is an intimate part of the family romance which remained for an American author to meet head on.

It is not the irony of *Benito Cereno,* though, which as one of the great American detective stories withholds its horror from the reader as cunningly as it does from Captain Delano, but an irony that gapes from the outset like an open wound that has few, if any, secrets remaining. The problem with *Pierre,* as Raymond Nelson suggests, is that "the parody, like the presence of a narrator, appears to have no place to go."[15] This is attributable in part to Melville's questionable attempt to make his own fantasies those of his country (if only in an attenuated sense), a project that clearly succeeds in *Moby-Dick* but in *Pierre* is the constant subject of doubts forced upon the reader by a narrator who often seems nearly as mad as his protagonist. Although he reassured his publisher, in the face of critical attacks on *Moby-*

Dick, that *Pierre* would be "a regular romance, with a mysterious plot to it, & stirring passions at work, and withall, representing a new and elevated aspect of American life,"[16] Melville's remarks only extend his burlesque further, defining in advance the desultory climate into which the book had to be received and ridiculing the tastes that would find no place for it. There is nothing "regular" about Melville's incest-romance, and the "American life" it represents is so "elevated" as to barely escape being sublimated out of existence along with the Glendinning family line.

II

"Death of the Father," writes Roland Barthes, "would deprive literature of many of its pleasures. If there is no longer a Father, why tell stories? Doesn't every narrative lead back to Oedipus? Isn't storytelling always a way of searching for one's origin, speaking one's conflicts with the Law, entering into the dialectic of tenderness and hatred?"[17] Whether or not we admit the universality of Barthes's proposal, we are compelled to ask if *Pierre* is not a book of the Father's death. There is no father, surely enough, when the book begins; but there is, in fact, more—an inordinately idealized memory of the father, fostered in part by Mary Glendinning. The case is curious, for Melville and Pierre are both twelve when their fathers die, though Melville's father died a shamed debtor. If the fictionalized father has any basis in biography, it would seem only to reveal that whatever allegiance Melville had to his aristocratic inheritance (which was, though, particularly through his mother), he had a simultaneous desire to destroy it, perhaps because he could not live up to the fame of his grandfathers (both, like those of Pierre, military heroes), perhaps because of the failure of his father, or perhaps because, like Hawthorne, he felt his own craft and career a disgrace. The father is dead in *Pierre* but hardly missing; he is a source of anxiety precisely because he has been transformed in Pierre's memory into an impossible ideal that only becomes human after it is inscribed with a deep flaw. Pierre's father is perhaps initially an overcompensation for Melville's, an elevated representative whose memory must be torn apart and made believable in the tragedy of his becoming the father of a bastard. Once the "unclouded, snow-white, and serene" marble shrine of his father has been stripped "of all overlaid bloom" and buried "beneath the prostrated ruins of the soul's temple" (*P,* 68–69), the paradox of Pierre's resolve to save Isabel and protect his father's sacred public memory lies in the fact that his very desire to keep the father's name untarnished insures that it will die out with Pierre. In a striking transfiguration of the totem drama, Pierre augments the father's power and keeps his memory unblemished by sacrificing himself instead.

Pierre may not be a story of the death of the Father, but it is still something quite different from *Moby-Dick*, which is the most paternity-ridden book possible. *Moby-Dick*'s narrative leads back to Oedipus, no doubt, could the whale only be caught; *Pierre*'s narrative does not lead back to Oedipus only because it does not need to: *Pierre* virtually *is Oedipus*—as much an American *Oedipus* as it is an American *Hamlet*. In view of this, it is worth comparing two famous passages, the first from *Moby-Dick*, the second from *Pierre*, in order to gauge one important difference between the books:

> Ahab's larger, darker, deeper part remains unhinted. . . .far beneath the fantastic towers of man's upper earth, his root of grandeur, his whole awful essence sits in bearded state; an antique buried beneath antiquities, and throned on torsoes! So with a broken throne, the great gods mock that captive king; so like a Caryatid, he patient sits, upholding on his frozen brow the piled entablatures of ages. Wind ye down there, ye prouder, sadder souls! question that proud, sad king! A family likeness! aye, he did beget ye, ye young exiled royalties; and from your grim sire only will the old State-secret come. (*MD,* 161).

> Not yet had [Pierre] dropped his angle into the well of his childhood, to find what fish might be there; for who dreams to find fish in a well? . . .Ten million things were as yet uncovered to Pierre. The old mummy lies buried in cloth on cloth; it takes time to unwrap this Egyptian king. Yet now, forsooth, because Pierre began to see through the first superficiality of the world, he fondly weens he has come to the unlayered substance. But, as far as any geologist has yet gone down into the world, it is found to consist of nothing but surface stratified on surface. To its axis, the world being nothing but superinduced superficies. By vast pains we mine into the pyramid; by horrible gropings we come to the central room; with joy we espy the sarcophagus; but we lift the lid—and no body is there!—appallingly vacant as vast is the soul of a man. (*P,* 284-85).

Two instructive transformations have taken place in the later book. No longer is the figure of the father under investigation, but rather the son, Pierre himself. Moreover, the "State-secret" buried deep within Ahab's ravings is now revealed as an illusive lacuna; his bearded root, throned on a broken torso, is gone from the sacrophagus into which Pierre descends: indeed, Pierre does lack a Moby Dick. The *Moby-Dick* passage, as many readers have noticed, figures the terrible burden of history, of the civilized and familial transmissions whose weight is heavy even for an American Ahab, who staggers "beneath the piled centuries since Paradise" (*MD,* 444). What should be noted, then, is that with the disappearance of the "grim sire" from the pyramid of genealogy, the "entablatures of ages" have become merely "superinduced superficies." The burden of the past remains, certainly, but it has been deflated and turned into redundant impedimenta that restrict the search and yield not an embedded authority but only its comic absence. The royal father—captive and mangled, but in *Moby-Dick* a king nonetheless—has been replaced by an empty coffin; Pierre finds no "family likeness" and nothing in its stead. If *Moby-Dick* can be read as the longest dream in American writing of a crisis in paternal authority, of doing in the dismembering father, *Pierre* is in some sense the fulfillment of the dream. Pierre's father is gone before the book begins, and the sarcophagus passage announces that freedom—one so often sought by revolutionaries, frontiersmen, and other lunatic Americanists—in all its horrible splendor. *Pierre* may then be a more American book than *Moby-Dick,* could such a distinction be drawn.

This is obviously too simplistic; we can hardly reduce either book to single passages, however powerful and climactic they are. Perhaps we will also seem to have come upon the *Pierre* passage, which is usually reserved as a critical ace, prematurely. I introduce it here because the fact of vacated authority is implicit in *Pierre* from the start; while *Moby-Dick* ends with Ishmael orphaned, *Pierre* begins with its hero already half so and on the verge of surrendering the other half by taking his mother concomitantly as a sister and a wife, by in effect *becoming the father.* Melville complained in a letter to Evert Duyckinck in 1849 that "we are all sons, grandsons, or nephews, or great-nephews of those who go before us. No one is his own sire."[18] As the passage quoted above suggests, this was one of the problems *Moby-Dick* attempted to work out. In *Pierre,* however, Melville's fantasy of becoming "his own sire" is played out not only in Pierre's incest but also in Melville's doubling of himself as the author Pierre-Vivia plagiarizing from his own experiences and writing the book we read. Pierre begins by assuming the paternal role of authority held alternately by Ahab and the whale in *Moby-Dick,* and that assumption is constitutive for the book. While the earlier book is thematically Oedipal, *Pierre* is deliberately a replication: that "club-footed Evil One"—the devil of doubt whom Pierre is able to banish in his allegiance to Isabel but who returns to goad him once he has renounced his mother—is his own Oedipal double. With "corpses behind . . . and the last sin before" (*P*, 206), Pierre, having destroyed the enshrined memory of his father, has only to undertake "the nominal conversion of a sister into a wife" in order to transmute and complete his "previous conversational conversion of a mother into a sister" (*P*, 177) and thus work out his own sure fate. We cannot minimize the differences between Oedipus and Pierre, but the general parallel of outline is significant. What Geoffrey Hartman says of Oedipus can be usefully applied to Pierre. By killing his father

and marrying his mother, Hartman points out, Oedipus "simply elides individual identity, and is allowed no being properly his own. The oracle takes
away, from the outset, any chance for self-development. Oedipus is redundant: he is his father, and as his father he is nothing, for he returns to the
womb that bore him." In the career unfolded from a prophecy, "Oedipus
coverges on his fate like an epigram on its point or a tragedy on its recognition scene. The etiologic distancing collapses, the illusion bursts, the
supernatural leaves the natural no space."[19] Though complete elision of self
may seem too strong a claim, Pierre undergoes much the same ordeal,
mechanically carrying out his own fate. But it is not the case alone that
Pierre and Oedipus, in supplanting their fathers, become "nothing"; they
also become everything since redundancy is as clearly excess as it is loss.

"For surely," Melville writes immediately preceding his remarks about
Pierre's conversion of a sister into a wife, "no mere mortal who has at all
gone down into himself will ever pretend that his slightest thought or act
solely originates in his own defined identity" (*P,* 176). Pierre's Oedipal action is complicated by the fact that his incestuous desires for his mother are
deflected into those for his sister, which in turn are motivated as much by
the need to vindicate his father—by legitimizing Isabel *as* his sister—as by
an impulse to displace him. In doing both, Pierre's redundancy is doubled
over once again. While the actions he takes make him on the one hand "his
own sire," they also, on the other, do not originate in his own "identity,"
since that identity—sanctioned by Pierre's overly sacred memory of his
father—can only be sought in its own disavowal. His redundancy, moreover,
unlike that of Oedipus, is not a hidden fate to be recognized only when it is
too late, but is an announced intention all along. The collapse of illusion
Hartman finds in the career of Oedipus has, in effect, already taken place
when *Pierre* gets underway. Not an oracle whose message will eventually be
correctly interpreted, but Melville himself precludes Pierre's "chance for
self-development." But the collapse of that illusion is an important one: for
Pierre, the father is not exactly missing and hence easily replaced (or unwittingly murdered), but is so internalized by Pierre's actions as to be his
haunting double. Pierre's sacrificial totemization of the father does not
allow the giving way of the natural to the supernatural; rather, it attempts to
legitimize the *unnatural.* Pierre is his own sire, but he is also, in effect,
Isabel's; he becomes, as the notorious Enceladus episode near the end of the
novel suggests, "doubly incestuous" (*P,* 347).

Pierre's doubly incestuous fulfillment of his fate continually impinges
upon the melodramatic, if not on sheer circus, though we should be nonetheless alert to the peculiar and real powers generated by scenarios in the
book that are overly theatrical, farcical, or parodic. While Pierre's resolu-

tions—both to acknowledge Isabel publically yet withhold her recognition out of charity for his mother, and "to screen [his] father's honorable memory from reproach" yet enter into "open vindication of [his] fraternalness to Isabel"—are "impossible adjuncts," which when "once brought together. . .all mutually expire" (*P*, 171), that mutual expiration is integral to the redundancy, the self-fathering, and ultimately the suicide, which it is Pierre's fate to play out. Those resolves issue in annihilating paradox, but as Dorothy Van Ghent has noted in an essay on *Don Quixote*, "paradox" and "parody," despite their initial and etymological similarity, have this difference: unlike paradox, parody "is able to intertwine many feelings and attitudes together in such a way that they do not merely grapple with each other antagonistically but act creatively on each other, establishing new syntheses of feeling and stimulating more comprehensive and more subtle perceptions." Parody offers "not a platform for derision" but "a field for the joyful exercise of perception."[20] Derision is hardly to be closed out in the case of *Pierre*, and we will want eventually to return to the question of the etymological kinship between *paradox* and *parody* and add a third kindred term that bridges the gaps between antagonism, derision, and joyful exercise—namely, *parricide*. But what Van Ghent's remarks point up is that *Pierre*, also a book whose hero's best intentions attentuate the distinction between the sacred and the gross in a constant skirmish with hallucination, gains its power precisely through the imposition of grotesque artifice and energizing contradiction. In the "pious imposture" of marriage Pierre undertakes in order to rescue Isabel and preserve his father's honor (*P*, 173), it is not clear whether he is "Orpheus finding his Eurydice" or "Pluto stealing Proserpine" (*P*, 59). And while the conclusion of Pierre's poetic career is more in keeping with the madness and dismemberment of Orpheus, we might still incline toward Pluto, particularly if we were to invoke the case of one of Pierre's fictional descendants—Quentin Compson, who like Pierre bears a thrice-repeated ancestral name, witnesses and participates in the dissolution of his family dynasty, identifies himself with Christ (*P*, 106, 162), and completes his career in suicide. There is another point of resemblance, of course, one which Faulkner's appendix to *The Sound and the Fury*, in its striking mixture of eschatology and quixotic melodrama, concisely illustrates:

> QUENTIN III. Who loved not his sister's body but some concept of Compson honor precariously and (he knew well) only temporarily supported by the minute fragile membrane of her maidenhead as a miniature replica of all the whole vast globy earth may be poised on the nose of a trained seal. Who loved not the idea of incest which he would not commit, but some presbyterian concept of its eternal punishment: he, not God, could by that means cast himself

and his sister into hell, where he could guard her forever and keep her forevermore intact amid the eternal fires. But who loved death above all, who loved only death, loved and lived in a deliberate and almost perverted anticipation of death as a lover loves and deliberately refrains from the waiting willing friendly tender incredible body of his beloved, until he can no longer bear not the refraining but the restraint and so flings, hurls himself, relinquishing, drowning.[21]

Pierre does not drown, not in water at any rate, though perhaps in the black tresses of Isabel's "long hair [which] ran over him, and arbored him in ebon vines" after their mutual suicide (*P,* 362). Nor does his rescue of Isabel (as does Quentin's of Caddy) take place in the ostensible name of forestalling her promiscuity, yet his incestuous compulsion does verge on presbyterian masochism even while it appears to be overtly erotic. The perilous conflict between the sensual and Adamic chastity that both the plot and the style of *Pierre* hold in paradoxical suspension may also bear the ambivalent marking that Freud assigns to the drama of the "rescue-motif," though in more complex performance than Freud indicates. While the fantasy of rescuing the father, says Freud, may usually be read as a means of defiance or a form of rationalization in which the son "puts his account square with him," the rescue of the mother, since it is she in particular who "gave the child life," often "takes on the significance of giving her a child or making a child for her—needless to say, one like himself." In a rescue fantasy in which he wishes to give his mother a son like himself, the son "is completely identifying himself with the father. All his instincts, those of tenderness, gratitude, lustfulness, defiance and independence, find satisfaction in the single wish *to be his own father.*"[22] Pierre's rescue charts an oblique course between the father and the mother, but by funneling the desires contingent upon the fantasized rescue of either one or the other into a sister who necessarily recapitulates the characteristics of both, it both accentuates the inherent conflict between the two and condenses the paradoxical drives of that conflict into a more subtle reading of the Oedipal drama. Though Pierre, for all his troubles, ends only as "'the fool of Truth, the fool of Virtue, the fool of Fate'" (*P,* 358), his knight-errantry, like that of Don Quixote or Quentin Compson, has a respectable tradition. As Murray notes in his essay on *Pierre,* the sister was often taken as the object of courtly love "because the incest barrier served to reinforce the knight-errant's resolution to adhere to the ideal of chastity."[23] Yet even though it is posed as a choice between "Lucy or God," Pierre's resolution to "become as immortal bachelors or gods" (*P,* 180–81) flirts more dangerously with the problem of chastity and impinges more noticeably upon the lurid than upon the courtly. Far from putting his account square with the father and mother,

Pierre finds that "the account of love" is "endless" (*P*, 34), as inscrutable and fathomless as the sarcophagus of authority, and that "love's museum is vain and foolish as the Catacombs, where grinning apes and abject lizards are embalmed...[the] decay and death of endless innumerable generations" (*P*, 197).

Hawthorne longs, we recall, for a glimpse of that face which always evaporates when its veil is lifted, leaving him with the feeble comfort of his own mirrored reflection, the very sign of his shattered narcissism and loss of identity. The double in the mirror represents the dismemberment of the subject's self-presence, and Hawthorne's craving to lift the veil which covers the maiden Priscilla or Nature herself may be read as a function of that crisis of perception in which the threat of castration is unfolded: what he *perceives* represents, by excision of the fantasized or expected maternal phallus, a threat of his own bodily integrity. By transferring the threat from the organs in question to the organs of perception whose capacity has consequently been called into question, the face that is both Madonna and Medusa contracts the threat to perception and turns the comfort of the double into an uncanny harbinger of mutilation or death. We will want shortly to recall the *crisis of perception* so crucial to Hawthorne and consider the severe manner in which it configures Pierre's anxieties as a writer (and thus affects the question of *parody* and *parricide*), but need only note here that Pierre too is haunted by a feminine face, one whose absence has made him a "bachelor before his time" and induced in him anxiety about being the last of the Glendinning line.

Like Priscilla's face in *The Blithedale Romance*, "whose impalpable grace lay so singularly between beauty and disease,"[24] the face of Isabel, whom Pierre has seen at the Miss Pennies's sewing circle, is one "ever hovering between Tartarean misery and Paradisaic beauty" (*P*, 43). The apparition of the face, as though screened by the rustling foliage, high among the branches of the huge paternal pine-tree at whose "roots of sadness" Pierre sits (*P*, 40–41), contrasts ironically with Pierre's earlier desire to cap "the fame-column, whose tall shaft had been erected by his noble sires," but which will remain for him but "a crumbling, uncompleted shaft" (*P*, 8). As the nominal head of a family that has "by degrees run off into the female branches," whose most recent female issue is illegitimate as well, and whose true power is held by a dominating mother, Pierre has no male companion surnamed Glendinning "but the duplicate one reflected to him in the mirror" (*P*, 7–8), the uncanny harbinger of his own threatened identity. In the melodrama of rescue Isabel only takes Pierre's Oedipal complex one step further, for by transferring his incestuous desires from his mother to his sister, Pierre doubly insures the end of Glendinning propagation. Early on, the face of Isabel accosts him "as some imploring, and beauteous, impassioned, ideal Madonna's haunts the morbidly longing and enthusiastic, but ever-baffled artist" (*P*, 49); but after Isabel's letter declares her the daughter of his father, Pierre, recalling Ahab's vow to "strike through the mask" of the white whale, be there "naught beyond" (*MD*, 144), and mixing the books' metaphors, unveils another aspect of the face: "Lo, I strike through thy helm, and will see thy face, be it Gorgon!" (*P*, 66). Only a moment before reading Isabel's letter, Pierre starts "at a figure in [his] mirror" which bears "the outline of Pierre, but now strangely filled with features transformed, and unfamiliar to him; feverish eagerness, fear, and nameless forebodings of ill!" (*P*, 62). However beautifully seductive, Isabel will remain a Medusa for Pierre, a continual reminder of his own shattered self and that of his father before him. In the place of "the long-cherished image of his father," which has now been "transfigured before him from a green foliaged tree into a blasted trunk" (*P*, 88), Pierre has the father's daughter, his own sister; his resolve concisely enacts the ambivalence of the Oedipal sacrifice—both to supplant and overthrow the father and to protect his revered memory by becoming his *representative,* even, in Pierre's case, becoming the father himself.

The destruction of the sacred status of Pierre's father and the ironic splintering of himself which his own doubly incestuous desires introduce combine to make every action Pierre undertakes ambiguous. His resolves contradict one another irreconcilably, and every attempt to fall upon a valid origin dissolves as surely as his own fragmented identity, for the mutilation of his father's memory has made Pierre's own "body only the embalming cerements of his buried dead within" (*P*, 94). If one small flaw is enough to wreck the brief Glendinning dynasty, how, Pierre wonders, is one to fathom the furthest reaches of moral and genealogical imperative? "But the magnificence of names must not mislead us as to the humility of things," Melville remarks in the ironic attack on English peerage. "For as the breath in all our lungs is hereditary, and my present breath at this moment, is further descended than the body of the present High Priest of the Jews, so far as he can assuredly trace it; so mere names, which are also but air, do likewise revel in this endless descendedness" (*P*, 9). The Glendinning name collapses, and along with it goes the security of ethical decision itself; since any event "is but the product of an infinite series of infinitely involved and untraceable foregoing occurrences," so "every motion of the heart" is imputable not to any immediate cause but only "to a long line of dependencies whose further part is lost in the mid-regions of the impalpable air" (*P*, 67). Genealogical source and ethical motive become lost in an inexplicable tangle of obscurity and ambiguity opening out over an abyss, a sarcophagus without a body. To descend into the heart of a man like Pierre is to descend "a spiral stair in a shaft, without any end, and where that endlessness is only concealed by the spiralness of the stair, and the blackness of the shaft" (*P*, 289). Such a descent stops, if at all, at the silence and veritable blankness of the genealogical sublime. It is the sublimity of family romance where, as Melville earlier cribs from Burke, "the extreme top of love, is Fear and Wonder" (*P*, 35). But it is also "The American Sublime," as in the poem of that name by Wallace Stevens, a locale of frightening burlesque where one goes "Blinking and blank" and the Adamic sublime

> comes down
> To the spirit itself,
>
> The spirit and space,
> The empty spirit
> In vacant space.[25]

Pierre's sublimation of the ancestral also has traffic with that womb of Nature in which Thoreau and Hawthorne kept hoping to find their proper *home*, but which would only reveal itself off to the side, like the uncanny itself. Melville provides a figure similar to Thoreau's and Hawthorne's when he remarks in the Hawthorne essay that the Truth that Shakespeare puts in the mouths of his "dark characters" like Hamlet and Lear would be madness for any other man; such Truth "is forced to fly like a sacred white doe in the woodlands; and only in cunning glimpses will she reveal herself."[26] For Pierre, the desire to return to his former *Heim* is constitutive for his incest fantasies and the constant figuring of places of power and authority as gaps, lacunae, or abysses. Not the phallus of signification, but its absence, the wholesale demolition of the *object* of reference, is *Pierre's* locus of truth. Between his two meetings with Isabel, Pierre goes to meditate beneath the "lengthened egg" of the Memnon Stone, whose mysterious inscription "S. ye W." ("Solomon the Wise") seems "to point to some period before the era of Columbus' discovery of the hemisphere" (*P*, 132–33), the Eden of America. Yet Pierre's desire for return is as much Oedipal as it is Adamic; the suicidal impulse of his incestuous desire is played out as he "slid[es] himself straight into the horrible interspace, and [lies] there as dead" (*P*, 134). Pierre's purported analogy with Memnon is loose at best. Like Memnon, who is slain by Achilles as he aids his uncle Priam in the Trojan war, Pierre will "with enthusiastic rashness [fling] himself on another's account into a rightful quarrel," but it is doubtful that he too will become immortal as a result. More important is that Melville finds embodied in Memnon's fable "the Hamletism of the antique world,"

just as Pierre's fable embodies a Hamletism of the American world; for if
"the English Tragedy is but Egyptian Memnon, Montaignized and moder-
nized," *Pierre* is but the same Americanized. "Shakespeare had his fathers
too," Melville adds; indeed, Melville also had his (*P*, 135). The "horrible
interspace" of the Memnon Stone is not only Pierre's personal womb but
also the literary womb into which Melville enters. He will risk finding but an
endless shaft, though, for the melancholy music of Memnon's memorial
statue (thought of old to be the young prince's mournful voice, but actually
caused by the dawn wind of the Nile whistling through the stone) is now
"lost among our drifting sands" in "a bantering, barren, and prosaic,
heartless age" (*P*, 136), just as the name of Pierre will presumably be lost,
along with Memnon and Hamlet, in the swirling, endless descendedness of
the air of names.

Though "the world is forever babbling of originality," Melville remarks
at a later point, "there never yet was an original man, in the sense intended
by the world...the only original author being God." If Pierre's rescue-
compulsion revolves around an ambivalent desire to be "original," both to
usurp and protect the father and to father himself on the mother, his
paradoxical resolves hold these desires in Hamlet-like suspension. While
Melville adds, "never was there a child born solely from one parent...self-
reciprocally efficient hermaphrodites being but a fable" (*P*, 259), we are inclined to suppose that Pierre and Isabel—even more clearly than Paul and
Eve in *Home as Found*, where the Platonic hermaphrodites are introduced
by way of *Twelfth Night*—are figures whose incestuous relationship nearly
parodies Freud's invocation of the *Symposium* myth in *Beyond the Pleasure
Principle*. Freud hesitates to bolster his reading of sexual instincts as
transfigurations of a death wish with Aristophanes' myth, "were it not that
it fulfills precisely the one condition whose fulfillment we desire. For it
traces the origin of an instinct to *a need to restore an earlier state of
things*."[27] It may be that Freud's own "desire" is as much at stake as
Cooper's or Melville's (or our own) in these matters, but we should note that
the episode of the Memnon Stone—which anticipates the mummified
"Egyptian king" whose unwrapping reveals but an empty sarcophagus (*P*,
284-85)—dramatizes the fact that Pierre's desire to reciprocate himself by
becoming "his own sire" can only exchange parricide for suicide and replace
sexual pleasure with an eroticism of death. And although the inscription of
Solomon's name on the stone tempts us to recall the passage from *Song of
Songs* that so acutely characterizes Cooper's incestuously enclosed garden
("A garden enclosed is my sister, my spouse: a spring shut up, a fountaine
sealed"),[28] we should note too that Isabel's mysterious music has so "be-
witched" and "enchanted" Pierre that he feels "caught and fast bound in

some necromancer's garden" (*P*, 128), though with the grotesque twist that his own father is playing the part of Rappaccini. Perhaps the Memnon Stone, like the other symbolic landscapes in *Pierre*, cannot be so reliably pinned down, but functions as the receptacle for the many associations that the fantasy of reading can bring to it. Still, it has explicit connections with Isabel and the deadly eroticism she promises, and it is necessary to pick out a few more of the "subtler meanings which lie crouching behind the colossal haunches of this stone" (*P*, 135), if only to multiply the episode's ambiguities.

Two other texts make the link between the Terror Stone and Isabel more comprehensible. After Melville's death J. E. A. Smith related the supposedly true story behind the Memnon Stone in an article in the Pittsfield *Evening Journal*. According to Smith, Melville was picnicking at the stone with a group of friends, when one of the ladies, apparently Sarah Morewood, "crept into that fearful recess under the rock" and hid there a music box. Soon "there issued from its depths sweet and mysterious music" which "completed in Mr. Melville's mind the resemblance to the Egyptian Memnon suggested by the size and form of the rock."[29] The music box more clearly connects the Stone with the haunting music of Isabel's guitar, which like the stone has a secret inscription inside—her name, *"Isabel"*—that has the power to send her into a mysterious erotic trance: "The secret name in the guitar thrills me, thrills me, whirls me, whirls me; so secret, wholly hidden, yet constantly carried about in it; unseen, unsuspected, always vibrating to the hidden heart-strings—broken heart-strings; oh, my mother, my mother, my mother!" Kneeling before what seems to Pierre the "vestibule of some awful shrine," Isabel breathes "the word *mother, mother, mother,*" and the guitar, shrouded beneath "her dark tent of hair," responds with a magic melody (*P*, 149–50). Pierre's insertion beneath the Memnon Stone takes place between his two interviews with Isabel, mythologizing the beautifully seductive and hallucinatory passages concerning Isabel and her guitar that close each interview. The interview chapters are fine stylistic achievements, the prose approximating the lithe and haunting music which Isabel and her guitar make, each phrase delicately floating on the air of the page: "And still the wild girl played on the guitar; and her long dark shower of curls fell over it, and vailed it; and still, out from the vail came the swarming sweetness, the utter unintelligibleness, but the infinite significancies of the sounds of the guitar" (*P*, 126). Like the pure *figure* Thoreau finds in the unintelligible but infinitely significant Indian tongue, Melville's language nearly gives way here to incantation, to music itself, as the "Mystery of Isabel" is simultaneously articulated and swallowed up in the rhythms of the utterance. The music of Memnon, itself born of air, would be the music of Isabel and her guitar, a mournful plaint that comes as the wind of his own mother, Aurora, passes through the shrine.

It is hard to know what to make of Melville's strange tableaus, since their very purpose is to resist explication and to dissolve into mysterious melody. Before attempting any further exposition, it would be well to recall another text, one that Melville, in all probability, read in December of 1849. The work is De Quincey's *Suspiria de Profundis,* a sequel to *Confessions of an English Opium-Eater,* which has often been remarked as an influential work for Melville.[30] Given its fragmentary and dreamlike character, the *Suspiria* as a whole may have suggested a number of things to Melville, but at least two passages seem of singular importance. Recalling in hallucinatory reverie his concurrently painful and erotic feelings while standing in the bedhcamber where his dead sister Elizabeth lies, De Quincey notes, "whilst I stood, a solemn wind began to blow, the most mournful that ear every heard. . . . Many times since, upon a summer day. . . I have remarked the same wind arising and uttering the same hollow, solemn, Memnonian, but saintly swell: it is in this world the one sole *audible* symbol of eternity."[31] This passage by itself, though suggestive, may perhaps not be enough to provoke consideration of the *Suspiria* as a direct source; yet coupled with De Quincey's latter chapter on "The Palimpsest" of the brain, it opens up a striking configuration. Comparing the brain to a manuscript erased and overwritten many times, De Quincey contends that life's buried griefs and joys can be relived when, in some "convulsion of the system, all wheels back into its earliest elemental stage." The illustration he goes on to provide is peculiar to himself, of course, but equally so to Melville, or at least to Pierre: "The romance has perished that the young man adored; the legend has gone that deluded the boy; but the deep, deep tragedies of infancy, as when the child's hands were unlinked for ever from his mother's neck, or his lips for ever from his sister's kisses, these remain lurking below all, and these lurk to the last. Alchemy there is none of passion or disease that can scortch away these immortal impresses. . . ." The haunting music that issues from the enclosures of guitar and stone evoke a kindred memory for Pierre, and we are inclined to suspect that De Quincey's palimpsest of the psyche lies behind Melville's figure of the empty sarcophagus buried beneath the mind's "superinduced superficies," or even that the Suspiria de Profundis (Sighs from the Depths) directly suggested not only Memnon's airy song but also the empty air of names Pierre must revel in. At the heart of the sacred womb, whether mother or sister, he may find mystery enfolded in its own music; or he may find, as De Quincey does in his further revery on mourning, the "Ladies of Sorrow"—"*Mater Lachrymarum,* Our Lady of Tears," "*Mater Suspiriorum,* Our Lady of Sighs," and finally "*Mater*

Tenebrarum—Our Lady of Darkness,'' who is ''the mother of lunacies, and the suggestress of suicides.''[32] If the maternal comfort Pierre seeks threatens, like De Quincey's, to split between Madonna and Medusa, it is not least because *Mary* Glendinning (and Isabel after her) is not only a Holy Mother but a night*mare* as well, the succubus of Pierre's concurrently enticing and repulsive dreams, the first figure of his melancholia.

De Quincey's scenario of the child's hands being unlinked from the mother or sister illuminates Pierre's peculiar romantic attachments, but we ought not lose sight of the fact that it is the initial loss of Pierre's father that promotes his descent into the sarcophagus of his memory, that it is the hand of the father from which young Pierre is disengaged. In a scene strikingly reminiscent of the childhood dream narrated by Ishmael, in which he half wakes to find his hand held by some ''nameless, unimaginable, silent form or phantom'' (*MD,* 33), Pierre recalls that while he held the one hand of his dying father, the other hand, as ''ashy white as a leper's,'' ''emptily lifted itself, and emptily caught, as if at some other childish fingers''—those belonging to the missing child he calls to in his dying words, ''My daughter!—God! God!—my daughter!'' The memory of the scene has remained a ''sunken seed'' in Pierre's psyche, covered over by ''other and sweeter remembrances,'' but ''the first glimpse of Isabel's letter cause[s] it to spring forth, as if by magic,'' and once more the empty hand lifts and falls, and the words of the ''plaintive and pitiable voice'' echo in his memory (*P,* 70–71). The conjunction of ''my daughter'' and ''God'' in the dying words of Pierre's father, emphatically repeated by Melville, is not in the least fortuitous, for *Pierre,* like Thoreau's *Week,* is distinctly concerned with the feminization of Truth, and I want to argue that this drive is integral to Melville's *parody.*

Having dealt in his early novels with primarily masculine communities where the feminine emerges only as a muffled, if sometimes violent, homoeroticism (as in the ambiguous sperm squeezing aboard the Pequod or in Ishmael's childhood dream, where the phantom hand is transformed into the arm of Queequeg that is wrapped about him in bed), Melville turned in *Pierre* to a society extraordinarily feminized, one in which psychological and philosophical authority undergoes a concomitant transfiguration. *Pierre's* lack of a Moby Dick entails replacing the authority of God the Father with that of God the Mother, the *Mater Tenebrarum,* or at least with a God whose authority is strangely hybrid, emasculated and feminized. The hand of the dying father that clutches emptily for his daughter is ultimately transformed into the empty authority of God: ''how could [Pierre] fail to acknowledge the existence of that all-controlling and all-permeating wonderfulness, which...is so significantly denominated The Finger of

God? But it is not merely the Finger, it is the whole outspread Hand of God; for doth not Scripture intimate that He holdeth all of us in the hollow of His hand?—a Hollow truly!" (*P*, 139). The finger becomes a Hollow, the phallus a gap, the Word Silence—the Silence that "is the general consecration of the universe. Silence is the invisible laying on of the Divine Pontiff's hands upon the world. Silence is at once the most harmless and most awful thing in all nature. It speaks of the Reserved Forces of Fate. Silence is the only Voice of our God" (*P*, 204). R. P. Blackmur is uncannily exact when he remarks that the author of these sentiments is "at home in his words and completely mastered by them."[33] We will need to return to the question of mastery, crucial as it is to parody, but should note here that, indeed, being "at home in his words"—at *Heim* in them—is precisely what Melville, or Pierre at any rate, desires and what his feminization of authority entails. The truth about the father ironically becomes for Pierre the Truth of the Father, as the Word is replaced by Silence and the uncompleted shaft of fame is inverted to become an empty sarcophagus. Like the Silence that empowers Cooper's Silent Pine or Thoreau's landscape of the Mother, Melville's revolves around incest and the loss of paternal authority. And Emily Dickinson might well have been reading *Pierre* when she wrote in 1873, "Silence is all we dread. / There's Ransom in a Voice— / But Silence is Infinity. / Himself have not a face."[34] "Himself" has no face for Melville either, but precisely because "Himself" is in question: the face belongs to Isabel, the lady of his sorrows and mother of his lunacy, an "empty echo...of a sad sound, long past" (*P*, 38). Pierre cannot "get a voice out of Silence" (*P*, 208), and if the book he writes makes no more of an advance upon Truth than Billy Budd's stammering or Bartleby's excruciating reticence, it is because the most awful Truth is ironic; it is the absence of the Word that, like the Memnon Stone, encloses Pierre in its own "Mute Massiveness" (*P*, 134) and harbors the reserved powers of fate in which the *mute* and the *mutilated* go hand in hand.

III

"If a frontier man be seized by wild Indians and carried far and deep into the wilderness, and there held a captive," Melville suggests, he must "exclude from his memory...the least images of those beloved objects now forever reft from him," for if he fails to "succeed in strangling such tormenting memories" he "shall, in the end, become as an idiot" (*P*, 307). Pierre is not Thoreau, but his tale at times sounds strangely like a captivity narrative; unfortunately for him, he is unable to exclude his beloved objects from memory and in the end approaches a thoroughly *natural* state of idiocy. We saw how Thoreau's rendering of the captivity of Hannah Dustan in the *Week* is inversely replicated in his own narrative, such that the violence of the mother, the Medusa of Nature he can look at only at hazard, turns back on him uncannily. In his journey into the landscape of his infant dreams, he relives the threat of his mother that he be skinned alive in order to be born again on the road, though his penetration of Nature entails a counter-violence by which the feminine and silent landscape is inseminated and engrafted by his load of thought and commodities.[35] Thoreau, of course, whatever benefits are generated by his profane cultivation, is nonetheless the victim of his own project, for it is precisely his *grafting* that obliterates the lost paradise, the zero state of Nature, in the same moment it is found. The truth of Nature can either be tilled nor told, since every attempt to domesticate the mistress only forces her into a deeper recess. Silence becomes Thoreau's purest *figure,* the trope of a fantasized moment lost in memory or lying in wait over the western horizon which cannot be written. The melodrama which engenders this *paradox* and the refraction of the Oedipal situation it contains are questions we must return to momentarily, but it is worth noting first that the captivity tableau Melville introduces to define Pierre's immobilization is not wholly incidental.

Few readers have been inclined to place *Pierre* in the American frontier tradition, and most have found it a complete anomaly even among Melville's own works. But in a section that directly follows Pierre's second meeting with Isabel, Melville provides an engaging metaphor for Pierre's obliquely American enterprise. Yoking together the impulse of wilderness exploration with Pierre's psychological trauma, Melville locates "the Ultimate of Human Speculative knowledge" in the "Hyperborean regions" of the frozen North where "the most immemorially admitted maxims of men begin to slide and fluctuate, and finally become wholly inverted." To reach such a region would be the summit of the Adamic drive, the revolutionary overturning of customary constraints. The example of "many minds forever lost, like undiscoverable Arctic explorers," should warn us that "it is not for man to follow the trail of truth too far, since by so doing he entirely loses the directing compass of his mind; for arrived at the Pole, to whose barrenness only it points, there, the needle indifferently respects all points of the horizon alike" (*P,* 165). Fussell is quite right to point out that Melville, having come to the heart of a metaphysical wilderness, "in one of his greatest moments proceeds to destroy a figure basic to his own apprenticeship."[36] But the destruction is also a fulfillment, horrifying though it may be, of the darker side of Adamic desire, one that codifies, for example, Thoreau's longing for an Eden in which one could "simply wonder," free from the "network of speculations" imposed by "reference and inference."[37] The paradise free from the entanglements of speculation and reference revealed in Melville's frontier hallucination is an abyss of madness and death; the maternal space is retained, but it has turned from a site of bliss and comfort to an enclosed fortress that repels the explorer's entrance by grotesque defense: "there is no China Wall that man can build in his soul, which shall permanently stay the irruptions of those barbarous hordes which Truth ever nourishes in the loins of her frozen, yet teeming North" (*P*, 167). A correlative of Pierre's loss of paternal authority and the book's lack of a Moby Dick, the frozen abyss of Truth is a landscape embodiment of Pierre's dismemberment; if for Thoreau and Hawthorne the entrance into Eden halts at a threshold beyond which language cannot go, because never free of speculation and reference, for Melville that entrance entails a vertiginous madness in which signification mutinies, referring, like the *figure* of Silence, everywhere and nowhere at once. The *Heim* of Nature becomes a house of horrors or of unknowing bliss, it is hard to say which.

Language without reference, properly no language at all, would be music or, at the extremity, Silence. The frigid Truth of the Arctic, where the compass goes haywire and one is swallowed up in the loins of madness, is the last stop of the mock death Pierre revels in whether beneath the Memnon Stone or in the Church of the Apostles, where Isabel's guitar accompanies him in his frustrating authorship: she "played her guitar till Pierre felt chapter after chapter born of its wonderful suggestiveness; but alas! eternally incapable of being translated into words; for where the deepest words end, there music begins with its supersensuous and all-confounding intimations" (*P*, 282). The womb of Truth is the locus of the nonreferential, the purely Adamic; as a place where signification has been mutilated or erased, it would denote—were denotation possible—the absence of paternity. Pierre's desire to father himself, then, has a motive akin to that which drives Thoreau and Hawthorne, and perhaps Cooper, into the deepest recesses of Nature. The trauma that accompanies Pierre's incestuous rescue-fantasy is more clearly marked, though, and his paradoxical position brought home with a vengeance, in the dream of Enceladus that he has toward the end of his doomed career. In the "phantasmagoria of the Mount of Titans" Pierre indeed "reads his own peculiar lesson" of the disastrous project he has undertaken—that he bears a "doubly incestuous Enceladus within him" (*P*, 342, 347). The glittering sterility of the hillside, "thickly sown with a small white amaranthine flower," first recalls the "amaranthineness" of the first object of Pierre's desire, Mary Glendinning (*P*, 5); but the illusive landscape slowly gives way to a precipice where "long and frequent rents among the mass of leaves revealed horrible glimpses of dark-dripping rocks, and mysterious mouths of wolfish caves" (*P*, 342–43). At length the landscape that begins as the *mons* of the Mother is transfigured into a Medusan nightmare where "grim scarred rocks...shot up, protruded, stretched, swelled, and eagerly reached forth; on every side bristlingly radiating with a hideous repellingness," and splintered trees, "the melancholy trophies which the North Wind" has "wrested from the forests, and dismembered...on their own chosen battle-ground," lie in ruin. Lording it over "this spectacle of wide and wanton spoil" is "Enceladus the Titan," "writhing from out the imprisoning earth" and endlessly throwing his mangled form against the "unresounding wall" of the Mount of Titans (the Greylock of *Pierre*'s dedication) in an assault on his paternity as futile as that of the Oedipal Pierre. With Pierre's "own duplicate face" emblazoned on his "armless trunk," the "American Enceladus" is a fitting emblem for the American Pierre lost in a wilderness of paradoxical resolves. Like the Enceladus, Pierre, in his attempt "to regain his paternal birthright," has become "doubly incestuous," entering into union first with the mother and then with the sister in a fantasy of self-fathering (*P,* 344–47).

As the hermaphroditic landscape of Enceladus makes clear, Pierre's version of American Nature is as treacherous as that of Thoreau or Hawthorne, and Pierre's replication in the stone figure of Enceladus marks the ambivalence of that Nature. In the loins of Truth one is frozen, stiff; or, beneath the stone—if one is named Pierre: Peter, *petros,* "stone"—he is stone istself, at once erect and dismembered or dead. "To be turned to stone symbolizes not only erection but also castration," writes Norman O. Brown, following Freud. "This is the Rocky Law of Condemnation and double Generation and Death; which makes the Loins the place of the Last Judgment....Coitus successfully performed is incest, a return to the maternal womb; and the punishment appropriate to this crime, castration."[38] Pierre, himself the stone, replaces the crumbled marble altar of the father. As we noted in the case of Hawthorne, some hypothetical transgression—one mutually comprised of original sin and the threat of castration—marks a crisis in referentiality, a cleft in the relationship between sign and object, image and reality. This is doubly the case in *Pierre,* where the "irrevocable sin" (*P,* 43) of the father fuels Pierre's own incestuous fantasy and informs the book's plunge into a wildly ironic, often insane, treatise on the disjunctions of language. At the extremity, though, both Melville's philosophizing and his prose spin off into an incantatory barrage, a near approximation of sheer sound, a chaotic music in which referentiality is swallowed up in the "Descartian vortices" of madness. The return to the womb, the *Heim* of Truth, risks mutilation and even embraces it as a reward. It is an escape from reference, from the phallus of authority, the signifier of law, language, and history. In the Eden of the Mother, absence is power, the power of bliss or madness, the loss of articulation that so empowers the nearly sacred authority of Billy Budd's stammering; it is finally the power of Silence itself, "the only Voice of our God" (*P,* 204). Actualizing the "sort of suicide as to the practical things of this world" that adherence to the Christlike, reference-free, chronometrical ideal of Plinlimmon requires (*P,* 210–15), Pierre's fantasy enacts, in however psychotic a fashion, the darkest Oedipal side of the American Adam.

Pierre is Peter, the rock of himself upon which he builds a blasphemous church. Instead of "flying in the marble face of the Past" (*P,* 174) he has usurped the place of his Past; caught indeed between a rock and a hard place, Pierre's paradoxical resolves have ensured a suicidal petering out of the Glendinning line. As a replication of Oedipus, Pierre has in effect become the father—the *père*—and parricide and suicide have become virtually equivalent. Pierre's inherent transmogrification enacts the ambivalence so crucial to the busts that haunt Cooper and Hawthorne and validate their representative authority. Like the mutilated Enceladus, he carries out the displacement and dismemberment of the Father but finds himself dismembered in turn, the final reward for an accomplished return home. The paradox of the totemic sacrifice which Hawthorne's marble heads and haunting portraits hold in energizing suspension becomes an annihilating travesty in *Pierre,* for if the totem sacrifice is ironic by definition—seeking at once to slay the father and revere his authority in deferred obedience—Pierre's paradoxical resolves, since he has himself assumed the place of the father, can only generate the final irony: suicide. Irony invokes an object of reference only to call it into question; in extremity it mutilates its own discourse and hollows out its own authority, leaving a lacuna in the stead of signification. Irony is the truth of the Arctic, where maxims are inverted, an authority of the maternal space of absence and Silence entered only at risk.

Irony, like "castration," works by paradox, and in a special way, for paradox is *para-doxa:* the setting side by side of contradictory laws or discourses, the son beside the father, say. If the Oedipal drama is ironic or paradoxical, then, it is not only because the murder and incest are perhaps unwitting (or unconscious) but also because the mutilation of the father's discursive power is integral to the desire enacted, as is the consequent risk to the discourse offered in its place. When the Oedipal drama is implemented in full view of the irony of the situation, with conscious abandon in the face of impending destruction, we are close to *parody.* This is not to say that parody is or need always be fully conscious nor that it is not subject to the same irony celebrated in the totem meal—that the murder of the father only uncannily augments his power—for indeed, as the case of Cooper makes clear, *imitation* must always entertain the eventuality that it be taken as both obedience and mockery. *Parody, paradox,* and *parricide* have, then, a complex relationship that requires more attention, but I want first to suggest that parody has not just the same structural conflict as paradox, but that as *para-oide,* the setting side by side of *odes* or songs, parody has a peculiarly vested interest in the mutilation of *doxa:* it strives for music, a discourse in Melville's scheme properly no discourse at all, one in which referents have been excised, "castrated," or feminized. Since *Pierre,* as several readers have noticed,[39] is an attack on the feminine reading public of Melville's day, an attack that parodies that sentiment throughout the course of its narration and reaches a peak in the review of young Pierre's preposterous career as a sentimental author, the feminization of *Pierre* (and Pierre) is of crucial importance to the question of its status as parody.

Articulation at its greatest power, then, is mute, empty of reference; it resides in the silent space of Nature and the Mother. We might be tempted to trace Melville's fascination with maternal muteness back to Maria Melville's forcing her children to sit silently about her bed while she napped; but whatever the "source" of Melville's concern, it is clear that he takes the issue seriously, and moreover, that he, like Thoreau in particular, takes it to be peculiarly American. One thinks of Melville's poem "America," which we might well situate in a diptych as the feminine counterpart to the traumatic scene in *Benito Cereno* (1856) in which Babo flourishes his razor about the throat of Don Benito, his shaving apron the flag of Spain.[40] In "America," where the "speechless" Mother represents the American spirit aghast at the destruction of civil war, it is the American flag that has become a "shining shroud":

> She sleeps, but sleeps, she is not dead.
>   But in that sleep contortion showed
> The terror of the vision there—
>   A silent vision unavowed,
> Revealing earth's foundation bare,
>   And Gorgon in her hidden place.
> It was a thing of fear to see
>   So foul a dream upon so fair a face,
> And the dreamer lying in that starry shroud.[41]

Battle Pieces would come fifteen years after *Pierre,* though; for a more immediate analogue to the strange version of authority offered in the novel, we should recall one of the "Fragments from a Writing Desk" that appeared in 1839.[42]

The first-person narrator of the story receives from one "Inamorata" an "elegant little, rose-coloured, lavender-scented billet-doux," inviting him to follow her messenger, who will lead him to her. A tantalizing catch-me-if-you-can game ensues, the narrator following his guide into a mysterious sylvan sanctuary where his mind becomes "haunted with ghostly images" and "the fictions of the nursery [pour] in upon [his] recollections." He is led at length into an edifice of Arcadian decadence, in which "mirrors of unreal magnitude, multiplying in all directions the gorgeous objects, deceived the eye by their reflections." The beautiful "inmate" of the boudoir, dressed in white and roses, reveals the "prettiest little foot you can imagine; cased in a satin slipper, which clung to the fairy like member by means of a diamond clasp," and the narrator falls entranced "at the feet of [his] fair enchantress." Gaining no response when he kisses her hand, he "imprint[s] one long, long kiss upon her hot and glowing lips" and cries, "Speak! Tell me, thou cruel!...Am I loved,—even wildly, madly as I love?" His seductress remains silent, and the horrible truth at last comes home to him: "I flung her from me, even though she clung to my vesture, and with a wild cry of agony I burst from the apartment!—She was dumb! Great God, she was dumb! DUMB AND DEAF!" The story is no master-piece and would be relatively inconsequential did it not prefigure *Pierre,* where the figure of the immensely seductive but finally terrifying mute woman, the enchantress without a voice who draws in and dismembers her lover at the same time, is transfigured into the only voice of God. Her muteness becomes the immobilizing inarticulacy buried in the frozen loins of Truth, the same voice that the author Pierre, utterly mad, presumably discovers once his "soul had been accosted by the Wonderful Mutes, and through the vast halls of Silent Truth, had been ushered into the full, secret, eternally inviolable Sanhedrim, where the Poetic Magi discuss, in glorious gibberish, the Alpha and Omega of the Universe" (*P,* 244–45).

Reading, writing, and speaking—all modes of articulation—appear continually in *Pierre* as activities that lead indifferently to the truth of mad-ness or the madness of truth. Pierre's great difficulties involve his willingness to believe what he reads, whether Hamlet and Dante, Isabel's letter, Plin-limmon's pamphlet, the philosophical gibberish of the Apostles, or his own plagiarized writings. Yet only by reading will he uncover the truth buried in the palimpsest of his brain. In the scene in which Pierre recalls the words of his dying father, a scene that fosters his willingness to believe in Isabel and insures his *paradoxical* career, Melville is curiously ambivalent about reading and writing. The narrator first berates Pierre for thinking that "the receipt of one little bit of paper scratched over with a few small characters by a sharpened feather" can topple that "strongest tower of delight," his father's sacred memory. Such a note, the narrator entreats, is easily written; indeed, "the brisk novelist, Pierre, will write thee fifty such notes, and so steal gushing tears from his reader's eyes." Yet only half a page later, the narrator provides the very model for Pierre's psychological delvings, one Freud might well have read with enthusiasm:

> Ah, fathers and mothers! all the world round, be heedful—give heed! Thy little one may not now comprehend the meaning of those words and signs, by which, in its innocent presence, thou thinkest to disguise the sinister thing ye would hint. Not now he knows; not very much even of the externals he consciously remarks; but if, in after-life, Fate puts the chemic key of the cipher into his hands; then how swiftly and how wonderfully, he reads all the obscurest and most obliterate inscriptions he finds in his memory; yea, and rummages himself all over, for still hidden writings to read. Oh, darkest lessons of Life have thus been read; all faith in Virtue been murdered, and youth gives itself up to an infidel scorn. (*P*, 69–70)

It is uncertain here, as indeed it is everywhere in Pierre's tortuous career, whether what is taken for the truth actually belongs to the text of memory or is inserted there by the "reader," the remembering adult. It is a problem Freud could not resolve, and it is one that leaves Pierre's resolution forever uncertain and in the end drives him to madness and suicide.

When Pierre as actor and Pierre as author have become virtually indistinguishable he sees at last "that all the great books in the world are but the mutilated shadowings-forth of invisible and eternally unembodied images in the soul; so that they are but the mirrors, distortedly reflecting to us our own things; and never mind what the mirror may be, if we would see the object, we must look at the object itself, and not at its reflection" (*P*, 284). Language, then, cannot embody the object, but can only mutilate it, a lesson Hawthorne's mirrors would have taught Melville; yet what is precisely at stake in *Pierre* is whether the sexual crisis has not dissolved belief in the *object* altogether, whether authority has not taken sanction in a labyrinth of words to be read, displacing the *object* of the Father, his Word. Only two paragraphs later we are met with the passage in which Melville adds that Pierre's "reading" of himself, were it to work through the abysmal strata of "superinduced superficies," would find only an empty sarcophagus containing "no body." Looking for the object itself, in one's self, yields no better results than reading; the two are, in fact, hardly unlike, for as Pierre knew early on (but apparently has forgotten), "the profounder emanations of the human mind...never unravel their own intricacies, and have no proper endings; but in imperfect, unanticipated, and disappointing sequels (as mutilated stumps), hurry to abrupt intermergings with the eternal tides of time and fate" (*P*, 141). More clearly than Ahab's, Pierre's tale is a "stump speech," one which, "ruefully contemplating [its] own amputation" (*MD*, 232), contrives—indeed, conspires in—its own sacrificial dismemberment. The statue "planted on a revolving pedestal, show[ing] now this limb, now that; now front, now back, now side," that Melville introduces as a figure of the "canting showman" of his art (*P,* 337), might on closer inspection appear more like the limbless Enceladus, flailing helplessly in the throes of a grotesque *parody.*

Parody in *Pierre,* partaking of the *ode* of the feminine in the paradoxical resolve of the incestuous rescue fantasy, takes Freud's admonition that "the distortion of a text resembles a murder"[43] to a ludicrous extreme. That dismemberment, even if it is accompanied by an ambivalence that places commemoration alongside slaughter in the account of desire, may be carried out either by reading or by writing. In Pierre's case, the reading of Isabel's letter destroys the sacred text that appears as the memory of his father. Ironically enough, the "sweetly-writ manuscript" of his life, whose only flaw is the omission of a sister "from the text," is terribly disfigured by the correction of this detail. Yet as we have suggested, *Pierre* is precisely concerned with replacing paternal authority with one maternal, with substituting for the phallus of the Word that absence denoted by Silence—the only "voice" of God harbored behind the "mutilated stumps" of discourse. In *Pierre,* then, reading and writing are conjunctively Oedipal: they seek to, or cannot help but, do away with the question of the Father in order to reach the truth possessed by the Mother. But since Melville can only carry out his project in a form he wants to discredit—one that offers but "the mutilated shadowings-forth of invisible and eternally unembodied images in the soul"—he must remain in the same paradoxical predicament as Thoreau, forever on the frontier of Nature's deepest recess trying to write himself in by a self-defeating process. The suspicion arises, then, that the fantastic alliance that Pierre enters into first with his mother and then with Isabel is one central to the incest of fiction itself and more particularly to the incest of *parody* and our determination of it as *readers.* With this in mind, let us read a short tale which Melville wrote in 1855, several years after the enormous and nearly unqualified public failure of *Pierre.*

"The Tartarus of Maids"[44] is one of the great documents on the social and psychological implications of the industrialization of the American Eden. But besides delineating the "deflowering of New England," as Marvin Fisher has contended,[45] the story has much to say about Melville's own fantasies about his writing. In one of the chapters of *Pierre* parodically recounting Pierre's early career as a writer of sentimental tripe, we are told that speculators once came to Saddle Meadows "to survey its water-power, if any, with a view to start a paper-mill expressly for the great author, and so monopolize his stationery dealings" (*P,* 264). In *Pierre,* the remark takes its place among the extensive Carlylian burlesque that compares Pierre's writings to fashionable clothes run through the mill and the tailor's shop in preparation for the public; but with "The Tartarus of Maids" in the background, the paper-mill may invoke a more startling configuration. The narrator of "Tartarus," a seedman whose "demand for paper" has become great with the growth of his trade, visits a New England mill in order to purchase envelopes. What he finds is an industrial hell where the factory maids have become automata at the mercy of a grim machinery, whose "glittering scythes" and "erected sword[s]" symbolize the deflowering and destruction of young American womanhood. Though the narrator goes to buy seed envelopes—which when "folded square," filled, and stamped "assume not a little the appearance of business-letters ready for the mail"—he actually observes production of a "rose-hued note-paper" not unlike the billet-doux that the narrator of the "Fragment" receives from his dumb Inamorata. "At rows of blank-looking counters sat rows of blank-looking girls, with blank, white folders in their blank hands, all blankly folding blank paper"; the conenction between the blank paper and the pale faces and bodies of the girls is repeated several times, turning the mill into a grotesque altar to the sacrifice of virginity. As the narrator's ironically-named guide "Cupid" remarks, "The Devil's Dungeon is no place for flowers." Several other points recall, moreover, the function of the feminine as we have seen it in Pierre: the narrator's journey begins with an explicitly sexual entrance into the mill's ravine through a "sudden contraction of the gorge" known as "the Black Notch"; amid the snowy, frigid landscape, whose "whole hollow gleamed with the white," stands the "whited sepulchre" of the mill, filled with white maids cutting and folding white paper; the girls "mutely" serve the manic machines, "the human voice [being] banished from the spot"; and the awful blankness of the place and its workers finally leads the narrator to recall "John Locke, who, in demonstration of his theory that man had no innate ideas, compared the human mind at birth to a sheet of blank paper."

One must agree with Richard Chase that the seedman "performs [an] allegorical intercourse upon a frozen world body" and that the paper-mill of Tartarus is a horrifying kind of Gorgon,[46] a figure that stands at once for the crude industrial disfiguring of New England's landscape and women, and for the narrator's (call him Melville) own implication in the sacrifice. Pierre's delving into paternal authority leads only to an empty sarcophagus, a perfect figuration for the *tabula rasa* of Locke, which the narrator of the "Tartarus" finds at the heart of the paper-mill. Since for Pierre the activity of writing ends with "mutilated sequels," and since his own reading is constantly presented as a simultaneously erotic and terrifying search for a sexual secret, we are tempted to link the gruesome machinery of the "Tartarus," which deflowers its maids, with the very act of writing, which makes the paper-mill necessary in the first place. A crude irony opens up between the young author Pierre's need for a paper-mill and the fact that he writes absurd love sonnets for an avid feminine audience, and the irony is only more startling in that the Truth Pierre seeks in his mature career is presented as one specifically maternal. Pierre's attempt to reach that vacancy in the cold loins of Truth contains and complicates the grim white tableaus of "Tartarus"; the Truth appears as the blank white page which the paternity of authorship covers up and disfigures: reading unsuccessfully seeks out that frigid Truth, and writing only further obliterates it. The link between the seedman and the author, moreover, is hardly incidental: the writer fills the envelope of his book with his *seeds,* inseminates the blank page of the Mother, the body of Nature, while overthrowing the authority of the Father figured in previous writing. As Thoreau and Whitman discovered, and as Melville certainly had noticed in *Moby-Dick,* an author's *production* has its own genealogy and its own commerce. But for a writer whose sense of retribution is as strong as Melville's, the punishment for such an Oedipal act could not go unserved: his efforts must have commerce with a Truth which is represented at once as an enticing virgin and as a frightening Gorgon, a Truth that is, as Melville would put it in *The Confidence Man,* "a thrashing-machine,"[47] the metaphysical equivalent of the paper-mill of "Tartarus."

IV

The elision of Pierre's identity, announced from the beginning and doubled in Melville's own apparent "identification" with Pierre, is determinant for *Pierre*'s constant threat of disintegration. Pierre, we are told, has in his relationship with his mother "habituated his voice and manner to a certain fictitiousness in one of the closest domestic relations of life" (*P,* 177); that act has prepared him to become eternally entangled "in a fictitious alliance" with Isabel, and "the same powerful motive which induced the thought of forming such an alliance, would always thereafter forbid [the] tacit exposure of its fictitiousness" (*P,* 175). The question of Melville's attitude toward his own "fiction" in *Pierre* is not to be divorced from the issue of incestuous alliances in the book. The fiction of an autobiographical (if fantastically so) story supports and complicates the fictional incest that Pierre (and Melville through him) engages in. The doubled fictionalization is, moreover, at the heart of the parodic in *Pierre;* what Hartman's analogy between Oedipus's career and the play's convergence on its recognition scene points up about *Pierre,* is that exactly because Pierre's recognition is already achieved and consciously subsumed in his intention—he is so "eager

to involve himself in such an inextricable twist of Fate, that the three dex-
trous maids themselves could hardly disentangle him, if once he tie the com-
plicating knots about him and Isabel" (*P,* 175)—he and his parody have virtually no place to go. There is, in one sense, no Moby Dick to keep chasing
(though in another sense that is precisely what Pierre is up to), no secret to
be unraveled: the result is an excessive, anguished parody, at once Melville's
striptease of gift-book sentimentality and a mockery of his own authorial
desires.

This is not to say *Pierre* is not serious, which it certainly is; but neither is
it to say without qualification that the book is a success, which it just barely
is. The difficulty with assessing parody is that, since one of its objects is to
mock the norms by which literature is judged, judgments about it are often
swallowed up by the book's own devices, precluding criticism out of hand.
Richard Poirier points out that in self-parodic works the plot does not issue
"from the interplay and pressure of individual human actions" but seems to
exist "prior to the book."[48] One might object to applying this definition to
Pierre; certainly Pierre acts and interacts under pressures from the other
characters, and his decisions carry the story along in a vague sort of way. But
as the comparison to Oedipus suggests, the plot *is* prior to the book, not just
in Melville's mind (as any plot might thus be said to be prior) but also in
Pierre's: once he longs for an omitted sister and romanticizes his father as explicitly as he does, the rest of the book seems almost foolishly inevitable.
The plot is an excuse for Melville's philosophizing, a convenience which is
not really awkward but does little aside from keeping the characters on
stage. One feels, oddly enough, that the plot of *Pierre* both could have been
no other way and could have been any way at all; it is both unimportant and
inevitable, the perfect vehicle of parody. Melville would seem to have admitted as much when he turns, fairly late in the book, to Pierre as author,
writing a book presumably very much like *Pierre.* The book Melville writes
seems designed to incorporate the book Pierre writes, and it is safe to say
that without this device *Pierre* would barely work at all. By turning his hero
into the author of the book he acts in, Melville effectively hollows out the
question of authority that so haunts the book. His own status as author is fic-
tionalized and mocked, and the plot becomes, to follow Poirier a step further, "a self-generating, even possibly self-generated formula of myths and
conspiracies whose source is as mysterious as the source of life itself."[49] The
source of life in this case is the source of Pierre's actions, that is, the motivation for an act that can have no conceivable outcome but disaster for all involved. Pierre's "rescue" of Isabel is not wrong; rather, it has no clear goal
and is founded not on a certain regard for the truth but on another apparent
fiction. The whole movement of the plot only guarantees that Pierre's self-

fathering will only entangle him further and further in its Medusan coils. Once the sacred representation of Pierre's father has been reduced to a "snake's nest" (*P*, 196), the book and its mechanical characters, like "the temple-polluting Laocoon and his two innocent children, caught in inextricable snarls of snakes" (*P*, 184–85), can only merge and strangle in a "noose of equivalents,"[50] where sister has become mother, son has become father, and fiction and reality have become as inextricable and abominably entwined as Pierre and Isabel at the moment of their fateful resolve: "they coiled together, and entangledly stood mute" (*P*, 192).

It is at this point of mute crisis that *Pierre*'s action is, for all practical purposes, complete. The remainder of the book seeks only to maintain the fiction of their relationship from destruction, whether at the hands of Plinlimmon, Lucy, Glen Stanley, or Pierre himself. The usurpation of the father's place in the very name of saving the father leaves Pierre the scapegoat of his own ritual; at the extremity of the "Cretan labyrinths" to which his "life's cord" leads him, Pierre's self-generation can only pass beyond the pleasure principle to suicide. "Men are what their mothers made them," Emerson writes in "Fate" (1860). "When each comes forth from the mother's womb, the gate of gifts closes behind him...he has but one future, and that is already predetermined in his lobes, and described in that little fatty face, pig-eye, and squat form."[51] Neither Pierre nor Oedipus presents such a ludicrous figure, though their encounters with fate are as surely contrived at the gate of gifts. The fictive illusion that Oedipus must discover, however, appears as an initiating function for Pierre, and with its etiology exposed at the outset, his story collapses into itself with sure fatality. Emerson adds, in the same essay, that "man is the arch machine," who "helps himself on each emergency by copying or duplicating his own structure" to such an extent that it is nearly impossible to find "the indisputable inventor. There are scores and centuries of them. 'The air is full of men.'"[52] For Pierre, the air is full of names, and the emergent flaw in his paternity has thrust him into a melodramatic duplication whose fatality is registered in the elision of identity not only between Pierre and his father but also between Melville and Pierre. The crisis of authority that envelops Pierre is reflected in the story's own mimicry of itself and Melville's of himself: the tale of Pierre, like Pierre himself, is redundant, turning back on itself and becoming its own sire in a deliberate and wild replication. Though "the dread of tautology" is a "continual torment of some earnest minds," Melville remarks at one point, "not to dread tautology at times only belongs to those enviable dunces, whom the partial God hath blessed, over all the earth, with the inexhaustible self-riches of vanity, and folly, and a blind self-complacency" (*P*, 227). Clearly enough, Melville's own dread of tautology is severe; it operates at an enervating pitch throughout *Pierre* to render the story at once its own sire and its own murderer, and at the limit of irony, tautology and parody are indistinguishable, as are suicide and parricide: they are one another's doubles.

The doubling in *Pierre* is dizzying indeed. Pierre is of "double revolutionary descent" (*P*, 20), as was Melville; his resolve to take up with Isabel leaves him "doubly an orphan" (*P*, 90) and "twice-disinherited" (*P*, 199); and as the Enceladus dream reminds him, he has been "doubly incestuous." Moreover, nearly everything in the book proceeds by pairs of opposites: Lucy and Isabel; the two portraits of Pierre's father and the two hands of the dying man; the "two antagonistic agencies" struggling for "mastery" of Pierre's consciousness (*P*, 63); America as Canaan or Circassia (*P*, 33); Plinlimmon's chronometrics or horologicals (*P*, 210–15); Pierre and his double cousin, Glen (*P*, 289); the two books Pierre writes, one of ink, one of blood (*P*, 304); the portraits of the Cenci and the Stranger, which bring Pierre face to face with the problems of incest and parricide (*P*, 351); the "double-doom" of Pierre's own "hereditary liability to madness" (*P*, 287); and so on and so on, all pairs issuing in paradox, contradiction, or ambiguity. In such a welter of doublings, often frustratingly mechanical, it is easy to lose heart, if not interest. Perhaps the most notable instance, though, occurs when Pierre, having learned the truth about his father and become aware of the "reciprocal identification" between his father's portrait and Isabel's face, "ejaculate[s] that wonderful verse from Dante"— "See! thou art not double now,/Nor only one!" (*P*, 85). What is striking is that the exclamation can refer to Pierre and Isabel, to his father and Isabel, or to him and his father, for all have merged in fantastic entanglement, neither single selves nor quite yet identical. Yet the doubling and tautology that infect the book throughout are integral to Pierre's rescue of his father and Isabel, and what is more, to Melville's attack on his own profession. By 1856, Melville's struggle with the genealogy of imitation would peak in the character of Bartleby, who, "as if long famishing for something to copy," seems "to gorge himself on [the] documents" of his employer, and with "no pause for digestion," writes away "silently, palely, mechanically."[53] Pierre stops barely short of such catatonia, but his imitation of Hamlet and Oedipus is equally ridden with the anxiety of past authorship. As in the case of Cooper, where Judge Cooper and Shakespeare at times approach totemic equivalence, Pierre's replication of his actual father and his literary fathers registers the ambivalent strain of that paternity. But Melville's hero makes more explicit the irony of the totem meal—and it is a *meal*, as the example of Bartleby indicates—for in *Pierre* rescue and parody, reverence and sacrifice, are entwined. It belongs to the function of parody that the object of imitation is an ancestor, whether actual or textual, who is both a figure of celebrated power and the butt of a burlesque. At extremity, the two are merged, neither identical nor yet separable, no more or less so than son and father in an incest fantasy.

But *Pierre* only properly becomes parody in retrospect. Continually we try to take Pierre's actions seriously, to believe that something may come of them besides madness itself. Only after Pierre is introduced as an author who has written a book suspiciously like the one we have been reading are we sure that the irony will never stop, *can* never stop. The ironic strain that has built throughout the novel and which is the most obvious yet transparent kind of doubling possible, suddenly swallows up the character of the author. I hinted before that the relationship between "Melville" and "Pierre" is intricate. Though there is almost always a tone of sentimental irony present, the voice of the narrator varies seemingly at random. At times there is narration about Pierre; at times narration about his thoughts; at times interior narration of his thoughts, though unquoted; at times quotation of these thoughts; and at times just the voice of Pierre speaking or of the narrator expostulating. The shiftings between these voices, sometimes clever, sometimes clumsy, on the one hand make the identification between the author Pierre and the author Melville more negotiable; yet on the other, the narrator discounts omniscience, and there is thus a rift between the two voices—though one that is, of course, ironic. Paul de Man has remarked that the moment that the difference between the persona of the author and the persona of his fictional narrator is asserted, is the moment the author asserts "the ironic necessity of not becoming the dupe of his own irony and discovers that there is no way back from his fictional self to his actual self."[54] This difference is implicit from the outset of *Pierre,* though, and it is exactly because we never believe that Melville is speaking that the sudden inversion—whereby the author is made the subject of the narrator's inspection and quotations from his work are offered that could have come from any page of the book—both collapses the distance and reopens it on the other side of irony, which is the true domain of parody. Melville's struggle to maintain the ironic voice of his narrator, who has been flagellating his author all along, can only blow up in his face; the inversion only makes clear that the actual self has been the travestied hero of the book all along, that there has at no time been any intention of returning to an "actual self" since there has never been one to start with. Early on the curious narrator remarks that Pierre has "spent long summer afternoons in the deep recesses of his father's fastidiously picked and decorous library; where the Spenserian nymphs had early led him into many a maze of all-bewildering beauty" (*P,* 6). By the time he sits down to read the flawed text of his memory, the beautiful maze of the library and the "Cretan labyrinth" of his infancy have merged, and when Pierre at last sits down to pen the "blasphemous rhapsody" that we read (*P,* 356), the book of the self and the self of the book have, like father and son, become entangled nearly to the point of mutual exclusion.

If irony is the vertiginous "consciousness of madness," as de Man notes, "a reflection on madness from the inside of madness itself" that "asserts and maintains its fictional character by stating the continued impossibility of reconciling the world of fiction with the actual world,"[55] we will have to mark *Pierre*'s irony as an advance in reflection, a parodic madness that reflects on its own reflection and does not so much impossibly distance the fictional from the actual as erase the actual altogether, making the author himself a character in an apparently self-generating fiction. The narrator's voice attacks Pierre to the point that its only avenue of escape is no escape at all but a willing disfiguration of itself, a submission to its own figurations and a gasped admission that Pierre, like one of Beckett's involuted narrators, might well have generated that voice himself. Pierre's elision of identity—his incestuous desire to become his own sire—is doubled in the novel's narrative strategy, which ultimately forces the character under scrutiny to usurp the place of the author and father his own fictional self. *Parody* is a form of *parricide* to the extent that it places the son beside, and even allows him to displace, the father; but when that parody turns back upon itself, mixing father and son, author and character, in hallucinatory reflection, murder cannot be told from suicide: tautology is complete, and the text has taken its own life. Written from such a position as that from which Pierre writes—"solitary as at the Pole" (*P,* 338)—Melville's book is the redundant replica of Pierre's, who finally sees "the everlasting elusiveness of Truth; the universal lurking insincerity of even the greatest and purest written thoughts. Like knavish cards, the leaves of all great books were covertly packed. He was but packing one set the more; and that a very poor jaded set and pack indeed" (*P,* 339).

Incipient confidence man that he was, Melville remarked while at work on *Pierre,* "I am keeping one eye shut and wink at the paper with the other."[56] It is the remark of an ironist, no doubt, an author dealing a deck at once stacked and empty, but one mimicked by his own hero, who "blindly [writes] with his eyes turned away from the paper;—thus unconsciously symbolizing the hostile necessity and distaste, the former whereof made of him this most unwilling states-prisoner of letters" (*P,* 340). At the extremity of his labors, Pierre's eyes finally "turn downright traitors to him" and "absolutely refused to look on paper. He turned them on paper, and they blinked and shut. The pupils of his eyes rolled away from him in their own

orbits'' (*P*, 341). That the ocular disturbance which Pierre suffers is so similar to that of young Nathanael in Hoffmann's ''The Sand-Man,'' whose
anguish Samuel Weber has read as the ''crisis of perception'' induced by the
threat of castration, may not be merely an uncanny coincidence.[57] For Hawthorne the crisis gets mythologically entwined with the crises of original sin
and parricide, with the sacrifice of mimesis that his craft enacts: in the world
of romance, a world of transgression in which speculation skews the relation
between object and name, reality and image, *mimesis* is utterly fantastic and
uncanny, a narcissistic Eden lost in memory or a Swiftian utopia to be
gained. Such mimesis is, of course, ironic, indeed, nearly parodic. But then
the crisis of perception is itself ironic, at once invoking an object of reference
(a Moby Dick) and taking it away in the same act. ''Castration'' offers a
paradox, one that is the obverse reflection of the totemic *parricide;* the
writing of the philosophical *parodist* partakes of both, for his assault on
authority will hazard the eventuality that the discourse that is mimicked will
increase in power, while his own text will only stray into blind alleys and,
turning upon itself, willingly enact its own disfiguration. The writer in such
a crisis might well avert his eyes from the page or lose sight altogether, for it
belongs to his craft that the only truth resides in the Silence of the blank
page, while each stroke of his pen paradoxically augments the shaft of the
Father at the same time it encroaches upon the madness of suicide.

The only ''object [that] is in a constant relationship with pleasure'' for
the writer, says Roland Barthes, ''is not the language, it is the *mother
tongue.* The writer is someone who plays with his mother's body. . . in order
to glorify it, to embellish it, or in order to dismember it, to take it to the
limit of what can be known about the body. . .''[58] Barthes seeks to
distinguish the oral (maternal) from the written (paternal), granting the
voice the same kind of anteriority as Thoreau, for whom the writer's *stylus*
performs a masculine cultivation of the home of Nature and the Mother, in-
scribing her with the figures of production and disfiguring her landscape in
the same act of *grafting*. Thoreau plays with the mother tongue, but he
plays even more deliberately with the figure of Silence, the true body of the
feminine and, as for Melville, the feminine body of Truth. Without pressing
the distinction between oral and written too far, can we not yet say that
Pierre is a text about playing with the body of the Mother? An erotic and
mysterious music, finally giving way to Silence, is substituted in place of the
Word of the Father: the object of reference that belongs, however tentatively, to discourse is excised, leaving vacancy in its stead. This is the parricidal point of *Pierre*'s parody—to play at last with a body where the object
has disappeared into a ''Descartian vortex,'' where discourse, taken to its
ironic and paradoxical extreme, is made to collapse into itself, but which as

long as it lasts skitters on the border of pure figure—what cannot but must be *read*. Parody hides the object, reveals it as a fantasy, and finally destroys it. As a "Pierrody" and "Pierricide" of itself, *Pierre* tells us how to read it—as the body of the Mother; as a membrane, but nothing else; as a tissue which conceals only further ambiguous tissue, revealing for the reader as for Pierre only "a black, bottomless gulf of guilt, upon whose verge he imminently teeter[s] every hour" (*P,* 337). The book doubles Pierre's own lesson, opening a Descartian vortex of reading where the body has been removed from the sarcophagus of the text; or rather, where the text *is* the sarcophagus of the body, an opening into which the reader, if he be an "admiring reader" of *Pierre,* will enter at the risk of his own ironic disfiguration.

"The best ode may be parodied, indeed is itself a parody," writes Thoreau in the *Week,* only a few pages before his reenactment of the Hannah Dustan captivity. What that ritual plays out, as we noted earlier, is the hazard broached by the writer who would transgress the frontier of Nature and look upon the pure figure of Silence, the hazard run by one who, in tracing "the interval from Eve to my own mother," at last experiences "that old threat of his mother fulfilled, that he shall be skinned alive," and consequently for whom "the talent of composition is very dangerous,—the striking out the heart of life at a blow, as the Indian takes off a scalp."[59] Melville's parody also runs in the face of the Medusa, and like Thoreau's androgynous craft, its feminization of truth turns violently back upon itself, mounting paradox upon paradox, dismembering or scalping its own discourse in the act, until Pierre's pen becomes "the beak of a vulture in his hand" and the escalating madness of his writing presses upon him to the point where he would fain "behead himself, to gain one night's repose" (*P,* 305). More clearly even than Hawthorne, who published his story of the artist Holgrave, his authorial double, in part as a means of throwing off the haunting tales that possessed him, Melville may have conjured up Pierre, *his* authorial double, as a means of turning the book before him into the "receptacle for his own rubbish" (*P,* 258) and mocking himself in public decapitation. Just as Pierre replicates his father, the progenitor of a bastard daughter, he also in the end replicates Melville, the progenitor of a bastard book. This seems to be what Murray had in mind when he remarked that "*Pierre* is a literary monster, a prodigious by-blow of genius,"[60] for Melville's renunciation of the "home of his fathers" (*P,* 3) and embracing of the home of the Mother had to proceed by way of a parodic fantasy in which his own double would both rescue and slaughter him, a fantasy in which his self and his book have so tautologically merged that, like Poe's William Wilson, he becomes witness to his own suicide in the mirror of his book. Plagiarizing from his own experiences to such ludicrous extremity, Melville is indeed "at home in his words and completely mastered by them."

No more than Pierre can place himself in the father's stead without becoming his own victim, can Melville completely escape self-sacrifice through the scapegoat of his author-hero. Certainly the device makes *Pierre* work, and impressively, but the extremity of Melville's mockery may only help us to see more clearly how close Cooper, Thoreau, and Hawthorne had come to the limits of parodic sacrifice, where the platform of derision and the scaffold of public scrutiny are so nearly the same. Their willingness to assume an important role in the authorial spectacles they undertook is a measure of serious commitment even as it is a sign of the fact that rebellious and experimental power must always be qualified by tribute to the vanquished. Like his character Redburn, who after concluding in his attempt to trace his father's route through Liverpool that just "as [his] father's guide-book is no guide for [him], neither would [his]...be a true guide to those who come after [him]," Melville might finally have agreed that "nearly all literature, in one sense, is made of guide-books," that indeed, "every age makes its own guide-books, and the old ones are used for waste paper."[61] A writer who took such a belief fully to heart, however, would not write at all; if he takes it as an index of the ironic position in which the craft of authorship places him, he will be alive, as Melville and his contemporaries were, to the precarious and powerful nature of the authority that was open to them in nineteenth-century America. For even while they found the success of their experiments hedged by the lure of sacrament, they were able and willing to risk themselves, and put their own authority at stake, in the interests of the commemoration that would be achieved. If family romance became romance with a vengeance, it became as well the requisite memorial from which their own acts of authorship took their best and most lasting power.

Notes

Preface

1. *The Complete Works of Ralph Waldo Emerson* (Boston: Houghton, Mifflin, 1903), 4: 254.
2. *A Future for Astyanax: Character and Desire in Literature* (Boston: Little, Brown, 1976), p. 10.
3. *Totem and Taboo, The Standard Edition of the Complete Psychological Works of Sigmund Freud,* trans. and ed. James Strachey et al. (London: Hogarth, 1953), 13: 140–50.
4. *Beginnings: Intention and Method* (New York: Basic Books, 1975; rpt. Baltimore: Johns Hopkins University Press, 1978), p. 83.
5. *The Writings of Henry David Thoreau* (1906; rpt. New York: AMS Press, 1968), 1: 368.
6. *Writings,* 7: 61.
7. The first to document the importance of the concept of the "virgin land" was, of course, Henry Nash Smith, in *Virgin Land: The American West as Symbol and Myth* (Cambridge, Mass.: Harvard University Press, 1960). A recent and impressive addition to Smith's work is Annette Kolodny, *The Lay of the Land: Metaphor as Experience and History in American Life and Letters* (Chapel Hill: University of North Carolina Press, 1975).
8. *Works,* 5: 273.
9. *Fathers and Children: Andrew Jackson and the Subjugation of the American Indian* (New York: Vintage-Random, 1976), p. 49.
10. Ibid., p. 70.
11. *The Complete Poems of Emily Dickinson,* ed. Thomas H. Johnson (Boston: Little, Brown, 1960), p. 677.
12. "The Uncanny," *Standard Edition,* 17: 249.
13. Ibid., p. 245.
14. Quoted in Hugh Kenner, *Gnomon: Essays on Contemporary Literature* (New York: Astor-Honor, 1958), p. 125.
15. *A World Elsewhere: The Place of Style in American Literature* (New York: Oxford University Press, 1966), p. 9.
16. *The Letters of Herman Melville,* ed. Merrell R. Davis and William H. Gilman (New Haven: Yale University Press, 1960), p. 78.
17. *The Scarlet Letter, The Centenary Edition of the Works of Nathaniel Haw-*

thorne, ed. William Charvat et al. (Columbus: Ohio State University Press, 1962), 1: 9–10.

18. *Selected Shorter Writings of Mark Twain,* ed. Walter Blair (Boston: Houghton, Mifflin, 1962), p. 226.

19. *The Education of Henry Adams,* intro. D. W. Brogan (Boston: Houghton, Mifflin, 1961), pp. 229, 302.

Chapter One

1. *The American Adam: Innocence, Tragedy, and Tradition in the Nineteenth Century* (1955; rpt. Chicago: University of Chicago Press, 1971), p. 99.

2. Arvid Schulenberger, *Cooper's Theory of Fiction: His Prefaces and Their Relation to His Novels* (Lawrence: University of Kansas Press, 1955), p. 50.

3. "Cooper, Leatherstocking, and the Death of the American Adam," *American Quarterly* 16 (1964): 419–31. Noble's argument could only be strengthened by further consideration of *Home as Found,* in which Natty has nearly been turned into a mythical god. In this respect *Home as Found* is a much more significant sequel to *The Pioneers* than to *Homeward Bound* (in which Cooper got so sidetracked by his sea adventures that he had to resort to an additional volume to tell the story of the Effinghams at home in America), and one might well consider it an integral part of the Leatherstocking series.

4. *James Fenimore Cooper* (New York: William Sloane, 1949), p. 116.

5. *Studies in Classic American Literature* (1923; rpt. New York: Viking Press, 1964), p. 41.

6. "A long absence from home, has, in a certain degree," Cooper wrote in *The American Democrat* (New York: Knopf, 1931), published in 1838, the same year as *Home as Found,* "put the writer in the situation of a foreigner in his own country; a situation probably much better for noting peculiarities, than that of one who never left it" (p. viii). As a handbook on American social and political institutions, *The American Democrat* should be read alongside *Home as Found.* Though the latter has usually been considered a crabbed personal document and seldom treated seriously as literature, there have been several discussions of it as an autobiographical document and social satire. The most useful and generous are John P. McWilliams, Jr., *Political Justice in a Republic: James Fenimore Cooper's America* (Berkeley and Los Angeles: University of California Press, 1972), pp. 216–35; Marvin Meyers, *The Jacksonian Persuasion* (1957; rpt. New York: Vintage-Random, 1960), pp. 74–97; Stephen Railton, *Fenimore Cooper: A Study of His Life and Imagination* (Princeton: Princeton University Press, 1978), pp. 183–93; and Lewis Leary's introduction to the edition of *Home as Found* cited below in note 7. Cooper also published *The Chronicles of Cooperstown* (Cooperstown, N.Y.: H. & E. Phinney, 1838) in the same year as the novel, and though it alludes in a general way to some of the personal controversies behind *Home as Found,* the facts and names are not specified.

7. All parenthetical page references are to *Home as Found,* intro. Lewis Leary (New York: Capricorn Books, 1961).

8. *The Letters and Journals of James Fenimore Cooper,* ed. James Franklin Beard (Cambridge, Mass.: Harvard University Press, 1968), 3: 278–79. Letter for the *Freeman's Journal* (16 August 1837).

9. Ibid., 4: 271. Letter for the *Brother Jonathan* (4–8? April 1842).

10. *The American Scene,* intro. Leon Edel (Bloomington: Indiana University Press, 1968), p. 91.

11. Ibid., p. 54.

12. Ibid., p. 165.

13. *The American Democrat,* p. 164.

14. *The Jacksonian Persuasion,* p. 74.

15. *The American Democrat,* p. 54.

16. *The Eccentric Design: Form in the Classic American Novel* (New York: Columbia University Press, 1963), p. 87.

17. *The American Democrat,* p. 110.

18. *Democracy in America,* trans. Francis Bowen, rev. and ed. Phillips Bradley (1948; rpt. New York: Vintage-Random, n.d.), 2: 74.

19. *Political Justice in a Republic,* p. 201.

20. *An American Primer* (San Francisco: City Lights, 1970), pp. 31, 34.

21. *Names on the Land,* quoted in Daniel J. Boorstin, *The Americans: The National Experience* (New York: Vintage-Random, 1965), pp. 299–300.

22. *The American Democrat,* p. 175.

23. Ibid., pp. 112, 115.

24. One suspects by this point that the book's initial epigraph from *Much Ado About Nothing* (III, iv)—" 'Good morrow, coz.' / 'Good morrow, sweet Hero.' "—not only introduces the meeting between Eve and her cousin Grace Van Cortlandt but also sets the ironic stage for Eve's discovery of her true cousin-"hero," Paul.

25. *The Deerslayer,* intro. Quentin Anderson (New York: Collier Books, 1962), p. 62.

26. *Regeneration Through Violence: The Mythology of the American Frontier, 1600–1860* (Middletown, Conn.: Wesleyan University Press, 1973), p. 499. "Deerslayer" is not, of course, the end of Natty's name changes, even in that novel. He must yet slay a man and thus become "Hawkeye." Joel Porte, *The Romance in America: Studies in Cooper, Poe, Hawthorne, Melville and James* (Middletown, Conn.: Wesleyan University Press, 1969), remarks that, in contrast to Natty's Indian names, "ordinary paleface names, traditionally and conventionally handed down from one generation to the next have *no* meaning, no inherent logic that unites them with the thing named" (p. 35). While this is certainly true in the case of Natty, we want to recognize that the question was no simple one for Cooper, that the handing down of a paleface name—that of "Effingham," say, or "Cooper"—was also of tremendous importance.

27. "Introduction," *Home as Found,* p. xix.

28. Judge Cooper died in 1809 from pneumonia, which he apparently contracted after being struck on the head from behind by a political opponent, someone whom Cooper could no doubt easily associate years later with the demagoguery plaguing Cooperstown-Templeton and the town's ignorant response to Judge Cooper's will. See *Letters and Journals*, 1: 16*n*1.

29. Ed. Willard Farnham, *The Complete Works*, ed. Alfred Harbage (Baltimore: Penguin, 1969), p. 949.

30. *The American Democrat*, p. viii.

31. I draw in the following paragraphs on *Moses and Monotheism, Standard Edition*, 23: 80–83; and *Totem and Taboo, Standard Edition*, 13: 140–61. William Wasserstrom, in "Cooper, Freud, and the Origins of Culture," *The American Imago* 17 (1960): 423–37, reads *The Prairie* in light of Freud's theory of the primal horde's rebellion. While *The Prairie* brings Cooper closer to the kind of primitive group Freud discusses, the yoking of the taboo of incest and the notion of social contract is more forceful, even if from Cooper's standpoint paradoxical, in *Home as Found*.

32. *Three Essays on the Theory of Sexuality, Standard Edition*, 7: 225–27; *Totem and Taboo, Standard Edition*, 13: 33.

33. *The American Democrat*, p. 91.

34. *New York*, ed. Dixon Ryan Fox (New York: William Farquhar Payson, 1930), p. 29.

35. *Political Justice in a Republic*, p. 133.

36. *The Pioneers*, aftwd. Robert E. Spiller (New York: Signet-New American Library, 1964), p. 222.

37. *Letters and Journals*, 4: 76. Letter for the Philadelphia *Public Ledger* (27 September–10 October 1840?). Cooper's confusion about "son" or "grandson" apparently stems from his not having decided exactly what the Effingham genealogy was. Since Paul is the great-grandson of Colonel Edward Effingham of *The Pioneers* (396) and the present John and Edward are sons of brothers, the only explanation is that Oliver Effingham, who marries Elizabeth Temple in *The Pioneers* and from whom Edward and Eve are descended, has a brother who is never mentioned, from whom John and Paul are descended.

38. *Letters and Journals*, 4: 256. Letter for the *Brother Jonathan* (22–25? March 1842).

39. For the English tradition of the enclosed garden, see Stanley Stewart, *The Enclosed Garden: The Tradition and the Image in Seventeenth-Century Poetry* (Madison: University of Wisconsin Press, 1966); for the enclosed garden in the American Puritan tradition, see Peter N. Carroll, *Puritanism and the Wilderness: The Intellectual Significance of the New England Frontier, 1629–1700* (New York: Columbia University Press, 1969).

40. *Cooper's Landscapes: An Essay on the Picturesque Vision* (Berkeley and Los Angeles: University of California Press, 1976), pp. 99–100.

41. *The Lay of the Land*, pp. 97–98.

42. *Notions of the Americans, Picked Up By a Travelling Bachelor* (Philadelphia: Carey, Lea, and Carey, 1828), 1: 104–5.

43. *Cooper's Landscapes*, p. 61. It is also worth recalling that *Home as Found* was published in England under the title *Eve Effingham*.

44. *James Fenimore Cooper: The American Scott* (New York: Barnes and Noble, 1967), p. 157.

45. *Pierre; Or, the Ambiguities*, ed. Harrison Hayford, Hershel Parker, and G. Thomas Tanselle (Evanston: Northwestern University Press, 1971), p. 7. The parallel is of course not exact; it should be noted too that Cooper remained quite close to his surviving sister, Anne, as his letters indicate.

46. "The Romantic Dilemma in American Nationalism and the Concept of Nature," *Harvard Theological Review* 48 (1955): 247. For a discussion of Cooper's changing attitudes toward and uses of landscape in *Home as Found*, see Nevius, *Cooper's Landscapes*, pp. 107–11; and Donald A. Ringe, *The Pictorial Mode: Space and Time in the Art of Bryant, Irving, and Cooper* (Lexington: University Press of Kentucky, 1971), pp. 83–84, 195. See also Cooper's essay, "American and European Scenery Compared," in *The Home Book of the Picturesque: Or American Scenery, Art, and Literature*, ed. Motley F. Deakin (1852; rpt. Gainesville, Fl. Scholars Facsimiles and Reprints, 1967), pp. 51–69.

47. Samuel Eliot Morison, *The Oxford History of the American People* (New York: Mentor-New American Library, 1965), 2: 236.

48. *The Pioneers*, p. 60.

49. *The American Adam*, p. 101. The key to the Hamlet question of course occurs, as we have seen, almost literally *in* the margin.

50. Quoted in Robert E. Spiller, *Fenimore Cooper: Critic of His Times* (New York: Milton, Balch, and Co., 1931), p. 227.

51. *Beginnings*, p. 22.

52. *Representative Men, Works*, 4: 42.

53. *Poetry and Prose of Alexander Pope*, ed. Aubrey Williams (Boston: Houghton Mifflin Co., 1969), p. 122. For the "maze" of sin in *Paradise Lost* see, for example, 2: 561; 9: 161; and 10: 830.

54. *Walden, Writings*, 2: 177.

55. Ed. Charles T. Prouty, *The Complete Works*, p. 332.

56. Trans. Michael Joyce, *The Collected Dialogues of Plato*, ed. Edith Hamilton and Huntington Cairns (Princeton: Princeton University Press, 1961), pp. 542–44.

57. *Standard Edition*, 18: 57–58 and *passim*.

58. *An Apology for Poetry*, ed. Forrest G. Robinson (New York: Bobbs-Merrill, 1970), p. 18.

59. *Letters and Journals*, 4: 238. Letter for the *Brother Jonathan* (7–11? February 1842).

60. See, for example, *Letters and Journals*, 4: 73: "In a work *professing* to be a fiction, no one has the right to suppose any part true, that cannot be *shown* to be true. Writers of fiction do, certainly, often introduce circumstances more or less true, but an intelligent reader understands that an ingenious blend of fact and fancy contributes to the charm of this species of composition." Letter for the Philadelphia *Public Ledger* (27 September–10 October 1840?).

61. *Adventures of Huckleberry Finn*, ed. Henry Nash Smith (Boston: Houghton Mifflin Co., 1958), p. 3.
62. *The Eccentric Design*, p. 106.
63. *Writings*, 1: 418–19.
64. *Pierre*, p. 204.
65. "Introduction," *Home as Found*, p. xxv.
66. *Notions of the Americans*, 1: vii.

Chapter Two

1. *The Pioneers*, p. 41.
2. Unless otherwise noted, all citations from Thoreau are indicated parenthetically in the text and refer to the Walden Edition reprint of the 1906 edition of *The Writings of Henry David Thoreau*, cited above, vols. 1–20.
3. *Home as Found*, p. xxix.
4. *The American Scene*, p. 463.
5. *Discourse on the Origin and Foundations of Inequality among Men*, trans. and ed. Roger D. and Judith R. Masters (New York: St. Martin's Press, 1964), pp. 92–93.
6. *The American Notebooks*, ed. Claude M. Simpson (Columbus: Ohio State University Press, 1972), p. 354.
7. *Frontier: American Literature and the American West* (Princeton: Princeton University Press, 1965), pp. 330–31.
8. *Hawthorne* (Ithaca: Cornell Univesity Press, 1966), p. 10.
9. For a provocative reading of Thoreau's self-emptying figure of Nature's "bottom," see Walter Benn Michaels, *"Walden's* False Bottoms," *Glyph I: Johns Hopkins Textual Studies* (Baltimore: Johns Hopkins University Press, 1977), pp. 132–49. Paul de Man has characterized Rousseau's use of the term "nature" in a fashion which, if it does not apply directly to Thoreau, does illuminate the problems of his enterprise: "Rousseau calls natural any stage of relational integration that precedes in degree the stage presently under examination.... [The 'natural' stage] conceals the fact that it is itself one system of relations among others, and presents itself as the sole and true order of things, as nature and not as structure. But since a deconstruction always has for its target to reveal the existence of hidden articulations and fragmentations within assumedly monadic totalities, nature turns out to be a self-deconstructive term. It engenders endless other 'natures' in an eternally repeated pattern of regression." See "Political Allegory in Rousseau," *Critical Inquiry* 2 (1976): 652.
10. "Some Green Thoughts on a Green Theme," *Triquarterly* 23–24 (1972): 626.
11. *Gulliver's Travels and Other Writings*, ed. Louis A. Landa (Boston: Houghton Mifflin Co., 1960), pp. 150–51.
12. *Works*, 1: 34–35. Rousseau had reached a similar conclusion: "As man's first motives for speaking were of the passions, his first expressions were tropes. Figurative language was the first to be born. Proper meaning sees them in their true form. At first only poetry was spoken; there was no hint of reasoning until much later." See *Essay on the Origin of Languages*, trans. John H. Moran (New

York: Frederick Ungar, 1966), p. 12. Nietzsche had certainly read Emerson, and he strikes close to Emerson's economic rhetoric when he writes that "truths" are no more than "metaphors which are worn out and without sensuous power; coins which have lost their pictures and now matter only as metal, no longer as coins." See "On Truth and Lie in an Extra-Moral Sense," *The Portable Nietzsche*, trans. and ed. Walter Kaufmann (New York: Viking Press, 1954), p. 47.

13. "Introduction a l'oeuvre de Marcel Mauss," Marcel Mauss, *Sociologie et Anthropologie* (Paris: Presses Universitaires de France, 1966), p. L.

14. *Tristes Tropiques,* trans. John and Doreen Weightman (New York: Atheneum, 1974), p. 333. Lévi-Strauss might well have been reading Thoreau when he notes elsewhere of his vocation that the anthropologist "acquires a kind of chronic rootlessness; eventually, he comes to feel at home nowhere, and he remains psychologically maimed" (p. 55).

15. *Consciousness in Concord: The Text of Thoreau's Hitherto "Lost Journal,"* with commentary by Perry Miller (Boston: Houghton Mifflin Co., 1958), p. 192.

16. *Pierre; Or, the Ambiguities,* p. 165.

17. *A Grammar of Motives* (1945; rpt. Berkeley: University of California Press, 1969), p. 303.

18. "Some Green Thoughts on a Green Theme," p. 606.

19. *Moby-Dick,* ed. Harrison Hayford and Hershel Parker (New York: W. W. Norton, 1967), p. 171.

20. *Meditations on Hunting,* trans. Howard B. Wescott (New York: Charles Scribner's Sons, 1972), pp. 57–58, 152.

21. *Basic Writings of Nietzsche,* trans. and ed. Walter Kaufmann (New York: Modern Library, 1968), pp. 418–19. Cf. Emerson's remark in "Circles" on the "truth" which cannot be "fully understood" by the thinker: "The last chamber, the last closet, he must feel never opened; there is always a residuum unknown, unanalyzable." See *Works,* 2: 286.

22. *The Prairie,* intro. Henry Nash Smith (New York: Holt, Rinehart, and Winston, 1950), p. 452. Natty's final utterance also echoes his own forceful ejaculation of "Here!" in the trial scene of *The Pioneers* (p. 353).

23. *Go Down Moses* (New York: Modern Library, 1955), p. 326.

24. Thoreau's "bottoms" should also be considered in the context of the scatological obsessions many critics have noted in his work. See, for example, Michael West, "Scatology and Eschatology: The Heroic Dimensions of Thoreau's Wordplay," *PMLA,* 89 (1974), 1043–64. The theorizer "in arrears" who sets out to discover the country "in the rear of us" may be on a similarly curious mission.

25. *A World Elsewhere,* p. ix. Of Thoreau in particular, Poirier observes that the abstractions to which he feels subservient ("nature," for example) "refer us not to anything with a settled existence but rather to something of which the style itself is the synecdoche" (p. 84).

26. *The Lay of the Land* (Chapel Hill: University of North Carolina Press, 1975).

27. On Thoreau's ambiguous relationships with women, particularly Ellen Sewall, Lidian Emerson, and his sisters Sophia and Helen, see Perry Miller, *Consciousness in Concord*, pp. 80–103. It is worth noting, also, that Nietzsche too grew up in a household of women. The best (though at times heavy-handed) psychoanalytic reading of Thoreau is Richard Lebeaux, *Young Man Thoreau* (New York: Harper and Row, 1975).

28. *The First and Last Journeys of Thoreau*, ed. F. B. Sanborn (Boston: The Bibliophile Society, 1905), 1: 106–7.

29. *Works*, 1: 15.

30. *Decennium Luctuosum* (1699), in *Narratives of the Indian Wars, 1675–1699*, ed. Charles H. Lincoln (New York: Charles Scribner's Sons, 1913), p. 264.

31. *Regeneration Through Violence*, p. 523.

32. *Narratives of the Indian Wars*, p. 266.

33. *Complete Poetry and Selected Prose*, p. 135.

34. *Narratives of the Indian Wars*, p. 266. Hawthorne must have found the violence of the woman more uncanny than Thoreau, for in his version of Mather's story, Hannah becomes a "raging tigress" and a "bloody old hag" who slaughters not only Indians, but Indian *children*. See "The Duston [sic] Family," in *Hawthorne as Editor: Selections from his Writings in* The American Magazine of Useful and Entertaining Knowledge, ed. Arlin Turner (University, La.: Louisiana State University Press, 1941), pp. 131–37.

35. *The Complete Poems*, ed. Elizabeth Story Donno (Baltimore: Penguin Books, 1972), p. 100.

36. *Consciousness in Concord*, p. 193.

37. *Complete Poetry and Selected Prose*, p. 79.

38. *Consciousness in Concord*, p. 116.

39. *Works*, 6: 113, 85, 87.

40. "The Symbol of the Hieroglyphics in the American Renaissance," *American Quarterly* 26 (1974): 115.

41. *"Walden's* False Bottoms," p. 136.

42. *Frontier*, p. 218.

43. *Beginnings*, pp. 317–18.

44. *Tristes Tropiques*, p. 411. Absence of "meaning" is not quite correct, though; the "unintelligible," that which is endowed with *mana* and hence at once has very much meaning and none at all, would be more appropriate.

45. *The Works of Walt Whitman*, 2: 424.

46. *Discourse on Inequality*, p. 92.

47. *The Collected Poems of Wallace Stevens* (New York: Alfred A. Knopf, 1954), pp. 526–27.

48. *Tristes Tropiques*, p. 389.

49. *Frontier*, p. 335.

50. William Elery Channing, *Thoreau: The Poet Naturalist*, ed. F. B. Sanborn (Boston: C. E. Goodspeed, 1902), p. 164.

51. "'Incessant Tragedies': A Reading of *A Week on the Concord and Merrimack Rivers*," *ELH*, 44 (1977), 517. Cf. Sherman Paul, *The Shores of America:*

Thoreau's Inward Exploration (1958; rpt. Urbana: University of Illinois Press, 1972), p. 198: "To ascend the river to its fount was to get to the beginning or youth of time, to the summit where water was mist and mingled with light, and all was a golden age. Thoreau was retraveling time to his springtime, and it was against the sense of this achievement that the descent was so rapid, that suddenly his golden age had turned to autumn."

52. *Early Essays and Miscellanies,* ed. Joseph J. Moldenhauer et al. (Princeton: Princeton University Press, 1975), p. 136.

53. Thoreau might at this point have been reading Rousseau, who remarks of the savage man that "the spectacle of nature becomes indifferent to him by dint of becoming familiar." See *Discourse on Inequality,* p. 117.

Chapter Three

1. *Writings,* 17: 452.

2. Unless otherwise indicated, all quotations are taken from *The Centenary Edition of the Works of Nathaniel Hawthorne,* cited above, 12 vols. to date, employing the following abbreviations: *SL, The Scarlet Letter; BR, The Blithedale Romance; HG, The House of the Seven Gables; MF, The Marble Faun; MM, Mosses from an Old Manse; TT, Twice-Told Tales; SI, The Snow-Image; AN, The American Notebooks;* and *WB, A Wonder Book.*

3. R.W.B. Lewis writes that Hawthorne, seeing *"through* time rather than over it or around it," "enlisted his language on the side of the actual in such a way that he was able to look within occurrences for signs of *re-*currence, to probe the action for what it *re-*enacted. He listened for echoes." See *The American Adam,* p. 120.

4. *Studies in Classic American Literature* (1923; rpt. New York: Viking Press, 1964), p. 65.

5. *Writings,* 1: 162.

6. *Complete Poetry and Selected Prose,* p. 417; Whitman's ellipsis.

7. In "Foot-Prints on the Sea-Shore" Hawthorne notes, in the Thoreauvian spirit, that "by tracking our foot-prints in the sand, we track our own nature in its wayward course, and steal a glance upon it, when it never dreams of being so observed" (*TT,* 454). When Hawthorne says of Hester Prynne that it is "marvellous, that, with the world before her," she chooses to linger about her place of shame (*SL,* 79), he recalls the ending of *Paradise Lost* and places those steps and footprints in a more precise mythological context: "The World was all before them, where to choose / Thir place of rest, and Providence thir guide: / They hand in hand with wand'ring steps and slow, / Through *Eden* took thir solitary way" (12: 646–49).

8. *Moses and Monotheism, Standard Edition,* 23: 135.

9. *Totem and Taboo, Standard Edition,* 13: 145.

10. *Moses and Monotheism, Standard Edition,* 23: 43.

11. I borrow the phrase from William Carlos Williams, *In the American Grain* (New

York: New Directions, 1956): "[History] portrays us in genuine patterns, like effigies or the carvings on sarcophagi. . . . It is concerned only with one thing: to say everything is dead. Then it fixes up the effigy. . . . It is an obscenity which few escape—save at the hands of the stylist, literature, in which alone humanity is protected against tyrannous designs" (pp. 188–89).

12. *Works,* 1: 9.
13. "The Scarlet Letter: Through the Old Manse and the Custom House," *Virginia Quarterly Review* 51 (1975): 444.
14. *The Sins of the Fathers: Hawthorne's Psychological Themes* (New York: Oxford University Press, 1966), p. 31.
15. *Hawthorne as Editor: Selections from His Writings in* The American Magazine of Useful and Entertaining Knowledge, p. 90.
16. *Writings,* 2: 64. The obsession of Hawthorne and his contemporaries with stone busts and monuments must also owe a good deal to the contemporary developments in cemetery grounds and funeral decorations. On this subject, see Neil Harris, *The Artist in American Society: The Formative Years, 1790–1860* (New York: George Braziller, 1966), pp. 199–208; and Ann Douglas, *The Feminization of American Culture* (New York: Alfred A. Knopf, 1977), pp. 208–13.
17. *Writings,* 7: 61.
18. Quoted in Horatio Bridge, *Personal Recollections of Nathaniel Hawthorne* (New York: Harper and Bros., 1893), p. 127.
19. Cf. the exultation of Miriam and Donatello following their crime in *The Marble Faun:* "They flung the past behind them. . . or else distilled from it a fiery intoxication. . . . For, guilt has its moment of rapture, too. The foremost result of a broken law is ever an ecstatic sense of freedom. And thus there exhaled upward (out of their dark sympathy, at the base of which lay a human corpse) a bliss, or an insanity, which the unhappy pair imagined to be well-worth the sleepy innocence that was forever lost to them" (*MF,* 176).
20. Roy R. Male finds in *The Scarlet Letter* a dialectic between "speculation," which is masculine and rending, and "investment," which is feminine and mending. The one is inclined to gamble, the other to conserve; "to speculate is to erect a kind of watchtower *(specula)* from which one can get a detached perspective and 'take stock.' To invest, on the other hand, is to accept the bond." For Male, Hester is an investor and a mender; the only trouble with this interpretation is that "speculate" is a word continually connected with Hester. See *Hawthorne's Tragic Vision* (Austin: University of Texas Press, 1957), pp. 72–74.
21. *The Classic: Literary Images of Permanence and Change* (New York: Viking Press, 1975), p. 110.
22. Quoted in G. P. Lathrop, *A Study of Hawthorne* (Boston: Houghton Mifflin, 1881), p. 227.
23. *Dr. Grimshaw's Secret,* ed. Edward H. Davidson (Cambridge: Harvard University Press, 1954), p. 122.
24. *Standard Edition,* 17: 236.
25. Ibid., 17: 235–36.

26. Ibid., 17: 241, 247–49.
27. Ibid., 17: 245.
28. *Nathaniel Hawthorne: The Poetics of Enchantment* (Ithaca: Cornell University Press, 1977), p. 147.
29. *The Complete Works of Nathaniel Hawthorne* (Boston: Houghton Mifflin, 1904), 11: 437.
30. Quoted in Lathrop, *A Study of Hawthorne,* p. 105.
31. "The Uncanny," *Standard Edition,* 17: 231.
32. *The Poetics of Enchantment,* pp. 39–80.
33. *Studies in Classic American Literature,* p. 85.
34. *Writings,* 11: 45. See chapter 2 above.
35. "The Sideshow, Or: Remarks on a Canny Moment," *MLN,* 88 (1973), 1122, 1112, 1119, 1131–32. Weber bases his interpretation upon what he finds to be Freud's misreading of Hoffmann's "The Sand-Man." In Freud's narration of the climactic scene on the tower, Nathanael looks through a spyglass and sees Coppelius, the figure associated throughout the story with the castrating father, and is thus thrown into a state of madness. In Hoffmann's text, however, Nathanael peers *sideways* through the spyglass and sees not Coppelius, but his betrothed, Clara; it is in her that the danger lurks, Weber points out, for as soon as Nathanael sees her in the glass, his trauma returns: "his eyes began to roll in their orbits and sparks showered from them. . . ." Freud, then, misses what is most uncanny in the story, "for it is not the visible figure of the castrating father that comprises the remarkable essence or non-essence of castration, but rather the glimpse of that almost-but-not-quite-nothing, a glance which is therefore itself almost blind, but not quite, for it 'sees' the difference that reveals and conceals itself in the same movement." The *side-glance* of Nathanael reveals the precise nature of the uncanny—that it is always off to the side, lurking in the wings, but, like the "castration" it may represent, cannot be exactly "seen" (pp. 1120–22). We cannot quarrel with the ingenuity of Weber's reading and should concur in its emphasis on the role of Clara, which Freud completely ignores; yet it seems overly corrective to rule out Coppelius entirely, for surely the ambiguity of what Nathanael "sees" also embraces the visible figure, itself taken in by a *side-glance.* To cancel the possibility of a visible *representation* underplays its function as a phantasm almost in the field of vision but suddenly not there, like the maternal phallus itself.
36. "Nathaniel Hawthorne," in *A Library of the World's Best Literature,* ed. Charles Dudley Warner (New York: The International Society, 1897), 18: 7054.
37. "The Uncanny," *Standard Edition,* 17: 244.
38. Ibid., 17: 244.
39. Trans. Benjamin Jowett, *The Collected Dialogues of Plato,* p. 466.
40. *Totem and Taboo, Standard Edition,* 12: 65.
41. *The Interpretation of Dreams, Standard Edition,* 5: 339–40 and section vi, *passim.*
42. "I. A. Richards and the Dream of Communication," *The Fate of Reading* (Chicago: University of Chicago Press, 1975), p. 32.

43. Ibid., pp. 35–38.
44. *Nathaniel Hawthorne: An Approach to an Analysis of Artistic Creation,* trans. Derek Coltman (Cleveland: The Press of Case Western Reserve University, 1970), p. 43. Cf. Miriam's sketch of Judith and Holofernes in *The Marble Faun,* chap. 5.
45. "Medusa's Head," *Standard Edition,* 18: 273.
46. *Narratives of the Witchcraft Cases, 1648–1706,* ed. George Lincoln Burr (New York: Charles Scribner's Sons, 1914), p. 274.
47. Quoted in Lathrop, *A Study of Hawthorne,* p. 321.
48. Quoted in Richard Rudisill, *Mirror Image: The Influence of the Daguerreotype on American Society* (Albuquerque: University of New Mexico Press, 1971), p. 38. The pioneer study of the daguerreotype's influence on *The House of the Seven Gables,* and one to which I am indebted, is Alfred H. Marks, "Hawthorne's Daguerreotypist: Scientist, Artist, Reformer," *Ball State Teachers College Forum,* (1962): 61–74. For the psychological impact of the daguerreotype on Hawthorne, one might well compare Freud's characterization of the uncanny as "something which ought to have remained hidden but has come to light." See *Standard Edition,* 17: 241.
49. Quoted in Rudisill, *Mirror Image,* p. 54.
50. *The Classic,* p. 93.
51. *Illuminations,* ed. Hannah Arendt and trans. Harry Zohn (New York: Schocken Books, 1969), pp. 236–37.
52. "Salon of 1859," *Baudelaire: Selected Writings on Art and Artists,* trans. P. E. Charvet (Baltimore: Penguin Books, 1972), pp. 292–96. I have followed Charvet's translation except where indicated by the French word in brackets; for the French text, see *Oeuvres Complètes,* ed. M. Jacques Crépet (Paris: Louis Conard, 1923), 1: 264–72.
53. *Illuminations,* p. 221.
54. "Salon of 1859," p. 297. Baudelaire distinguishes photography as a technically valuable duplicating tool, so long as it does not purport to be an art; for Benjamin, of course, the two functions are not as easily separable.
55. Quoted in Rudisill, *Mirror Image,* p. 57.
56. *The Machine in the Garden: Technology and the Pastoral Ideal in America* (New York: Oxford University Press, 1964).
57. "Salon of 1859," p. 296.
58. *The Sins of the Fathers,* p. 173.
59. Quoted in Taylor Stoehr, "Hawthorne and Mesmerism," *Huntington Library Quarterly* 33 (1969): 42.
60. *Illuminations,* pp. 186–87.
61. *Hawthorne, Melville, and the Novel* (Chicago: University of Chicago Press, 1976), p. 13.
62. *The Interpretation of Dreams, Standard Edition,* 5: 338.
63. Somewhat less suspicious than I am of Hawthorne's intent and Holgrave's actions, Laurence B. Holland writes that although Holgrave draws back from taking mastery of Phoebe, "his abstention and verbal repudiation of his story-

telling do not cancel out or invalidate his effort, for . . . the effort and the restraint constitute, by prefiguring, the reciprocal and authentic bond of intimacy that will eventually mature between them. . . . If one were to claim that Holgrave in some measure 'betrays' Hawthorne's authority by exceeding limits that Hawthorne himself would respect, or by falling short of Hawthorne's more persuasive power and tact, one would have to recognize that to betray is also to reveal, as with secrets, the design of the author." See "Authority, Power, and Form: Some American Texts," in *The Yearbook of English Studies,* ed. G. K. Hunter and C. J. Rawson (London: Modern Humanities Research Association, 1978), 8: 9–10.

64. *Hawthorne* (Ithaca: Cornell University Press, 1966), p. 99.

65. Quoted in Beaumont Newhall, *The History of Photography from 1839 to the Present Day* (New York: The Museum of Modern Art, 1949), p. 27.

66. *Hawthorne,* p. 94.

Chapter Four

1. Samuel Beckett, *Malone Dies,* in *Three Novels* (New York: Grove Press, 1965), p. 254.

2. Quotations from *Pierre* and *Moby-Dick* are cited parenthetically in my text (abbreviated *P* and *MD,* respectively) and refer to *Pierre; or, The Ambiguities,* ed. Harrison Hayford, Hershel Parker, and G. Thomas Tanselle (Evanston: Northwestern University Press, 1971); and *Moby-Dick,* ed. Harrison Hayford and Hershel Parker (New York: W. W. Norton, 1967).

3. *Hawthorne, Melville, and the Novel,* p. 185.

4. *Studies in Classic American Literature,* p. 160.

5. *American Renaissance: Art and Expression in the Age of Emerson and Whitman* (1941; rpt. New York: Oxford University Press, 1968), p. 468.

6. *Selected Essays* (New York: Harcourt, Brace and World, 1964), pp. 125–26.

7. *Frontier,* p. 285.

8. *Herman Melville: Mariner and Mystic* (New York: George H. Doran Co., 1921), p. 63.

9. *The Machine in the Garden,* p. 305. For Marx's treatment of this three-chapter grouping, see pp. 302–10.

10. *The Savage Mind* (Chicago: The University of Chicago Press, 1966), p. 105. The absence of a Moby Dick may also help explain the way in which parricide gives way to suicide in *Pierre.* As Guy Rosolato, for example, has pointed out about the totemic sacrifice, the murder of the father is often accomplished indirectly and symbolically through the substitution of the scapegoat, whether animal or human, as a third, mediating term. In *Pierre,* however, the place of the third term occupied in *Moby-Dick* by the whale is vacant, and Pierre himself, as we will see, must fill it and thus become his own sire and his own victim. For an explication of Rosolato and a discussion of the triadic structure of sacrifice in Faulkner that illuminates a number of issues in *Pierre,* see John

T. Irwin, *Doubling and Incest/Repetition and Revenge* (Baltimore: The Johns Hopkins University Press, 1975), pp. 125–35.

11. "Introduction to *Pierre*, ed. Henry A. Murray (New York: Hendricks House, 1949), p. xxxvi.

12. *Notions of the Americans*, 1: 104–5. See also chap. 1, part iii, above.

13. Edwin Haviland Miller, *Melville* (New York: George Braziller, 1975), pp. 77, 88.

14. *Clarel, The Works of Herman Melville* (London: Constable and Co., 1924), 15: 250.

15. "The Art of Herman Melville: The Author of *Pierre*,*" Yale Review* 59 (1970): 203.

16. *The Letters of Herman Melville*, p. 150.

17. *The Pleasure of the Text*, trans. Richard Miller (New York: Hill and Wang, 1975), p. 47.

18. *Letters*, p. 78.

19. "The Voice of the Shuttle: Language from the Point of View of Literature," *Beyond Formalism: Literary Essays 1958-1970* (New Haven: Yale University Press, 1970), p. 348.

20. *The English Novel: Form and Function* (1953; rpt. New York: Harper and Row, 1967), pp. 22–24.

21. *The Sound and the Fury* (New York: Vintage-Random, 1956), p. 411.

22. "A Special Type of Choice of Object Made by Men," *Standard Edition*, 11: 172–73.

23. "Introduction" to Hendricks House *Pierre*, p. lvii.

24. *Centenary Edition*, 3: 101.

25. *The Collected Poems of Wallace Stevens*, pp. 130–31.

26. "Hawthorne and His Mosses," *The Portable Melville*, ed. Jay Leyda (New York: Viking Press, 1952), p. 408.

27. *Standard Edition*, 18: 57. See also chap. 1, parts iii and v, above.

28. Melville notes in a letter of 1851 to Hawthorne, "I read Solomon more and more, and every time see deeper and deeper and unspeakable meanings in him. I did not think of Fame, a year ago, as I do now. My development has been all within a few years past. I am like one of those seeds taken out of the Egyptian Pyramids, which, after being three thousand years a seed and nothing but a seed, being planted in English soil, it developed itself, grew to greenness, and then fell to mould.... I feel that I am now come to the inmost leaf of the bulb, and that shortly the flower must fall to the mould. It seems to me now that Solomon was the truest man who ever spoke, and yet that he a little *managed* the truth with a view to popular conservatism; or else there have been many corruptions and interpolations of the text." See *Letters*, p. 130.

29. Quoted in Hershel Parker, "Historical Note," Northwestern Edition of *Pierre*, p. 395.

30. Merton M. Sealts, Jr., *Melville's Reading: A Check-List of Books Owned and Borrowed* (Madison: The University of Wisconsin Press, 1966), pp. 55–56. The edition of De Quincey Melville owned is unidentified, but was purchased

in London; the *Confessions* and *Suspiria* often appeared together, as in the 1850 edition cited below.

31. *Confessions of An English Opium-Eater* and *Suspiria de Profundis* (Boston: Ticknor, Reed, and Fields, 1850), p. 159.

32. *Suspiria de Profundis,* pp. 220–29. For an excellent reading of De Quincey which examines his relationship with his sister in detail, see J. Hillis Miller, *The Disappearance of God: Five Nineteenth-Century Writers* (1963; rpt. New York: Schocken Books, 1965), pp. 17–80.

33. "The Craft of Herman Melville: A Putative Statement," *The Lion and the Honeycomb: Essays in Solicitude and Critique* (New York: Harcourt, Brace, and Co., 1955), p. 143.

34. *The Complete Poems of Emily Dickinson,* p. 548.

35. See chap. 2, part ii, above.

36. *Frontier,* p. 290.

37. *Writings,* 7: 61.

38. *Love's Body* (New York: Vintage-Random, 1966), pp. 49–133. Brown builds on Freud's "Medusa's Head," *Standard Edition,* 18: 273–74.

39. Most recently, Ann Douglas, *The Feminization of American Culture* (New York: Alfred A. Knopf, 1977), pp. 304–13.

40. *Selected Writings of Herman Melville* (New York: Modern Library, 1952), pp. 308–9.

41. *Collected Poems of Herman Melville,* ed. Howard P. Vincent (Chicago: Hendricks House, 1947), p. 106.

42. Reprinted in William H. Gilman, *Melville's Early Life and Redburn* (New York: New York University Press, 1951), pp. 265–71.

43. *Moses and Monotheism, Standard Edition,* 23: 43. See also Chap. 3, part i, above.

44. *Selected Writings,* pp. 195–211.

45. "Melville's 'Tartarus': The Deflowering of New England," *American Quarterly* 23 (1971): 79–100.

46. *Herman Melville: A Critical Study* (New York: Macmillan, 1949), p. 163.

47. *The Confidence-Man: His Masquerade,* ed. Hershel Parker (New York: W. W. Norton, 1971), p. 104.

48. *The Performing Self: Compositions and Decompositions in the Languages of Contemporary Life* (New York: Oxford University Press, 1971), p. 36.

49. Ibid., p. 36.

50. John Seelye uses this suggestive phrase to describe the paradoxical choice Pierre faces between Falsgrave and Plinlimmon. See *Melville: The Ironic Diagram* (Evanston: Northwestern University Press, 1970), p. 82.

51. *The Conduct of Life, Works,* 6: 16.

52. Ibid., 6: 22.

53. *Selected Writings,* p. 12.

54. "The Rhetoric of Temporality," *Interpretation: Theory and Practice,* ed. Charles S. Singleton (Baltimore: The Johns Hopkins University Press, 1969), pp. 200–1.

55. Ibid., pp. 198, 200.
56. *Letters,* p. 116.
57. See chap. 3, part ii, above. On the relationship between Melville's known difficulties with his eyes at the time and a possible castration anxiety, see Chase, *Herman Melville,* pp. 118, 125.
58. *The Pleasure of the Text,* p. 37.
59. *Writings,* 1: 328, 346, 326, 351. See also chap. 2, part ii, above.
60. "Introduction" to the Hendricks House *Pierre,* p. xciii.
61. *Redburn: His First Voyage* (New York: Anchor-Doubleday, 1957), p. 151.

Index

Adam, the American. *See* Eden, American; Frontier, the
Adams, Henry, xx
"America" (Melville), 172
American Democrat, The (Cooper), 7, 8, 11, 15, 18, 19, 188 n.6
American Notebooks, The (Hawthorne), 47, 98, 101, 103, 106-7, 138
Ancestral Footstep, The (Hawthorne), 90, 102
"Artist of the Beautiful, The" (Hawthorne), 135-36
Authority: defined as literary problem, xi–xx, 185; as genealogical problem in Melville, 145–46, 150, 153; and the past in Hawthorne, 86–88; as political issue in Cooper, 2–3, 36 (*see also* Cooper, imitation and authority in); in Thoreau, 56. *See also* Representation; Writing

Barthes, Roland, 154, 183
"Bartleby" (Melville), 167, 180
Baudelaire, Charles, 130–32, 135
Beckett, Samuel, 143–44
Benito Cereno (Melville), 153, 172
Benjamin, Walter, 127, 130–31, 134, 135
Bersani, Leo, xii
Bewley, Marius, 8, 36
Billy Budd (Melville), 167, 171
Blackmur, R. P., 167
Blithedale Romance, The (Hawthorne), 91, 92, 104–7, 137, 139, 160
Brodhead, Richard, 136, 144
Brown, Norman O., 170
Burke, Kenneth, 56

Cape Cod (Thoreau), 49, 79
Castration: compared to original sin, 101, 103, 105, 117, 160, 183; in Freud (*see* Uncanny, the); as metaphor in Thoreau, 64–65; as thematic problem in Melville, 144–45, 160, 170–72, 174–75, 183; tree as symbol of, in Cooper, 5, 35; and the uncanny in Hawthorne, 101, 103–15,

119–21. *See also* Oedipal conflict; Perception, crisis of
Channing, William Ellery, 81
Chase, Richard, 176, 202 n.57
Clemens, Samuel L. [pseud. Mark Twain], *Adventures of Huckleberry Finn*, 34–35; "The Art of Authorship," xix; *Pudd'nhead Wilson*, 126
Confidence Man, The (Melville), 177
Cooper, James Fenimore, xvi, xviii–xx, 72, 95, 103, 121, 146–48, 167, 171, 180, 185; *The American Democrat*, 7, 8, 11, 15, 18, 19, 188 n.6; American Eden in, 2, 17–22, 30, 35–37; on American language, 8–11, 38; *The Deerslayer*, 12; fiction as incest in, 28–29, 33–35, 38–40; figure of Natty Bumppo in, 1–2, 7–8, 12–13, 16, 19, 21–22, 27, 31–38, 189 n.26; *Home as Found*, xvi, 1–40, 42, 44, 56, 59, 60, 86, 87, 88, 136, 145, 151–52, 153, 163; home as metaphor in, 3, 12, 15, 17–24, 33, 40; *Homeward Bound*, 1, 11, 188 n.3; imitation and authority in, 6–7, 16–17, 22–40; incest in, 11–22, 24, 26, 30, 33, 36, 39–40; Indian language in, 12–13, 189 n.26; influence of *Hamlet* on, 13–15, 19, 25, 28; *The Last of the Mohicans*, 21; *Letter to His Countrymen*, 28–29; marriage as ritual in, 12–13, 17–22, 29, 39; names and naming in, 4–5, 9–19, 29–35, 37–39, 189 n.26; *New York*, 19; *Notions of the Americans*, 21, 39, 150; parody and satire in, 2–3, 25, 28, 31–33, 36–37; *The Pathfinder*, 12, 58; *The Pioneers*, 1, 2, 15, 20, 22, 24, 25, 27, 31, 34–35, 41, 88, 188 n.3, 190 n.37; *The Prairie*, 58; quotation as imitation in, 13–14, 28–35; relationship of, to original sin (Judge Cooper), 2, 4–5, 9, 14–17, 20, 26, 27, 29–31, 36, 39, 190 n.28; relationship of, to sister (Hannah Cooper), 19–22; stone busts in, 24–26, 28; symbols in, 6, 16, 24–25, 35–38; the totem animal in, 37–39; writing and authority in, 27–35, 39–40

The Johns Hopkins University Press

This book was composed in Compugraphic Garamond 49 by the Britton Composition Company from a design by Charles West. It was printed on 50-lb. No. 66 Eggshell Offset Cream paper and bound in Roxite A and G.S.B. Style 535 book cloth by The Maple Press Company.

Library of Congress Cataloging in Publication Data

Sundquist, Eric J.
    Home as found.

    Includes bibliographical references and index.
        1.   American literature—19th century—History and
criticism.   2.   Family in literature.   3.   Psychoanalysis
and literature.   I.   Title.
PS217.F35S8   810'.9'003   79-4949
ISBN 0-8018-2241-6